DIGNITY & DECENCY

RHAPSODIC MUSINGS OF
A MODERN ANARCHIST

COLLECTED WORKS OF STERLIN LUJAN

Discovery Publisher

Author: Sterlin Lujan
Editing: Carey Wedler
Cover Art: Joel Wright

616 Corporate Way
Valley Cottage, New York
www.discoverypublisher.com
editors@discoverypublisher.com
Proudly not on Facebook or Twitter

New York • Paris • Dublin • Tokyo • Hong Kong

TABLE OF CONTENTS

DIGNITY & DECENCY

RHAPSODIC MUSINGS OF
A MODERN ANARCHIST

COLLECTED WORKS OF STERLIN LUJAN

For my beautiful wife, Cecillia Lujan, who I could not have compiled *Dignity & Decency* without.

For Ross Ulbricht, who deserves better than being locked in a cage for life.

And for Nathan Freeman: a shining beacon of liberty who was taken from us way too soon.

Approbations

Anarchy isn't about wearing masks or throwing bombs. It's about treating others with dignity and decency. For those lucky enough to know him, Sterlin Lujan has already been showing us by example. Now the rest of us can learn directly from his words collected in one place.

Dignity & Decency is a great place to start for anyone interested in using voluntary human interaction to build a better world.

—Roger Ver

In *Dignity & Decency*, Sterlin reminds those familiar with his work why his message is so memorable and so necessary at this moment. Readers who are new to his writing will have the joy of discovering his vision of compassionate anarchism—a world where rationality, morality, psychedelics, and anarchism collide. This collection introduces his insatiable desire to reduce violence and promote peace while offering practical solutions to those who can feel that something is amiss in our world. Sterlin has an inimitable ability to communicate the message of anarchism, simplify the intricacies of cryptocurrency, and explain the psychology of spanking in a way that tends to build bridges and open hearts. The world is better thanks to his articulations of the concepts of liberty.

—Derrick Broze

Foreword

I t's no shock or secret that the past year has been tumultuous, entering the cultural lexicon as a time of doom, misery, division, and upheaval—of chaos, fear, and discord.

We have watched otherwise good humans caught in the trance of statism, propaganda, and panic cower to a barrage of sensationalism and fear propaganda to justify a creeping police state in the name of feeling safe. We've witnessed terrorized humans who trust the authorities issue harsh, hateful demands that those who aren't gripped by terror comply, shaming them for questioning narratives and urging the State to force them into submission.

Some believe the pervasiveness, crimes, and severity of statism are growing. Others say nothing has changed—that the true nature of the ruling class and the power it wields has simply been unmasked. Whatever your take, however, it's clear the current paradigm isn't working. The ruling class continues to abuse the rest of us, fueling empire, exploitation, and the false narrative that the true enemies are not those who would lord over us, steal from us, and kill us for resisting but our fellow humans, who are also victimized by statism. This false belief echoes a refrain familiar throughout human history. Something has to give.

Many anarchists have struggled with frustration and a sense of helplessness and hopelessness as we've watched so many millions, if not billions, of otherwise decent people fall prey to predatory rulers and systems. We've found ourselves caught not only in fear of what may come but anger and bitterness, which are extensions of fear, at these power structures, as well as toward those who blindly believe in them. Despite our diametrically opposed world views, many of us have been just as reactive as the statists we have come to resent, feeling disconnected from those we have unsuccessfully efforted to shake out of the statist trance. It has become all too easy to forget the reasons we arrived at anarchism in the first place: our deep reverence for freedom and peaceful coexistence.

Enter *Dignity & Decency*.

This collection of essays and observations embodies the anarchist spirit of voluntary relationships, optimism, problem-solving, and evolution. It contains rational, thoughtful explanations of the morality and mechanics of freedom, providing overwhelming and heartening examples of how humanity's evolution toward voluntaryism is both inevitable and accelerating. From cryptocurrencies and civil disobedience to the most fundamentally important task of disentangling statists from the mentality of authority worship, *Dignity & Decency* provides strategy and hope.

But most uniquely and importantly, Sterlin's work compassionately yet powerfully (and successfully) argues the case for cultivating love, empathy, and our own inner healing in our efforts to promote true liberty in the world.

It doesn't take much scrutiny to recognize the lack of empathy and emotional stability among statists and inherent to statist thought. Demanding your fellow humans submit to your wishes at the barrel of a government gun—even when they do not consent—is the antithesis of empathy, and the widespread emotional outbursts displayed by statists of all partisan predilections reflect deeper inner chaos and turmoil no doubt exacerbated by the never-ending onslaught of hate and fear porn shoved down the masses' throats.

Anarchists often snicker and scoff at these reactions, perhaps remembering a time when we were just as confused, chaotic, and controlled. Yet in our agitation at the audacity of statists and the government they bow to, too often we end up caught in the same emotional reactivity. We get angry, lash out, and let our justifiable disdain for the State and those who would control us overshadow our love for freedom. Unfortunately and ironically, this takes us out of alignment with our true nature and the nature of anarchism, which is inherently empathetic in its respect for the rights and liberties of other humans.

Within these pages are rational breakdowns not only of why anarchism is important and the only viable way forward for humanity but also of why compassion, healing, and kindness are essential on the path toward achieving it.

Some anarchists may confuse this with submitting to statism. If we have compassion for those who subscribe to it, surely we are letting them off the hook and consenting to having our freedoms and liberties trampled. But this is a false dichotomy. It is possible both to recognize the inhumanity and delusions of statism and refuse to let such nefarious beliefs build armor around your anarchist heart as you wholeheartedly, passionately resist.

Opening our hearts may be considered a weakness, but in a paradigm where evil thrives by shutting down the hearts of humans, by disconnecting us from our fundamentally loving nature and pitting us against each other in fear and polarization, we must embody the opposite of the State. We must embrace our own love and care and take responsibility for our own well-being both in the spirit of personal responsibility and out of concern for the evolution and survival of the human race.

And it is in these pages that Sterlin strikes a balance between the logic and reason of anarchism and the kindness, compassion, and self-awareness (and responsibility) it requires to truly help humanity unlock its potential.

It has been my honor and pleasure to participate in this project, and in the face of mounting discord and tensions, it has provided deep breaths of fresh air to my own journey in the pursuit of anarchism. I trust it will do the same for you.

—Carey Wedler
March 17, 2021

Introduction

Anarchy is blossoming. Not the "anarchy" of violence and chaos but the anarchy of dignity and love. The philosophy is evolving and maturing. Its seductive nature is infiltrating mainstream consciousness. Some people are getting confused by the message, but others are discovering a goldmine of truth within it.

The push toward more liberty is the frequency that powers the pulse of modernity, and it represents a renaissance of the conscience—a reforging of society, a shunning of the tyrannical impulse, and the creation of a new moral ethos. A wellspring of possibility has burst forth in the heart of humanity, ushering in an age of freedom.

Social and political movements are experiencing widespread growth. Some people think of the 1960s as the time when countercultural ideologies thrived in America. However, what is happening with emergent anarchist and voluntaryist movements dwarfs the hippie communities of the past.

Over the last few decades, there has been an information revolution via technological advancement, and throngs of people have been exposed to numerous novel ideas. Before the creation of the internet, people had little access to divergent philosophies and political theories. Historically, governments have controlled the flow of information and held dissident philosophies at bay. Now, more people are being exposed to anarchist thought. They are reading about different ways for society to function and finding honesty in alternative media. I have had the luxury of being a part of this awakening to new ideas, and it is all happening at a rapid pace.

Over the last decade, I have used technology, particularly social media and blogging platforms, to share my thoughts and ideas. Indeed, it was originally through the adoption of the internet and social media that I became acquainted with the anarchist community.

The freedom movement has taught countless people that human society does not need monarchs, politicians, bureaucrats, presidents, or government functionaries to operate. It has taught everyone that ideas should be accessible to the masses and that no one should have a monopoly on information. At its heart, this is what *Dignity & Decency* is about. It is about unleashing the courage to challenge the status quo. It is about sedition and treason, but it is also about warmth and compassion. The book contains a collection of ideas that have been extracted from various social media platforms and other incubators of my thoughts.

Over the years, I have articulated a number of ideas that have previously been considered taboo and heretical. I have called for the abolition of government. I have suggested that spanking children is an affront to morality and tantamount to abuse and that psychiatry is pseudo-medicine, while psychedelic medicine is real medicine. And most recently, I have been inspired by the crypto-anarchists who believe technology will subvert governments and bring economic and financial peace to humankind.

I have brought all of these ideas to a multitude of people and received inspiring feedback. When I began my campaign of illuminating the truth, I was heckled and denounced. Friends and family scorned me and denounced my ideas. Nonetheless, I persevered and pushed forward. In time, like-minded people found me, and we quickly built a rapport. Now, I can look around and not shy away from expressing ideas. I can stand up in a crowd and scream, "Down with government!" and everyone will applaud and cheer in agreement.

For some people reading this book, my success may seem like luck or coincidence. They may say, "So what? You found your corner of crazy on the internet!" Well, that is true to a degree. The anarchist movement still represents a minority of the population. However, since the members of this minority have joined hands, the number of people devoted to articulating truth has grown substantially. More and more individuals are embracing the tenets of anarchism. They are envisioning many ways to think and live and be. They are crafting a new paradigm, and it is anything but crazy.

One thing remains true, though: Governments are aggressively attacking the free flow of information online in whatever manner they can. It seems they may even be colluding with large tech platforms like Facebook to censor content. For instance, Alex Jones was silenced in August 2018, when multiple social media platforms removed all his content at once. Just two months later, Facebook and Twitter banned numerous independent news organizations, and similar purges continue today. Nonetheless, the internet will not be sucked into a statist wormhole. New platforms will be created, disseminated, and enjoyed; and ultimately, there will be no way to stop the spread of truth and anarchism.

That is the reason I wrote the present volume. I want to spread these ideas to more remote corners of the world and on the web despite attempts to censor and ban them. I want people of all creeds, colors, races, and mentalities to share in the revelations of an idea whose time has come.

The book is organized for the "info junkie." One can start reading any section depending on their personal belief system. It does not have to be read front to back. The ideal reader is likely not a full-fledged anarchist but someone who is skeptical and open-minded. If they read logically from Part 1 to 3, they should discover anarchist truths in a stepwise fashion. Along the way, they will learn how anarchists integrate compassion, rhetoric, psychology, and technology into their worldview.

Some ideas are similar but said in different ways to solidify a point because embracing anarchism can take considerable time if the person is unfamiliar with the ideas. My intent has been to capture the arguments and visionary elements of the philosophy in as many ways as possible, even if ideas tend to overlap or express similar principles. It's my hope that all of the examples and expressions leave the reader hungry for more and excited about the beauty and power of anarchism.

I have filled the present volume with truth, courage, justice, poetry, and love.

I hope it finds you well.

> "Nothing else in the world…not all the armies…is so powerful as an idea whose time has come." –Victor Hugo

Sterlin Lujan
January 16, 2021

PART 1: ANARCHOS PRINCIPIA

On Becoming an Anarchist

12/31/2015

When one becomes an anarchist, he does not fling explosive cocktails at common people. He does not don black attire, incite riots, or write anarchist cookbooks with recipes on burning buildings. One can indeed be an anarchist and commit trouble galore, but that is not the case on the whole. Modern anarchists are generally peaceful and pensive. They resemble most everyone and adopt similar passions, interests, hobbies, appetites, and other human behaviors. They simply vie for social and cultural change. They just want to be free.

They are not wild-eyed maniacs with violent histories or knife scars from gang fights. Everyone tends to have these preconceived notions and fantasies because governments have painted anarchists as an insane group of desperados who want to ignite the world in a conflagration of chaos. This is not true. It is a pernicious lie.

Anarchists would rather plant gardens of woodruff and wine cup flower and live peaceably in the woodlands while wooing nature. The figure of the anarchist is much less alarming than previously suspected. The anarchist is a figure of destiny, a symbol for what humankind seeks to become—the orgiastic manifestation of peace and truth brought to bear in a kaleidoscopic explosion of love and unity.

Indeed, the term "anarchy" is a humble term. It means "without rulers." It does not mean "blow things up" or "sow disorder." Anarchism is an apolitical philosophy that champions the individual and decries the monarch. Anarchy is the triumphant concept that people should live unobstructed by laws and rulers and instead be consumed by love and kindness.

Anarchism is the face of the future echoed in the cries of the people. It is written on the voices of the downtrodden and dominated. And ultimately, a person who believes in peaceful anarchism is one whose silhouette and character have often been shaped by cultural traumata and painful experiences of the past.

Here I will explore the depth of the anarchists' character and their motivations with the intent of creating more anarchists and showing people the color and poetic beauty of the anarchists' deep self and love of peace.

Traumata and Close Encounters with the State

Many anarchists are born out of the chaos of modernity. They are the product of an unwholesome environment characterized by an epidemic of violence against the population.

They were created by the myriad Molotov cocktails shot into the bosom of society by State machinery. When a grotesque monster like government grows into a raging behemoth, the play of nature starts to unwind on the stage of life, and the anarchists arise to contradict the brutality of these malevolent forces.

Many anarchists have indeed awakened as a result of talking to people. They have come into knowing the truth because other anarchists and activists started to paint the world with anti-authoritarian thoughts.

On the other hand, the rest of the anarchists were victims. They have experienced the tumult and torture of governmental culture, the lucid nightmare foisted firsthand upon them. That is what brought them into the fold.

They may have been accosted, harassed, kidnapped, caged, and ransomed by State enforcers. Some may have had their children taken for nonsensical reasons by CPS or other agencies of evil. Others may have come to acknowledge the perils of modern maliciousness by introspecting about their childhood. Perhaps they have done the math, pieced the puzzle together, and now comprehend the inhumanity they experienced at the hands of State education and indoctrination. Perhaps they were even drugged as children, called sick and dumb and dead. There are many reasons for their metamorphosis—and their change is understandable—as the world has become too unbearable for them.

It has been this traumata and experience of an agonizing society that has brought them to attention. The naughtiness of this dirty, rotten culture with its all-seeing government poisoning everything, has made them cognizant of the abuses and injustices they have suffered. It is these experiences that have colored their character and shaped their humanness. And that is why they now call themselves anarchists and why they fight to erase the culture of authority and make life livable for future generations.

In *Anam Cara: A Book of Celtic Wisdom*, John O'Donohue inadvertently exposed the nature and beauty of the anarchist soul.

> When love awakens in your life, in the night of your heart, it is like the dawn breaking within you. Where before there was anonymity, now there is intimacy; where before there was fear, now there is courage; where before in your life there was awkwardness, now there is a rhythm of grace and gracefulness; where before you used to be jagged, now you are elegant and in rhythm with yourself. When love awakens in your life, it is like a rebirth, a new beginning.

What happens when this grace and gracefulness unfolds in the anarchist's soul? What happens upon experiencing this rapturous metanoia? What occurs after these anarchists have unplugged and rid themselves of their fetters? What does their character contain?

The Contents of the Anarchists' Character:
A Matter of Principle

The anarchist is a person of sheer principle, of unyielding dignity and decency. Once they become what they may not have expected to be, they adopt a central thesis for living, a framework of interconnected thoughts to explore, invest in, and radiate outward. It is these traits that form the shape and contour of the freeman, which will allow him or her to act as a thought leader. Now they help the seed of anarchism grow and bloom within folks who have not directly experienced the hot steel of government violence.

Some anarchists have even attested to how the realization of anarchism has made them whole, how they have never felt so powerful, intelligent, and loving. Before their epistemological awakening, they were disconnected and confused. But after they embraced these truths, their minds expanded like the universe after the Big Bang. They gained an interconnected mental network of principles.

The basic principles they now accept are called axioms. They are self-evident truths. A person owns himself and the fruits of his labor. He owns his property. He has a right to self-defense and defense of his property. However, he also accepts non-aggression and shares that principle with his neighbor, for this is the dictum of cultural respect. It is antithetical to the barbarisms of socialism, communism, and statism. It is these principles that have lifted the fog of thought that previously encumbered the anarchist.

Ralph Waldo Emerson composed a beautiful poem called "Boston Hymn" in defense of the aforesaid principles, including individual liberty and self-ownership. The poem was meant to combat slavery, but it is just as relevant today. Here is a bit of it:

"But, lay hands on another To coin his labor and sweat, He goes in pawn for his victim For eternal years in debt. To-day unbind the captive, So only are ye unbound; Lift up a people from the dust, Trump of their rescue, sound! Pay ransom to the owner And fill the bag to the brim. Who is the owner? The slave is owner, And ever was. Pay him."

Principle-Building and Thinking for Oneself

An anarchist should also build his own principles and ally himself with the practice of thinking for himself. He must be his own form of art and work his art like magic for all to experience. It is his personal manifesto lived out for everyone to see so the entire world learns to turn itself toward him, explore his dimensions, and realize the glory of living decently and peacefully. It is a kind of sainthood, except its goal is to stimulate people to adopt self-efficacy, self-esteem, self-realization, and nonviolence. The goal is never to indenture people to him or enslave them as a cult figure would enslave the gullible.

Above all, the freeman leads by example. His beauty and bodacious grace shower all the world in what it should be—what it wants to be—in petals of peace and goodwill. In turn, people will react to this; they will listen, adhere, consider, contemplate, and learn of the advantages of truth over the despair and violence of government. It is within this crucible of principle and grandeur that everyone musters the courage to accept self-responsibility and self-dignity.

Conclusion: An Ode to Anarchists

The anarchist reverberates with a sparkle of truth within the winding tunnel of this destructive reality, which is a form of damnation. But it is a hell that can be doused with the purity and character of the freeman.

So, this is an ode to anarchists who had the strength to wake up. This is a compassionate way of saying thank you for turning away from the travesty of governmental evil. It is also a periscope turned inward for others to see the shimmering stature of the anarchist and hear the poetry and music of his soul. And hopefully, more comatose people will have that satori moment and begin to comprehend the anarchist mind—to feel the beauty and strength of the anarchist as a human being.

The goal is to place a yearning for freedom on display, to allow others to feel it so deeply it rattles their bones—touching their spirits so intimately it thrusts them headlong into understanding, thus spurring an eruption of truth in their heart. Future generations deserve this call for peace above all, as they are born anarchists; and deep down, their wish is to die as one, peacefully and serenely without ever knowing the demoniac slave master called government.

Philosophy for the Ages

December 4, 2011

Eating healthy and getting exercise are important to me, but I would never try to force anyone to live by my standards. Attempting to force someone to eat or behave in certain ways is immoral. If people want to live better lives, they will choose those paths of their own accord. Trying to push someone to live precisely as I do only cause resentment and hostility.

October 31, 2012

There's something I enjoy much more than winning a debate: the satisfaction that I argue from morality, personal values, and an honest sense of the golden rule.

December 18, 2012

Is kidnapping someone and holding them for ransom acceptable if they have a certain kind of plant in their pocket—simply because the law says so? Does "law" automatically equate to morality? And if the "law" did not exist, would you be okay with putting a gun to a person's head to kidnap him because of his fondness for smoking vegetable matter?

June 24, 2013

Your body is your own. It's nobody's right to command you to do what you don't want. It's nobody's right to ordain what you eat, drink, or inhale. It's nobody's right to coerce you into acting or behaving outside your own will and conscience. For someone to lord over your body and control your actions is slavery, and no political pretext or law can make the natural right to self-ownership void or nonexistent. The right to self-ownership is natural and fundamental to freedom.

June 28, 2013

Freedom without truth is like a plant without sunlight; the former requires the latter to grow and flourish.

July 16, 2013

Anarchists do not claim all hierarchies are bad or evil or even that hierarchies will cease to exist. Indeed, anarchists would not choose to do away with hierarchically structured businesses, chess clubs, or the Girl Scouts. Anarchy just refers to an absence of violent rulers. Removing rulers would be a conscious decision, just like people consciously choosing to do away with businesses, chess clubs, and Girl Scouts.

The beauty of humanity is that we do not have to accept hierarchies because free will and conscious choice allow us to live in a variety of ways or create different social arrangements.

August 3, 2013

If you understand that government, in all its branches, distinctions, offices, and namesakes, are the same as a violent mafia without regard for morality and life, then you're starting to understand the crux of the problem.

Rejecting government is more difficult than rejecting religion, but the fruits you will reap are more beneficial than the alternative. The clarity of mind and beauty of truth gained from this realization make living a principled life easier.

August 5, 2013

When cops assault or murder people, why are they not held to the same standards as other non-costume-wearing citizens?

I've watched tons of videos of cops assaulting and killing, and usually, the victims or their families only talk about "filing a complaint" or "suing" the officer. The police departments themselves generally only talk about "firing" or "suspending" the officer.

Why aren't the officers put in a cage like everyone else? Why the glaring hypocrisy when it comes to cops?

Could it be because cops are above the law, and the system is not for the protection of the people but rather to control and enslave them?

August 5, 2013

Do you believe you should be free to have absolute control over your own life? Or should you have masters who tell you how to live under threat of violence?

November 7, 2013

Statists claim anarchists want to promote chaos and disorder. But if anarchists wanted chaos and disorder, wouldn't they be happy with the current system, where there is no justice, no peace, and no order—where there is only assault and robbery by the government? If anarchists wanted chaos and disorder, wouldn't the current system be the anarchist's wet dream?

November 30, 2013

Someone once argued that anarchy is a kind of absolutist philosophy and that its adherents are stuck within its parameters.

False. Anarchism is the opposite of absolutism. Statism is absolutism. It is the absolute, do-as-I-say-or-I'll-shoot-you-in-the-face dogmatic answer to every scenario. Anarchism, on the other hand, embraces plurality. It's the free-wheeling notion that individuals have the right to choose, and that no person has a right to tell them otherwise. Anarchism shuns the absolutist stance and embraces the beauty of spontaneous organization.

January 10, 2014

The beauty of anarchism lies in spontaneous organization, which consists of heretofore unknown forms and structures. This notion is akin to the mind of a musical genius who composes great symphonies seemingly out of thin air, creating order in the organic madness of his notes and letting a pseudo-chaotic harmony swell and burst forth.

The same can be said of the storyteller who pens letters and words, letting his story tell itself without any artificial blocks or restrictions hamstringing him, clouding his judgment, or fettering his mind.

Anarchism, then, unleashes a creative elegance upon humanity and allows the seemingly random dance and play of many to crystallize into the philosopher's stone by way of the most natural and radiant alchemy imaginable.

January 18, 2014

You can't force someone to help others, and if you do force them to "help others," well, your society is based on the illusion of beneficence and decency. In reality, your society is violently absurd and delusional.

January 31, 2014

This cannot be stated enough: Self-ownership exists regardless of whether some asshole is lording over you at the point of a gun. You still have the choice to obey or disobey; however, the reality of self-ownership is why it is unnatural for another person to claim to rule you. No person can physically or logically control you and attempting to do so defies the natural truth of self-ownership. This is the reason slavery in all its forms must be shunned completely.

February 8, 2014

I know it sounds absurd to most people, but there is still a ruling class and a peasant class. Humanity has yet to evolve past barbarism, but thanks to philosophies like voluntaryism, this nonsense is coming to its long-awaited conclusion.

February 11, 2014

It irritates me when people say, "I have beliefs." I marshal evidence and work from first principles. I hardly call these things "beliefs." Indeed, the differentiating factor is intellectual rigor. Anarchists do not just pull truth out of their asses. There is a foundation for these ideas that builds on itself like calculus or biology. It's called evidence and logic.

February 11, 2014

Yes, I am an extremist.

1. Extreme acceptance of moral principles
2. Extreme rejection of the initiation of force
3. Extreme love for life
4. Extreme opposition to war
5. Extreme promoter of peace

The question is: why aren't you an extremist?

February 26, 2014

If you believe that anarchy will never work, why not ask a government to tell you how to live and what to do in the ungoverned aspects of your life? Why are these "anarchic" aspects of your life working, and why do you enjoy them? If you really believed anarchism could never work, you would vie for people to limit the chaos in your life by letting them tell you how to live and what to do.

Or, if you were truthful, you would just call yourself an anarchist already. Stop pretending that anarchy does not already exist in your life. Stop pretending you don't cherish freedom. Stop pretending you resent civilization by shunning freedom. Admit what you are and spread it consistently at every level. Anarchism is already a burgeoning part of you.

March 3, 2014

As atheism is a lack of belief in gods, anarchism is a lack of belief in the State. Through atheism, you can easily point out the natural world and its inhabitants but no gods. Through anarchism, you can point out men and buildings but no State. Therefore, the burden of proof falls on the people claiming gods or States exist.

Both entities—gods and States—are products of men's insecurities, need for control, and overactive imaginations.

April 13, 2014

Plenty of people question the non-aggression principle. They point out that it is impossible to "implement" overall and claim is incompatible with most people for varying reasons.

This argument, or lack thereof, is irrelevant. First and foremost, the non-aggression principle is just that: a principle. It is a code of behavior adopted by individuals for different reasons. It does not matter if everyone adopts it or not because once people learn and understand who the bad guy is—who is doing the aggression—the tenets of non-aggression become obvious. The good guys will use self-defense to thwart the attacks.

So let people naysay and shun the non-aggression principle and talk about how it will not work. People are going to follow it anyway.

The only ones who are not going to follow the natural and obvious path of non-aggression are those assholes who want to find justification to initiate force and hurt people.

April 25, 2014

Sometimes people refer to anarchists as "radicals." The notion that anarchists are radical should be accepted wholeheartedly.

Anarchists are radical conveyors of freedom, radical advocates for peace, radical defenders of self-ownership, radical lovers, radical humanitarians, and radical decent fucking people.

So, yes. I'm radical, too. If you're not radical, you might want to reexamine your worldview. You're probably doing it wrong.

September 26, 2014

Every time I argue an anarchist point with most people, I am met with this silly bromide: "This is the reality you live in, and the reality you want is a fantasy."

First, I know "this" is the reality we live in. That is precisely why I am working to alter your belief that this reality is acceptable and moral. The fact that you praise and worship this reality is a sign that you need to work on adjusting your thinking to a less violent and more peaceful philosophy.

Right now, the reality you accept is based on child abuse and rampant violence against everyone. No wonder the younger, more intelligent generations are so hesitant to breed. All of our forebears helped build a community based on hatred and simian aggression, which is incompatible with rearing peaceful youngsters.

Second, what I want is a fantasy in your mind because you've become so dependent on and comfortable with what you see as the truth, that change for peace has become too terrible and scary to contemplate.

Try to look at the core of this reality: an anti-human culture surrounds us, which is based on brutality galore. If you can observe it objectively for a moment, it will help you understand the anarchist position. It will help you see why anarchists want a freer world and why it makes more sense to shift the paradigm.

And you know what? It's inevitable that change will occur because so many people are sick and tired of all the unnecessary violence. Just accept reality. Start looking toward more peaceful solutions to problems because one day you won't have a choice.

It will be anarchism or extinction.

November 8, 2014

Voluntaryism[1] is a beautiful philosophy not only because it opposes government violence but also because it functions off the principles of harmony and freedom.

As a voluntaryist, you automatically let other people know you recognize their freedom to interact peaceably. You let them know violence will not be a consequence of their interactions so long as everyone involved maintains civility. It's one of the few philosophies that puts relationships and associations above all other agendas. It is the *sine qua non* of duty ethics. It gives absolute dignity to humankind's ability to work together.

Voluntaryism is the ultimate prescription for accepting people as self-responsible moral agents and having faith in them to make their own decisions. It allows people the freedom to fail or succeed as a result of those decisions.

There's not a philosophy that makes me feel more respectable and proud to espouse than voluntaryism. To accept and understand voluntaryism is to know that you've evolved and conquered the monkey brain. It is to know you are a being of love. Indeed, voluntaryism represents the future of the species, and inevitably, more people will come to know it. All other options have been exhausted.

January 17, 2015

To this day, I still run into people on pages and forums arguing that anarchism is a utopian pipe dream.

I am really surprised that so many of these government apologists have not confronted anarchists and had this idea demolished.

Anarchists do not believe that society will become a utopia after anarchism takes hold. That's a fact. It's just that most people have been indoctrinated with the idea of anarchism as a whimsical, teenage wet dream that can never happen.

---

1. For anyone who is unfamiliar, the phrase voluntaryism means a person who believes all human relationships should be as consensual as humanly possible. It means that the initiation of force is always morally wrong. It means every interaction should be based on voluntary consent rather than coercion or force. All voluntaryists are anarchists, but not all anarchists are necessarily voluntaryists. Sometimes I will use voluntaryism and anarchism interchangeably in this text, but my philosophical leaning is geared more toward voluntaryism as it is the more precise phrase. It is just more awkward to use regularly because it has so many syllables.

The truth is that anarchism does not make murderers and rapists vanish with a snap of the fingers. Anarchism is not a magic pill for society.

However, anarchism does suggest that a small group of men should not rule over the rest of society and that the initiation of force for personal ends is generally unacceptable.

But these ideas are not utopian, either.

They are no more utopian than wanting to get rid of chattel slavery, and there is nothing wrong with having strong convictions that evil things should be ousted and never looked upon again. Indeed, the idea that chattel slavery is normal, acceptable, and good is now obsolete.

June 30, 2015

Anarchism is peace. Government is violence. If one realizes this truth, he is more perceptive and forward-thinking than most people. Anarchism is also a psychological boon because it frees the mind to explore whole new concepts and ideas that are unknown to the statist. Both peace and novelty are totally lost on lovers of government.

July 25, 2015

Have humans become less violent in the modern age? Humans are less violent because they have made moral progress by determining certain behaviors to be evil—like chattel slavery, witch burning, and human sacrifice—despite once viewing them as socially acceptable.

Today, plenty of people are still evil. But like in the past, much of this violence occurs at the institutional level. In the 20th and 21st centuries, most of the mass violence has been caused by governments. Anyone who does not believe this should simply view the democide statistics. Democide is when governments slaughter their own people, which has been a significant problem.

Thus, for humans to take the next logical step in moral thinking, abolishing institutionalized power is the answer. Government is magnetic to psychopaths who love to kill without repercussions, so removing it would be akin to removing the Church's authority in an age where people believed in the divine right of kings and other superstitions that got people senselessly murdered.

August 12, 2015

Radical Idea: Government is irrelevant. Live your life as you see fit and by the thrust of your own consciousness regardless of arbitrary rules put forth by politicians. Try only to practice the golden rule and hurt others only in self-defense. This is social etiquette.

August 28, 2015

Some critiques of anarcho-capitalism and voluntaryism involve deceptive semantics and twisting definitions. In other words, there is a lot of equivocation and confusing rhetoric.

For instance, anarchists argue that a system based on initiatory violence is wrong and socially destructive.

Disingenuous people with a poor grasp of philosophy say, "But voluntaryism is a system based on violence! Self-defense is violence!"

These arguments are ludicrous and lack a clear understanding of anarchism. But it is not just a lack of understanding. These arguments are mainly linked to denial because folks twist language and alter definitions to trash anarchism. This is the epitome of intellectual dishonesty and sophistry.

Here is the skinny: Anarchism is not a system. It is not a centralized organization that advocates initiatory violence to run society. The term "initiatory" is the key. It means to start the use of violence, including physical altercation and destruction, as well as forms of coercion and fraud. So yes, there is violence involved in anarchism, but it is not founded on imposing violence to control others. Anarchism only contains the warning that violence will be used in self-preservation and protection. It is not based on telling people how to live, coercing behavior, or keeping people under constant duress and surveillance. Anarchism embodies self-defense and individualism, not collective control and utilitarian motivations.

The big difference between government systems and anarchic non-systems is simple: Anarchists say, "Live how you see fit so long as you don't harm me or my property." Statists say, "Live how I see fit, or you will suffer. I will throw you in a cage or kill you."

The delineation cannot be made clearer.

February 11, 2016

I tell people I have few beliefs. I believe in my wife, myself, and all of my loved ones. However, as for politics...I have no beliefs. I acknowledge facts. I see that the government enslaves and kills people, and so I opt to live free from that entity. This is not a belief so much as it is a designation based on uncomfortable truths. It is the reason why anarchists do what they do, and it is not based on the supernatural or imaginary. It is based on the evidence of the here and now.

May 27, 2016

Anarchism is the watercourse way. Like Tao, it is about balance and harmony. It appears too soft and peaceful for some, but it erodes statism like water erodes granite.

It appears chaotic, unsteady. But it is the natural way of things. It is the common denominator of peace. It provides not only a deep sense of spiritual and emotional attunement but also a calculated and logical precision.

Anarchism is the yin and yang of life, but people have tried to repress its full expression for far too long. Now it is breaking its way into conscious thought, clearing away the disequilibrium of government. It is just becoming integrated into awareness, like an epiphany.

Don't try to fight it. Accept the change. Accept growth.

Anarchism is the path, the tool, the word—a well that is used but never used up.

August 5, 2016

Anarchism is not politics. Anarchism is the rejection of politics; it is the rejection of implementing violence to solve problems.

Anarchism is the solution to most social ills and the insanity of religious violence. If any philosophy exposes the beauty of the human spirit, it is anarchism.

The philosophy represents the epitome of ethical thinking, and it demonstrates how sensual and loving a person can become. Those who have adopted anarchism usually harbor a sensitivity for other humans and seek to resolve problems with talk and love. They have no more use for forceful aggression because they have matured to the point of dispensing with their latent urge to control others.

Anarchism, in a sense, is an evolution in thinking. It is an evolution in feeling. It is the final phase in the metamorphosis from barbarian to fully civilized being.

If you are not an anarchist, consider taking the leap.

History may remember you.

October 31, 2016

Statism is a utopian fantasy that results in chaos and rule by political gangbangers.

Anarchy is a realistic philosophy that results in freedom of the individual and spontaneous order.

December 28, 2016

Abolishing the nation-state is the largest step humanity can take toward global peace.

Anarchy Is For Lovers

01/3/2014

Anarchy is all around us. Without it, our world would fall apart. All progress is due to it. All order extends from it. All blessed things that rise above the state of nature are owed to it. The human race thrives only because of the lack of control, not because of it. I'm saying that we need ever more absence of control to make the world a more beautiful place. It is a paradox that we must forever explain.

—Jeffrey Tucker

Many good-hearted people confuse anarchy with mayhem. They fear it causes widespread violence, blood, guts, and grenade explosions. They believe total freedom implies a dog-eat-dog and all-versus-all world, and that it injects the vilest form of social Darwinism into the community, leading to pandemonium.

The media pelts unwitting viewers with images to advertise this hell. Broadcasters portray punk-rock kids wearing Mohawks and jumpsuits. These punks wave black flags and carry bomb-filled messenger bags. They prepare to hurl Molotov cocktails through grandmother's window at a moment's notice.

Educational institutions, court philosophers, and government authorities paint anarchy under the same damnable light. They speak of the first humans having been embedded in a wild and anxious state of nature where lawlessness descended into the law of the jungle, and mobs engaged in desperado-style brawls and gunfights. As a result, rulers and court intellectuals urge citizens to accept Leviathan to defend against this constant scourge of human nature.

Today, well-meaning people continue to mistake anarchy for bloodshed, disorder, and chaos, but this is the opposite of the truth.

The truth is anarchy is for lovers.

Anarchists oppose strife and disorder. They shun fighters and bomb-lobbers. They disavow warmongers. They loathe slaveholders and tyrants. Instead, anarchists champion peace, nonviolence, and prosperity. Anarchism represents the *sine qua non* of human decency and freedom, and because anarchists promote such civility, this article intends to combat incorrect assumptions about anarchism, provide refutations to common arguments, and dispel old and tired propaganda.

"Resolve to serve no more, and you are at once freed. I do not ask that you place hands upon the tyrant to topple him over, but simply that you support him no longer; then you will behold him, like a great Colossus whose pedestal has been pulled away, fall of his own weight and break into pieces."

—Etienne de La Boétie

Without Rulers

Anarchy means "without rulers." It comes from the Greek *an* (without) and *archos* (chief or ruler). It simply means no masters. No tyrants. No rulers. No government.

Some believe anarchism denotes "without rules." This is false. Rules always exist in society, the marketplace, business, and private homes. Anarchism just describes the absence of authority.

Many people compare anarchy to a political system, but anarchism opposes systems. People do not implement anarchy. They do not place a key in an ignition, rev, and start it, nor does anarchy require men thousands of miles away to write laws and order men to cage and kill other men. It simply means freedom from institutional violence.

Spontaneous order develops as a natural consequence of this freedom. It suggests self-organization or order out of chaos. It refers to people's tendency to cooperate without central planning. Spontaneous order states that the human organism will act according to its will, and civilization and "rules" will emerge as a result.

An article from *The Economist* eloquently expressed spontaneous order.

What it means to say that an order is spontaneous is simply to say its stable macro-level patterns—those things that make a complex system a system, an instance of order rather than disorder or randomness—do not come about through design, planning or imposition, but arise instead from the interaction of micro-level elements operating according to certain basic principles or rules.

With knowledge of these self-organizing principles, there is no need to implement systems of governance and force people to behave in specific ways. People are capable of handling their problems and lives by choosing who they associate and work with.

To impose government on total freedom is to force artificial restrictions on human action, subvert peaceful people, and tear asunder voluntary association. Obstruction of liberty means jamming the gears of humane, prosperous, loving, and forward-moving societies—but before people accept this truth, they must disabuse themselves of the erroneous belief that anarchy equals mayhem.

People must submit themselves to the peace blooming inside what they misperceive as unchecked chaos and allow themselves to see the truth of the anarchist love for liberty.

Approaching the Argument

The following are common arguments marshaled against anarchism, as well as their refutations, which will help clarify the position.

Government apologists claim human nature undermines anarchy by turning the world into a *Mad Max: Beyond Thunderdome* bloodbath, but if human nature forces people into violence, then there is no hope for individual choices of peace and love. Yet many people prefer peace to war, love to hate, nonviolence to violence, and morality to immorality.

This suggests that peace and violence reflect opposite points of "human nature."

People are not programmed robots. One cannot argue that all humans commit violence because many do not; one cannot argue that all steal and kill because many choose to trade and love; one cannot argue that all want government because some do not. Humans exhibit unique personalities, and they are not all geared toward destruction and death. Committing violent or peaceful acts are independent choices. They are not preordained. People are conscious agents with the elbow room for free will.

Arguing against anarchy using the human-nature-equals-violence argument implies blind faith that a group of men has moral perfection. If men instead possess moral imperfection, and they gain power, this status gives them access to an unlimited supply of armies and weapons. Then they strive for the subjugation of humanity.

If evil humans desire to command power, an intelligent society should never relinquish its strength and weapons to these psychopaths at the expense of the many. Similarly, people often forget nurture and focus on nature when thinking about the consequences of anarchism, but nurture and nature work together. Biologists refer to this as the epigenetics of gene expression. The environment switches genes on or off.

For example, alcoholism may crop up in a person if they associate with people who drink, use drugs, or gamble. However, just because a genetic trait exists does not imply submission to that trait. Human psychological nature is not ironclad. It is malleable. It changes based on environmental stimuli.

The University of Utah website says this about epigenetics: "The genome dynamically responds to the environment. Stress, diet, behavior, toxins and other factors activate chemical switches that regulate gene expression."

From this knowledge, one can conclude that human tendencies shift according to nurturance and development. Humans express either violence or love according to their surroundings, which implies that anarchism does not automatically devolve into madness and chaos. Instead, society organizes according to people's individual choices (and will be both good and bad) with people solving problems of their own volition.

Those seeking to discredit anarchy go on to say, "We need government to protect us from murderers and robbers."

Besides being contradictory, this argument misses key points. For instance: Merchants and philanthropists do not run government. The people in positions of authority do not rely on business exchanges or charitable donations.

Government consists of people holding a monopoly on the "legitimate" use of violence over a geographical region, which means that they acquire their earnings by brute force rather than as a gift or through trade.

If government uses violence to accomplish goals, it metes out social justice in the same way as street gangs. Governments fail to protect and defend people from criminals and instead commit criminal acts against everyone, everywhere. The following question captures the argument from protection: "How can the State protect people from murderers and robbers when it is itself made up of murderers and robbers?"

The obvious answer is that it cannot and will not.

"Under anarchy, the poor and impoverished suffer the most due to the disorder caused by freedom since no one will help them because everyone is greedy," argue the communists.

This position devalues the fact that people organize regardless of government. Voluntary association and cooperation bud in the absence of political power. Goodwill and philanthropy remain an integral part of group dynamics. Charity does not vanish under freedom, and it may multiply because people no longer have their earnings extorted.

Already—without government—millions benefit from the generosity of kind people. To say that the poor and infirm will continue to suffer under anarchy is to say that people are incapable of helping. This argument suggests that without authority, people suddenly become less philanthropic—that people need a government gun to their heads to force them to share. More frighteningly, this position suggests that only the angelic men with political power maintain the ability to aid the suffering. But governments consist of criminals, not angels.

Thus, no sane person appoints them to care for the meek. Doing this would be like asking Jeffrey Dahmer to babysit children or run a nursing home. True concern is when peaceful and free people network and use their skills to care for the impoverished.

This occurs through charity and charitable organizations.

An article from *The Huffington Post* discussed novelist J.K. Rowling's donations. The article explained that Rowling lost her "billionaire" status by giving 160 million dollars to charitable causes. She accomplished this without a gun pressed against her temple.

The above example shows that people are capable of kindness and love without the threat of violence against them.

Dispelling Bad Arguments

Another common argument from well-meaning people goes: "In the absence of Big Brother, roving bands of gangs will rise up and rule over everyone. Therefore, abolishing government would be detrimental to society."

If government amounts to a group of violent criminals, then the fear that violent criminals might take over is illogical and circular. Using this argument is like saying that if people abolish slavery, it will return a decade later. If people remove an inflamed appendix, it will grow back and become inflamed again. If people eradicate human sacrifice, it will resurface tomorrow, on and on ad nauseam.

No one dying of cancer opts out of surgery for fear the cancer might return, especially if undergoing the operation might save their life. No one worries about imagined consequences if they benefit from taking immediate action. No one allows a violent, immoral group of tyrants to continue ruling based on the irrational fear that more will crop up in their absence.

The aforesaid complaint reeks of Stockholm syndrome and does not constitute a valid argument.

Further, if a moral action faces a practical one, the moral action takes priority because the "practical" one results in evil. Too many people fall for the charm of "practicality" because it appears logical even though choosing it allows for certain death, enslavement, rape, robbery, and genocide—all opposite of the love and morality that characterize anarchy.

For instance, some believed (and some still do) that owning human chattel during the 19th century was a matter of practicality and that simply releasing slaves would have been impractical because it would have caused economic ruin in the southern states. However, if people adhere to practicality, regardless of the truth, they de facto advocate slavery, which is an unacceptable position for decent, moral people.

When freedom advocates argue for total liberty, liberty haters often say, "Move to Somalia if you do not like it here." These folks assume Somalia is an alternate dimension wasteland, like something out of Stephen King's *Dark Tower* series. They assume violence and bloodshed arose out of the stateless environment and that Somalians murder each other for control of people and property.

In reality, the Somali government collapsed due to inherent corruption and instability. In the aftermath, gangs now murder each other to regain that power not because anarchy molds people into killers but because political power lures and charms psychopaths. If anything, the "argument from Somalia" validates anarchy.

The Somalia problem demonstrates that people go to great lengths to gain political power and that assaulting and murdering others highlights these lengths. Thus, if the idea of government-as-necessity turned into a myth, the roving gangs would be considered criminals rather than aspiring politicians and leaders.

To characterize the situation another way, American politicians are the kind of people who murder and pillage for power. They resemble the kind of people who are ravaging Somalia and attempting to impose their will. This state of affairs does not bode well for the defense of political authority.

In addition, although gang warfare consumes Somalia, the private sector blossoms. Outside of this rampant warfare, the market thrives. The standard of living continually increases while the cost of goods and services continually decreases.

In 1996, Robert P. Murphy wrote a brilliant article titled "Anarchy in Somalia" that referenced these statistics.

Somalia: How Has Life Changed?		
Index	1991	2011 (or latest)
Life expectancy	46 years	50 years
Birth rate	46	44
Death rate	19	16
GDP per capita	$210	$600
Infant mortality	116 deaths <1yr, per 1,000 births	109 deaths <1yr, per 1,000 births
Access to safe water	35%	29%
Adult literacy	24%	38%

Some statistical problems exist. Access to safe water decreased, which implies some unconsidered variables. The birth rate declined, which is ambiguous. The overall stats, however, showed that society does not crumble in a state of freedom. Civilization grows and begins to prosper. This represents spontaneous order arising from the muck of statist violence.

For the Love of Anarchy

As with Somalia, when people think "anarchy," they think "chaos," but anarchy drives people forward. Government stays out of many areas of people's lives, allowing them the freedom to make decisions. Sadly, people revile the idea of anarchy and label it dangerous and evil, anyway.

Stefan Molyneux expressed this fear: "We love the anarchy we live and fear the anarchy we imagine."

He was right.

Every time people brush their teeth, watch television, go for a hike, cook hamburgers, or make love, they are living anarchically. Everyone enjoys intimate time with their spouses and lovers; everybody embraces the freedom to join a chess club, bridge club, or Toastmasters; everyone chooses their work and career path, and everyone places emphasis and pride on their hobbies, tastes, likes, and dislikes with minimal government involvement.

Where Big Brother abstains, anarchy flourishes.

Condemning anarchy means condemning people's own lives and decisions. Shunning liberty means supporting sociopaths, warmongers, slaveholders, and tyrants. It damns humanity to the uncivil ghost town of oppression and denies the compassion and cooperation rooted in mutual respect and love; it ushers in the blood and bombs everyone fears.

Ideas of anarchy fester with images of mayhem, blood, and bombs due to the utopian dream of the centrally planned society, which rests on the notion that with enough threats and guns, societal bliss unfolds and blooms like a flower.

The truth contradicts this idea.

Truth expresses the fact human happiness, kindness, equality, and freedom correspond to the individual's ability to live his own life unburdened by controls and threats. Freedom is not the ugly state of nature portrayed by the tyrants and control freaks; freedom answers why so many people are trying to gain as much wiggle room in their lives as possible and why many have turned their backs on government.

Lovers thus value anarchism because chaos and violence represent the opposite inclination of love, which is hatred.

People must steer clear of hatred for the future's sake. If the responsibility unleashed by freedom fails to take hold, the consequences will bear hardest on children, who represent everyone's appreciation of liberty since the lovemaking that produces children occurs in a state of pure, uninhibited, and raw anarchy.

Nature of the State

March 29, 2011

Donning a uniform does not make you exempt from morality.

November 24, 2012

A few reasons why I support freedom from government:

1. I maintain that the initiation of physical violence and coercion is immoral.

Government is built on the initiation of physical force and violence for those who don't unquestioningly obey.

2. I believe people should keep the fruits of their labor. To take anything the laborer earns is a form of slavery.

Government takes a percentage of every laborer's hard work (taxation), thus enslaving people on a grand scale.

3. Governments trick people into believing their violence is righteous.

This makes living with friends and family difficult because they are propagandized into believing that the violence of government is a necessary evil, when in reality, initiating violence on another is never good or moral.

4. Governments wage wars against other governments and thus compel "citizens" to fight and die for their causes.

War is heartbreaking because it causes people fighting for governments, i.e., men who claim the right to rule, to believe they are fighting for their "country" and for "freedom." In reality, they are pawns in a game of thrones, losing their lives for no reason.

December 10, 2012

Insights from reading and watching *A Game of Thrones: A Song of Ice and Fire*:

No matter how noble or virtuous you pretend to be, playing a game of thrones—a game of power— will tear your virtues and principles asunder, and if you try to live by those virtues and principles, you will undoubtedly lose against the sociopaths. You can see this with the Starks of Winterfell.

Having power in the form of a State or government attracts the most wretched sociopaths like metal to a magnet. Even if characters change throughout the story to become what appears to be more virtuous, they still maintain that defending the State is a noble or necessary cause. You can see this in the

Lannisters, who are a bunch of evil sociopathic assholes who push 10-year-old children out of windows to protect their position in the ranks of power.

For me, *A Song of Ice and Fire* is ultimately about how absolute power corrupts absolutely and how those vying for power are after their own ends. They don't give two shits about the "common folk" or the "people." Their sole concern is the domination and physical subjugation of others.

July 17, 2013

I hate thieves because morally, stealing from a person is the same as stealing their time and energy; essentially, it's an assault on the person. This applies to all individuals, including those who call themselves "government" and wear fancy uniforms and suits.

August 9, 2013

Quit worshiping soldiers; and just maybe, one day, we won't have tyrannical overlords who send them to die for insane reasons. Support the soldiers by not condoning their activities and not condoning political wars, which amount to unfettered, wholesale murder.

August 11, 2013

Wake up.

Stop defending the government by condemning victims with the shameful guilt trip, "It's the law. You broke it, so face the consequences."

That's nonsense. If the politicians enacted a law tomorrow that mandated the immediate imprisonment or murder of thousands, would you cower down in obedience and continue to stress that it was the "law" and that those who break it deserve it? If you do this, you are complicit in those kidnappings and murders.

The "law" is not some commandment from a deity on high. It is an arbitrary command scribbled on a piece of paper by a sociopath in a suit and tie. Realize this truth and wake up before we drive our species into an early grave.

August 22, 2013

The phrase "war crimes" is misleading, as if to suggest war is generally valid but that there are crimes within warfare. In reality, *war is a crime*. War is mass murder cloaked in uniforms and rhetoric.

January 9, 2014

If nature causes people to be violent to any degree, government and military boot camps bring it out in its fullest, most despicable form.

January 31, 2014

What it tells me when people argue in favor of government: "I am perfectly okay with putting a gun to your head and making you do what I want, even if you are my friend or sister or father. Just because we are close or share blood does not mean you are safe from my violence."

The aforesaid theme shows how disingenuous and violent our relationships can be, and it makes me wonder how we can call the whole of our social relationships "civilization."

Relationships are too important and beautiful to be mired in the muck of statist violence. Let your friend or relative live as they see fit. You will see your relationship with them grow and prosper. It will also allow for the development of a truly civilized society—not the fake one that surrounds us like a bunch of barbarians masquerading in shawls and dresses.

February 10, 2014

The difference between politicians and leeches is that the leeches fall off when they've had their fill.

February 20, 2014

What is government by representation? Is it the idea that another man has your best wishes at heart, knows you inside and out, and wants to take care of you?

Representative government is a grand deception.

People are unique and different. No single person can represent anyone or act like he knows what you want in any way. "Representation" through government is a lie that makes you feel like you have choices. It is a front for servitude. It is the pretense that you can change things by talking to your representative.

A representative is like a slaver who allows the slaves to believe they're free because they imagine the slaver works for them. In reality, the representative does what he wants with his imagined power and authority.

Don't get caught up in the bullshit. You are your own person. You live for yourself. You don't need another to make decisions for you. Assert your existence and resist this subtle and demeaning method of cheating you out of being yourself for yourself. Reject human ownership through this pseudo-representation nonsense. Clench your fist. Walk your path. Never tell sociopaths your needs, wants, desires, or preferences. Take the power back by trusting yourself, shunning evildoers, and living with unrelenting rational self-interest.

June 28, 2014

War is murder and insanity. Think about it. Men get together and murder each other, and they do not even know each other. They have no grudge. They just follow the commands of their political masters. They just follow what their commander tells them about the other guys. War is a children's telephone game with bullets, and soldiers go about it unthinkingly because the other guy has been dehumanized. War is thus the incitement of hollow rage without cause. It is the most batshit crazy, medieval, caveman activity man has ever cherished... and it has to end. People have to stop listening to psychopaths. They have to stop believing that orders to murder other humans have validity. There's no real rage. There is no offense. Everyone must put down their weapons and consider how it all started. Think about the insanity of the very idea of "war."

June 30, 2014

There's a prominent idea that government protects you, but this is a myth. Government enslaves you through its racket. Can an entity that steals your labor, commands you, surveils you, IDs you, and keeps tabs on you be your rightful protector? No. They cannot protect you any more than a mafia protects a business. Government exists to take advantage of you by offering you mafia-style protection in which the government promises not to hurt you if you comply and give them part of your earnings.

Now, you can pretend that the "force" aspect of the equation is moot by citing your voluntary participation, but a mentally disturbed person can also cite that he freely gave his money to an armed bandit on the street. Does this make the action voluntary? Or is the mentally disturbed person just fabricating or imagining his cooperative participation? Don't fall for these tall tales anymore. Come to see reality and truth. It's the best option for starting our ascent toward a more peaceful, less insane civilization.

July 3, 2014

Government is the shallow water where the sharks congregate. If someone has a hunger for the helpless and ignorant, he will seek out government—this refuge, this shallow sea of blood where his feeding can go on without consequence and without end. Though the water feels right and good, we must resist the swim because of what lurks beneath. We must notice the waves of red, the bodies, organs, legs, arms, hands, and heads. And we must search for purer waters, or better yet, head for land and walk upright on our own two feet as we were meant to do. Don't swim anymore. There's a whole world waiting away from that evil gulf, that place of death. We are not prey, not victims of this silly idea that we only have one option in life: the swim.

April 2, 2015

If you are not an anarchist—that is, if you assume that government and power are necessary to force people to live in certain ways—then you might want to reexamine your assumptions about the world. Do you want to be told how to live and how to solve problems? Do you want to risk the vast corruptions of power that have led to the Maos, Hitlers, and Stalins of the world? Isn't it time to say enough is enough? Have the blood-soaked annals of history not taught you the lessons about the nature of government? Should you allow the continuous rape of your body and mind to protect the illusion that power is necessary? Is it not time to reconsider your religious devotion to power and start awakening to the awful truths of the world? After all, it is the knowledge of these truths that will help pave the way toward more freedom, peace, and love. The time is ripe; it is now or never.

July 14, 2015

Government is the ultimate archaism. It is the one institution that stifles humanity by keeping everyone in a state of perpetual primitivism. It disallows societal advancement by forcing the population to live by its antiquated and convoluted laws. It is bloodletting in an age of medicinal cures. It is the horse-drawn carriage in a world of automobiles. It is violence in the time of peaceful capitalism. It is the one cult that finally has to wither away and be lost in the shameful records of history. Let humanity move into this next phase of existence. The age of infancy and suckling at the teat has finally come to an end.

December 24, 2015

How disturbing is it that random strangers have "authority" to pull over cars and harass and possibly extort the occupants? You know we live in a twisted society when a roadside ransacking is approved under the color of some artifact called "law." If a random stranger pulls over another person to harass and extort them, it is considered a grievous crime, but if someone called a "police officer" does it, all of the sudden it is acceptable—commendable, even. How in the world is this activity even remotely sane? How is this predatory behavior considered a normal function of society?

There is nothing good or great about driving down roads with the fear that you might be legally harassed, extorted, kidnapped, or shot for peaceably doing what the hell you want. Oddly enough, however, some people cheer this behavior and laud the gangbangers who do it. We all have to start condemning the pernicious activity of highway shakedowns and berating the assholes who perform them. A civilized society does not congratulate abject thuggery simply because it is normal and lawful.

May 17, 2016

When a cop pulls me over, I am reminded of that oafish, ugly troll that lurks under the bridge in fairy tales, shaking down travelers. The troll slinks out from under the bridge and demands coins from the traveler, and if he refuses, the troll holds him upside down and empties the contents of his pockets.

That's what the cop is: that hideous, bullying troll that hides beneath the bridge and robs innocent people under the threat of a bludgeoning.

June 3, 2016

Government destroys people's ability to love and connect with each other and to see things clearly.

But why?

Bureaucracy and political talk are opposites of authentic communication and truth. They are based in fantasy.

Fraud and deceit characterize every word uttered by political creatures. All the evil governments commit is hidden behind jargon, legalese, and euphemistic speech.

Instead of murder, it is just collateral damage.

Instead of genocide, it is just war.

Instead of robbery, it is just a tax.

Instead of a kidnapping victim, it is a lawbreaking prisoner.

Instead of a war against people, it is a war against drugs.

The men and women uttering these twisted non-truths are hollow inside.

The political game has molded them into believing mayhem and destruction are acceptable ways of handling problems even though they conceal the reality of their actions behind fraudulent language.

This is why compassion dies with government: words are altered to obliterate reality, which alters the character of individuals, turning them into something monstrous and devoid of empathy.

Vladimir Nabokov summed up his feelings on psychopathic politicizing with these words:

"It is hard, I submit, to loathe bloodshed, including war, more than I do, but it is still harder to exceed my loathing of the very nature of totalitarian states in which massacre is only an administrative detail."

June 22, 2016

One of the greatest frauds about why governments exist is the belief that they provide safety. But governments unequivocally undermine safety with all their laws, regulations, and controls.

In reality, safety is an illusion; no one can guarantee the safety of another.

The only thing we can do is care for each other and demonstrate compassion and empathy. We can only help others as much as we care for them, and using the coercion and force of government thoroughly compromises this capacity for love and attachment.

July 9, 2016

After the Dallas shootings, false narratives about "anarchy" have been circulated by various media outlets and other fear mongers.

But ironically, combative reactions against government tyranny are not "anarchy" in the etymological sense of the term. The storytellers are simply trying to bolster the "anarchy is political disorder" trope.

In reality, all these killings have been a direct result of government and police brutality against innocent and downtrodden individuals.

"Anarchy," in their fraudulent use of the term, then, implies the opposite of its definition. It means destruction and chaos in the presence of government.

This is a false definition, of course, because anarchy just means "without rulers."

And without rulers, their twisted vision of anarchy as political disorder would not exist because there would not be a political order to incite these defensive attacks in the first place.

September 20, 2016

I am staggered every time I read something that tries to suggest democracy is categorically better than authoritarianism.

Let's be truthful: Democracy is a governmental system. It is therefore authoritarian. Any social setup that relies on forcing others to do the bidding of kings, politicians, or other sociopaths is by its very nature authoritarian. Democracy is not an exception to the rule. Just because it is touted as a form of freedom and justice does not mean that is true.

Just a glance at its condition around the world suggests that "democracy" has brought about a level of nastiness and slavery on par with many of the old regimes and other barbaric systems.

How did this happen? Democracy isn't any different than those other systems. It is still empowered by violence. It is still evil festooned with social justification. It is still the mechanism that allows the inhumane and indecent to rise to the upper echelons of society and treat the rest of humanity as beasts of burden and chattel.

So, no. Absolutely not. Democracy is not something novel or special. It is still a broken authoritarian system.

Let's work to change people's minds about it and get people geared up for real freedom, which will be devoid of government, authority, and vast power imbalances. Let's replace these systems with compassionate and peaceful institutions. Let's rework all these shitbrained values and create a world that is not so bloated with insanity and heartlessness.

The only non-authoritarian governmental "system" is no system.

October 14, 2016

What is the best way to create a society full of people who are incentivized to harass, assault, extort, and murder others?

Allow that society to be run by an organization called government, which specializes in all of the above.

That is called leading by example.

January 2, 2017

It does not matter whether the president is Republican, Democrat, black, white, female, male, or an alien from Zeta Reticuli.

All presidents run a system that is built on your subjugation. All presidents steal, kill, maim, and destroy.

This is the uncomfortable and unmentionable truth of governmental systems.

The system is always pro-violence and anti-humanitarian.

February 18, 2017

Many people say government is inevitable.

This has been the world's most destructive self-fulfilling prophecy.

February 25, 2017

Government is a criminal organization that siphons off the lifeblood of the population. It's a cancerous entity that deserves to be eliminated so humankind can push forward unimpeded by nonsensical regulations, rules, laws, and other uncivilized controls. A world without government or the governed will be a world of happiness and decency. It will be a world we can pridefully provide for our children without shame in our hearts.

March 8, 2017

Government is a magnet for psychopaths. So long as governments exist, the worst people in society will clamor to be recruited into its ranks.

In this way, government is cancer. Its malignancy is unparalleled, and it becomes more virulent as it spreads.

The cure for this disease is total ablation. It must be removed from the flesh of humanity. Once gone, humankind will finally begin to heal.

People will start to realize that organizational violence has been the catalyst for much of the evil in the world. They will also realize all violence, including family violence, once empowered and emboldened governments.

With government gone, every act of initiatory aggression will be laid bare for the unacceptable act that it is, and people will look back on all violent law-making organizations as historical mistakes. They will know that heretofore no government body should ever be accepted as legitimate, decent, or humane.

Governments will be shunned and condemned forever.

The Anatomy of Warfare and Terrorism

11/28/2015

Many people believe Islamic jihadists loathe freedom. They are painted as barbarians who despise Western civilization, who want to watch it burn, and who want to kill indiscriminately. There is truth to their hatred, but it is not a totally random and arbitrary hatred. That is an oversimplification. Their hatred is partly a product of tribal engineering.

Tribal engineering is the process by which culture transmits values and memes to its young to inculcate them with the idea that dying for their culture is acceptable. The West is not immune to tribal engineering, either. Western hate is similar to Muslim hate. Everywhere, people are trained by various culture doctors to loathe a politically manufactured boogeyman. The culture doctors include parents, educators, politicians, and religious leaders.

This "mind molding" is typical of tribal psychology. Once tribal leaders create enemies, they instill in the tribe a sense of fear and hatred toward those enemies. They spread this anger through education, religion, propaganda, sporting matches, and magazines like *Dabiq* or media stations like America's *Fox News*.

This cultural "education" prepares a person to kill and die for their country and ideology. The tribal engineers ready their countrymen for self-sacrifice in a kind of collective blood ceremony. Ayn Rand described this ritual. She called man the sacrificial animal and blamed altruism for it. Altruism is the idea of sacrificing oneself to aid others, even if it is detrimental to the self. She said collective altruism inspires men to lay down their lives and kill for the nation. They do this because they are okay with sacrificing individual values for collective values.

The Blood Sacrifice

Barbara Ehrenreich's book, *Blood Rites: Origins and History of the Passions of War*, elaborates on this topic. It delves into the ritualistic and psychohistorical aspects of warfare and terrorism, but it disregards traditional ideas of genetic predispositions toward violence. Instead, for her, warfare is a continuation of ritualistic sacrifice conducted by prehistorical and savage humans.

These early humans imagined themselves as predatory animals and mimicked their gory feeding frenzies. These uncivilized humans eviscerated and decapitated their victims at the altar as if they were prey. This is what the Aztec culture did to its victims of the blood debt. Ehrenreich writes:

> The body would be disposed of in various ways, such as feeding animals at the zoo or putting on display (the heads). There are some accounts of cannibalism, but it's uncertain if this was practiced to any great extent. There were other ways that humans would be sacrificed – shot with arrows, drowned, burned, or otherwise mutilated. Killing in a fight (like the Roman gladiators) also took place.

According to Ehrenreich, these blood debt sacrifices are the sociocultural roots of warfare. It is a form of collective tribalism that has an evolutionary basis relating to how humans were a prey species, and it has transformed into mass "sacrifices" called warfare or terrorism.

It is helpful to bear in mind that Ehrenreich primarily cited anecdotal and loose history as evidence. Nonetheless, the material offers an alternative way to view human warmongering and terrorism, which all cultures tend to have in common.

Blowback and Revenge

The cultural programming inflicted by radical Islam is compounded by another problem: Western imperialism. The American government has caused the deaths of thousands of innocents. The CIA has a term for the unintended consequences of this "collateral damage": blowback. It occurs, for example, when the agency sends covert operatives into a country with missions to destabilize governments.

These missions often cause civilian casualties and destruction to the nation's infrastructure. Women and children die by the dozens. The consequences of blowback do not include the emotional carnage wreaked by American bombing campaigns, which are known for hitting weddings and peaceful villages. This causes more blowback.

Blowback often involves retaliation against American acts of "terrorism." Radicals become infuriated that their families were murdered. Their prior cultural indoctrination is intensified, and they become jihadists who are further radicalized against Western "crusaders."

The terrorists who attacked the Bataclan in Paris in 2015, killing over 100 people, hinted at why they committed the atrocity. Survivors overheard the terrorists' words while they reloaded their rifles. The *Guardian* article, "'It looked like a battlefield': the full story of what happened in the Bataclan," caught the details: "The gunmen shouted that they were there because of Syria and Iraq and particularly François Hollande's airstrikes on Syria. They said they would 'make you understand' what women and children were suffering in those air raids."

Recruit Psychology

Terrorists fight in a guerrilla or urban tactical manner because they do not have a stable government army. But fascinatingly, terror organizations echo governmental military forces in recruiting strategy. They only differ in combat style and target acquisition. Nonetheless, the reasons why recruits sign up have startling similarities across cultures.

Young men who join either terrorist organizations or standing armies are tricked into it as a result of cultural engineering. Recruiters also play on young men's urge for wanderlust and excitement. They tell them about the awesome adventures the military and guerilla groups provide. The whole enterprise is painted under an idyllic, Marco Polo type of quest. But there is an even stronger reason why many recruits join organizations: monetary gain.

For example, in the United States, when someone asks a soldier why they signed up, they often say they did it for the money. Indeed, joining the military can be a lucrative career for a high school graduate. It includes adventure, as well as adoration from a herd of sycophants. Unsurprisingly, Islamic jihadists are also motivated by money. An article from *Yahoo Finance* described their financial motivations.

"According to Abu Khaled, a large number of people are joining ISIS because they need money. After joining the militants, people are paid in US dollars instead of Syrian liras. Abu Khaled said that ISIS also runs its own currency exchanges."

Religious Context and Cultural Annihilation

Part of what motivates people to cheer for terrorism or "war" is their fear of cultural annihilation or the destruction of their values.

For instance, in the West, people see "freedom" as an important value embedded in their culture. They talk about "freedom" incessantly, like it's a mantra, even though most people can't define it. They imagine that "freedom" is at stake, so they take up arms in its defense. It is vague and ambiguous cultural memes like "freedom" that spur hate, warfare, strife, and terrorism. Many people in the West are willing to die and kill for "freedom" regardless of what being free means to them. And arguably, they are not free in the slightest.

An American Psychological Association article called "Understanding Terrorism" examined this issue from the Islamic perspective.

In a more global sense, a fear of cultural annihilation may help fuel terrorist sentiments, says psychologist and terrorism expert Fathali Moghaddam, PhD, of Georgetown University's department of psychology. In "How Globalization Spurs Terrorism: The Lopsided Benefits of One World and Why That Fuels Violence" (Praeger, 2008), Moghaddam argues that rapid globalization has forced disparate cultures into contact with one another and is threatening the domination or disappearance of some groups—a cultural version of "survival of the fittest."

Besides globalization, religion in all societies has been a common predictor of warfare and bloodletting. Everyone knows that throughout history, religious crusades for God and country were terrifyingly commonplace. This religious warfare is still practiced today, but it is not only Islam that practices religious warfare. America does the same thing, except it is couched in the machismo of militarism and neoconservatism rather than jihadist sentiment.

Statism is a kind of religion. It becomes intimately intertwined with mono-theistic paths like Christianity or Islam, and this exacerbates the war trance and makes people excited and hungry to commit murder. Religious warfare is also a global phenomenon. It is not unique to jihadists, but it is certainly a major reason why they fight.

Conclusion: Anti-Culture, Dis-Education

The anatomy of terrorism and warfare is multifaceted and diverse. It is nearly impossible to understand when looking at it from a singular perspective. Almost all simple answers are false, but there are clear indicators that point toward terrorist or militaristic behavior. It has to do with culture, tribal engineering, and individual motivations, and no culture is immune to them.

People embedded in a certain culture can only see "truth" from their own perspective—from the information fed to them by their government, parents, and culture. But if they purposely unplug and examine reality objectively, they can see why young adults are spurred to kill and sacrifice their lives. In the case of the jihadists, culture, the desire to meet basic needs, and genuine anger motivate them.

The only way to end the insanity is to advocate for a total ceasefire, which can only occur if cultural myths are busted through a kind of anti-culture, dis-education program. People have to be informed about their biases, and they also have to be desensitized to various cultures. We must also replace the na-tion-state with a worldly community that advocates respect for all humankind.

But the only way to succeed is to spread information and speak with people. Pointing more guns, blowing children up, terrorizing nightclubs, advocating for government, and dehumanizing cultures only invites a vicious cycle of bloodshed and destruction. But with everyone's vigilance and compassion, we can stop terrorism and warfare. Stepping up to the pulpit and delivering proclamations of nonviolence and goodwill can catalyze a paradigm shift. It will also create lasting change for peace. The pen is mightier than the sword, indeed.

Indoctrination, Myopia, and Mind Control

August 29, 2011

Public education is perfect for children. They get to learn about all kinds of random facts, and they are taught discipline and how to behave properly in all contexts. It makes them good, well-mannered citizens. We should keep having to hand our money over to fund this benevolent enterprise!

August 15, 2013

So many people have their ideas handed to them on a platter and spoon-fed. These ideas are a mixture of personal beliefs, nonsense their parents taught them, and goop their governments brainwashed into them.

Too few people develop their thinking and behavior from core principles, and this is the tragic effect of a cannibalistic mind-eating culture.

August 16, 2013

Why is it that we feel better when we call something by a different name? Why should anyone feel better about murder when it's called "collateral damage"? Why should anyone feel better about torture when it's called "rendition" and "enhanced interrogation"? Why is theft suddenly acceptable when it's referred to as "taxation"?

Why do we so easily allow language to alter our perception of reality and seemingly turn evil into good?

August 16, 2013

People are so out of touch with reality they believe we have free markets. They fail to see government coercion at every bend and turn, so when some economic collapse occurs, like Detroit's bankruptcy, people rally to blame "free markets." This is the height of indoctrination and the pinnacle of absurdity.

November 10, 2013

There's nothing more aggravating than people who act out against peaceful ideas, secure in accepting the violent status quo and afraid of moving beyond their comfort zone.

Wake up. There's virtue, clarity, and happiness in peaceful principles.

November 21, 2013

I loathe what the Prussian model of education has done to people. It has created people who do not know how to think deeply enough to see fundamental contradictions in their own views of reality. It has also created broken people who simply bow to authority rather than questioning it.

January 11, 2014

There's a notion people harbor that I despise: it's this idea that people want to send their children to public schools just to get them out of their hair.

These are your children! They are your blood, and you want to get rid of them by sending them to a brain-deadening indoctrination camp?

Remember that children are *your* responsibility by virtue of your decision to have sex to create them. Do you feel no accountability for the pain and suffering you put your children through? Do you have no sense of care or concern for their well-being? Children are what mold our future. Please take note of how you treat them and where you send them.

January 15, 2014

The State trains you for moral illiteracy and prepares you for a life of docile servitude.

February 22, 2014

The State does not give a shit that speech is free because the slaves under the State, who suffer from Stockholm syndrome, will do anything in their power to silence people, including issuing threats of violence.

Friends, let us grow beyond that mindset. To inhibit speech is to regress. It is to edge on accepting violence to censor various opinions. It is tyranny rising.

March 3, 2014

There is a phenomenon in the psychology of cults that allows them to easily recruit people. It is called the "foot-in-the-door" phenomenon. The cult first approaches broken and helpless people, promising them a better life, and then subverts them to the religiosity of the cult. The State is even more cunning. They find you as you are exiting the womb, and they start propagandizing you and naming you as one of them before you have the cognitive capacity to defend yourself. It's the most vicious and evil method by which the cult sinks its claws into you. They have their foot in the door before you have yours upon solid ground.

March 4, 2014

The fear of freedom envelops us. We have been brainwashed to believe that freedom turns us into barbarians. But what if I said we are already a bunch of barbarians? No brainwashing necessary. Believe it. But know this: If we are barbaric cavemen with no ability to control ourselves, why would we want to give just a small minority of us barbarians power over the rest? That just sounds like a recipe for disaster, but it does not have to be like this. Even as barbarians, we can choose not to believe in authority and rulership. We can choose not to allow a couple of us to run roughshod over the rest.

March 11, 2014

I was reading about the "Rape of Nanking," a historical atrocity. Here is the gist: During the Second Sino-Japanese War, a group of men in military costumes (Japanese) occupied Nanking in China and raped and murdered the people there. The estimated dead range starts at 200,000 but could be higher, with scholars disagreeing on the exact number due to the desecration of bodies and lack of documentation.

Here are my thoughts on the matter:

End nationalism. End government. End belief in authority.

When you have this mixture of bullshit propaganda with absolute belief in rulers, you get a situation where military leaders can easily brainwash people into believing that the enemy is subhuman and deserving of death. This dehumanizing factor makes people feel good and justified in hurting and murdering others, even innocents.

The Japanese soldiers showed how they felt about their enemy in Nanking by sadistically raping innocent women and then desecrating their bodies in ways I won't mention here. They showed how they felt by randomly executing villagers and torturing people. Two Japanese officers even had a contest to see how many people's heads they could chop off in a certain amount of time... and they photographed it for pleasure.

Seriously, what kind of sick, psychotic individuals would do this? It is unimaginable, but it only happens because of myths and rhetoric that make people feel good about it. Barbaric acts like this must come to an end, but it will only stop when people stop worshiping cultural abstractions and pretending war is somehow necessary or desirable.

December 30, 2014

It irritates me when people my age or a generation or two younger find no interest in helping subvert the political world. I am especially irritated when people my age ask why I spend so much time arguing politics or trying to convince people of anarchism and freedom.

Here is the reason:

We have little time on this earth, and I don't intend to live life under the thumb of a bunch of soul-sucking, droll, and lifeless bureaucrats. I intend to do what I want and live life how I see fit, and I don't appreciate mind-numbing, low-IQ troglodytes telling me how to live life and what is best for me. I am a lover of freedom, and I intend to experiment with the varieties of life with all of my being regardless of their tired and pathetic attempts to stop me.

I don't see why people my age—who have had time and experience with technology and alternative media—can't see what is right in front of them. There is no excuse. They have not grown too old to change. They live on the internet. They have lived in violent and abusive family environments. They have been accosted by the bullies who call themselves peace officers. They have grown up in a hellhole of a world, which has already been ripped to shreds by warfare and dystopian Orwellian controls. They have basically experienced the same things as me, yet their maturity levels are juvenile, and they ignore the atrocities all around them.

I mean, my God, the evil is ubiquitous. If the people my age are still falling for the propaganda, they have either not done enough good acid or simply obeyed every authority figure their whole lives without question. Maybe they have not browsed a single naughty or illegal website in their life, where this information is spread wholesale without fail.

Because of their lack of responsibility, laziness, and desire to live in immutable comfort, they have chosen to let the world crumble without so much as a peep, and this is tragically irredeemable and inexcusable. If they're not thinking on at least libertarian terms by now and questioning all authority, they might as well put their diaper back on and start sucking a pacifier.

February 8, 2015

There are not only physical barriers to freedom because of State violence, but there are also cognitive barriers. Too many people believe they are already free. This is due to psychological warfare. When the ruling classes allow a certain amount of leeway for citizens, they believe they are "free," yet they are too complacent to acknowledge the bars that cage them, to recognize their serfdom. In this, they express loyalty to their captors in the form of Stockholm syndrome.

The same thing happened to human chattel in the antebellum South. Many slaves thought they were free. They were propagandized to believe this pseudo-truth. They were kept from education, and they vehemently reviled those who spoke against their servitude. As Johann Wolfgang von Goethe observed, "None are more hopelessly enslaved than those who falsely believe they are free."

This problem is the same problem anarchists face with government apologists. Thus, liberty lovers must fill their lungs with truth and breathe it out. At every footfall, they must demolish the lies invented by the State and disallow the twisting of innocent minds. They must maintain clarity and liberate the brain.

The time has come to open every human to the reality that no person may govern another; that ultimately, all people are sovereign creatures, governable only by their own will and conscience.

June 17, 2015

I despise political correctness, yet I am surrounded by it. Instead of focusing on the real causes of cultural poisons, people indoctrinated by government nonsense focus on politically safe notions of race, class, and gender, which revolve around not hurting feelings and accepting differences in people.

I get it. These issues are important for showing the importance of empathy, but they also benefit government propaganda schemes. When people remain obsessed with differences, they forget about the violence government regularly commits.

Isn't it convenient? If governments encourage people to focus on each other's differences and exploit people's emotions, then the rulers can get away with violating everyone's rights on a daily basis. They even get away with murder because people have become absorbed with a smorgasbord of emotionally charged distractions.

This is how totalitarian psychology works—and how political correctness blots out the elephant in the room.

September 23, 2015

You can tell how brainwashed and confused people are when they view monsters like Vladimir Lenin and Che Guevara as heroes. These guys were insane megalomaniacs who murdered and imprisoned anyone who opposed their violent ideologies. It is a testament to statist indoctrination that various populations see these men as martyrs and heroes. A lot of work has to be done to help people realize what kind of traits and actions deserve reverence. Murdering people for ideological purposes is certainly not something to be proud of; it is the epitome of anti-humanitarian and socialist thinking. It is the pinnacle and success of "education." It's time to reconsider what constitutes good and decent.

October 13, 2015

Step 1. Child-rearing: Destroy the child's emotional circuitry through culturally accepted abuses, including spanking and coercing—which occur throughout childhood—so the child only knows fear and resentment.

Step 2. Education: Funnel children through educational systems that elevate obedience and authority above learning, creativity, and individuality. Instill a sense of tribal loyalty and altruistic nationalism. Mold the person into good, upright citizen drones.

Step 3. Workforce: The individual is now ready to join the workforce, where his money can be stolen via predatory tax regiments without even a thought of its legitimacy because he is totally subservient to the system.

Step 4. War: Now that the individual is fully indoctrinated and emotionally detached, he can sign up to murder other human beings without moral trepidation or emotional impact. All his subsequent education and rearing prepared him for his duty. His life now belongs wholly to the State and its machinery. His soul is obliterated under the delusional pretense of fighting for freedom. Every country or tribe goes through similar motions, some with less freedom, but every murderous action is shrouded by cries of freedom, religion, a common enemy, or another obsession. It is shared psychopathy.

Step 5. Mental Anguish: If the individual returns from war, his violent deeds and experiences return to him in the form of "PTSD," which is simply how an emotionally frozen person deals with horror and atrocity. Metaphorically, it is a form of punishment for aiding and abetting evil and committing violence. It is the price these poor souls have to suffer for relying on their toxic culture to teach them "decent values."

Step 6. Vicious Cycle: If the individual survives and has children, the acculturation and indoctrination continue, perpetuating the cycle of social hell and damnation.

We must all work to change this culture and mentality, and I believe it starts with parenting. We should not have to see so much evil and destruction. We should not be training people for violence and hatred at a young age. It makes no sense.

Time to break the cycle.

December 3, 2015

If you do not "educate" children, State overseers become flustered and upset. They may even have CPS kidnap children as a result. But ironically, if you dis-educate children—that is, teach them how to think and that obedience to authority is destructive and anti-intellectual—the State will get angry for other reasons. Tribal engineers want children to be educated into a perfectly numb stupor where rote memorization and robotic repetition are of primary importance, and history told from the perspective of the oppressors represents truth. For these State vampires, this is even better than no education, for a child should not have his mind intact upon entering adulthood. As a matter of fact, if you dare to teach children how to reason first from principles and to think for themselves, the mind molders will consider your efforts a stain on "good" education because a child's free-grazing mind poses a threat to the integrity of the system.

The overseers do not want autonomous individuals walking the streets, for among these individuals the rising tide of revolt and dissent festers until it grows so agitated and pus-filled that it bursts into an uncontrollable urge to smite the system. Dis-education, then, is the mantelpiece of the human psyche. The mind yearns to work out problems on its own without interference. It is this vital energy of mind that strives for the abolition of traditional education and the injustices foisted upon children by insect lords who seek to collectiv-ize all uniqueness into a vast honeypot of sameness and rigidity.

But this is not the birthright of humankind. It is an amphitheater of torture and insanity. Deep down, it is not the quintessential desire of the human spirit. Complete sovereignty and creativity are the original aptitudes of all children. Do not let the culture doctors spoil them.

January 13, 2016

It is sad how people line up behind politicians like cattle. Why do these folks follow thugs and sociopaths? Do they not realize the system is a legally sanctioned mafia? Why do they idolize and worship these leeches as if they are actually going to do something to better the world? The backward way of things and people's inability to see what is right in front of them boggles my mind. I have a few ideas on how to help people wake up, but sometimes I just can't help being utterly dumbstruck by how gullible people are and how willing they are to follow killers and maniacs. It is just so glaringly obvious that it is sickening. Is this culture really so seductive that people can't even see how attached to brutality, hatred, murder, and insanity they are? Something has to give because sometimes I have trouble believing this is the actual world we live in. Do you understand how I feel?

January 24, 2016

I am constantly surprised and disturbed at how frequently people worship the police. I browsed the NYPD's Facebook page just to get a glimpse of the insanity, and there are hundreds if not thousands of comments with people giving thanks and licking the boot.

However, being a sycophant for thugs who routinely assault, rob, kidnap, and murder is nothing to be proud of. I try to open channels of peaceful commu-nication with these people to help disabuse them of the authority myth, but it is difficult to cheerfully communicate with folks who get wet and horny for rampant violence against the innocent.

There are a lot of entrenched interests and cultural challenges to break down, but I intend to press on through the haze of batons and bullets to shake people from their reveries. Our world depends on it. Our children's lives are at stake. With every new copsucker that emerges, a child in his or her crib risks death from a drug raid.

We must all continuously scream the truth at the top of our lungs until our voices drown out the excitement for violence and bloodshed.

Change is on the horizon.

February 16, 2016

Even though I have been an anarchist for seven years, the religious-like quality of statism still manages to surprise me and catch me off guard. A lot of the time when I am in public, I just observe the people in my vicinity. In some of these situations, these people banter ceaselessly about politics, presidential campaigns, voting possibilities, and as many intimate details of their political masters as they can muster. They do it in a Jim-Jones-is-speaking kind of way, and I can tell that they do not even consider their words. They just do it automatically, as if they were speaking in tongues and running on autopilot. It is as if the culture has burned itself so far into their souls that it has blotted out their ability to consider alternatives or wonder about the consequences of their political soothsaying.

In most of these situations, I am not able to justify intervening or feel that it would not be worth my time to engage with this audience. I try to pick and choose my battles, and an intelligent individual always selects the high ground if possible. Nonetheless, combating this kind of zealotry is difficult and time-consuming. I have rhetorical methods and processes to help decondition people and see the woofuckery of their ways, but it is always a challenge trying to topple someone's worldview and get them to see things more truthfully and realistically. I guess what I am saying is that I have matured in my approach to campaigning for anarchism and truth—but not everyone is ready to discard their dogmas, even if I use my most polished arguments and techniques to snap them out of their culture comas.

March 24, 2016

Kids in the West join the military for many of the same reasons kids in the Middle East join terrorist organizations. Excitement, money, revenge, and cultural machismo all play into their reasoning. Essentially, they are duped into believing their culture or race is superior.

It turns out that what Westerners call a terrorist attack is the same as what they call a military strike. Terrorism and military action are identical species, except the language is based on different perceptions of who is good and bad. This psychological befuddlement occurs so that one culture's leadership can propagandize its soldiers and serfs to see the other tribe as an evildoer, a terrorist.

The only real difference between terrorism and military action is the scale, the language used to describe the event, and the clothing worn by the attackers. The similarities are obvious: one society instills fear and misery into another tribe and then tries to harm or kill that tribe's people.

In both scenarios, innocent victims die by the dozens, and no one ever "wins." People suffer, economic devastation ensues, flags are raised, and evil politicians and oligarchs are rallied behind.

To stop needless killing, the culture of tribalism must be abolished.

June 20, 2016

The fact that people are willing to cross vast seas and mountainous terrain to murder people they know nothing about because they are following orders from people they know nothing about is the height of social absurdity, cultural violence, and incivility.

July 4, 2016

A gay man from Illinois burned an American flag on July 4, 2016. He was arrested and thrown in a cage for it. I don't agree that burning a flag changes people's minds or exposes the evil of government, but in the current environment, it acts as a form of emotional release.

To kidnap and cage someone for torching their own property is the epitome of fascism and only makes people angrier and more agitated, especially if they already feel marginalized.

Anyone who wishes to harm or punish someone for committing that act has some introspection and self-reflection to perform. If this "country" were truly free, people could do whatever they wanted with their own stuff.

It disgusts me that someone can be arrested and charged with a felony for something superficially harmful like destroying the flag.

It is time for some people to reevaluate what "freedom" means to them.

November 18, 2016

I was doing a little research on American warfare and came across the Haditha massacre in Iraq, where Marines killed 24 unarmed, innocent "civilians."

As I studied, I saw that it was compared to a worse atrocity during the Vietnam war when upwards of 500 innocent civilians were killed in the Mỹ Lai massacre in 1969.

Youths and children were summarily executed in both instances.

I also noticed that in both military murdering sprees, no one was truly held accountable, and servicemen tried to conceal evidence of their crimes. When everything came to light, justice was not served. In the end, no one went to prison or faced any other significant consequences. Only one soldier, 1st Lieut. William Laws Calley Jr., was convicted—only to have Richard Nixon commute his life sentence to house arrest, which lasted only three years. What a joke.

Why is it that when soldiers commit atrocious acts of murder in wartime they get a slap on the wrist, but if a "civilian" murders another civilian they are practically drawn and quartered by the legal system?

It is these little facts about the injustices of the world and the atrocities of government that make me so goddamn livid I can barely breathe.

If this kind of hypocrisy is to be stopped, government must be abolished, and the idea that warfare is acceptable must be removed from human consciousness.

Currently, people are of the mindset that those who wear uniforms and possess rank have some special moral immunity. They believe they can go out on murdering sprees without facing any repercussions.

It's like humans use political myths, fancy uniforms, and militaristic practices as outlets for their subconscious desires to brutalize and maim others. There is something so darkly psychological about these activities that lends direct reasoning to the anarchist goal of abolishing all of these insane cultural practices and rituals.

It's ironic to me that people condemn anarchy as a philosophy of mayhem and bloodshed, yet people's beloved government allows for some of the most egregious violence to take place without any repercussions.

Government is chaos. Government is violence. Government is death.

December 13, 2016

ZzZz.

Many people prefer the "simple life." They enjoy their television soap operas, their quaint routines, doing their Christmas shopping, hanging out with their family, and living day-to-day in a state of oblivious bliss.

They do not want their routine disrupted or encroached upon. They want to feel safe and secure in their cultural habitat of sterility and preoccupation.

When the world is crumbling around them, they pretend everything is okay. "Everything is fine," they say. And so they sleepwalk. ZzZz. Their programming is firmly in place as cops murder people everywhere, politicians siphon money from the productive classes, their family members are caged for nonviolent drug offenses, and the specter of unholy chaos hangs ominously over their blind tranquility.

ZzZz.

These things happen, but they fight back against truth. They are too afraid to wake up, too tired of reality, too scared to see light and fight back. ZzZz. Ashamed of the dastardly nature of the nation-state.

"Everything is fine," they say.

"It's okay. The simple life is working. No bad can happen. The government will take care of me. My lover will take care of me. Hold me tight. Rock me to sleep as the bombs fall and bodies scatter. ZzZz. My soap is on! Reality TV is on. "

Hypnotized. Flash fires in the background—decaying people in industrial prisons that contain panopticon vision.

"Maintain the simple life. Nothing is wrong. Stay safe and secure in bliss-filled ignorance. Shush now. Obey the State. Stay dialed into American Idol and show tunes. ZzZz. Our voices are hollow, short-lived, and inviolate to the powers that be.

"What matters is our simple life. The anarchists are nonexistent. This security is what matters. The bombs are mythological. The bureaucrats are wise. ZzZz. They know me. We are friends. ZzZz.

"Everything is good.

"What do you want for Christmas?"

April 20, 2017

Do not feel ashamed if you have broken immoral laws, like if you smoked a plant, ate a pill, or prostituted your body. You made a decision for yourself that harmed no one. It's not up to any specific person or government to tell you how to live your life. There is no greater self-fulfillment than doing what you want to do by snubbing the petty tyrants and control freaks. We only live this life once, and obeying shit laws is a waste of your life. Instead, live free and proud.

April 21, 2017

Public school is a nightmare. "Education" as it is conceptualized is indoctrination. But it is much worse. It is brutality; it is child torture that has been justified by a toxic, sleepwalking society.

Any place or institution that demands the obedience of youngsters while forcing them to attend is not just child abuse. It is also a grievous human rights violation.

If there is one reason why people need to wake up from the matrix of cultural hypnosis, it is to save the children from this brain-melting machine that everyone calls civilized. It is to extricate them from the straitjacket of toxic conventions and free them from the "teachers" who are megalomaniacal, insane masochists.

I wish what I was saying was overly dramatic or hyperbolic, but what these "education facilities" are doing is beyond wrong. It is a tragic affair to witness, and it must be abolished.

Unplugging from Destructive Cultural Artifacts

March 18, 2014

Bleh, "civil rights." What needs to be talked about are *human rights*. Civil rights are merely used as a springboard to divide and distract people. When you talk about human rights, you cannot distract people because it implicates the ruling class, and you cannot divide people because it applies to everyone. The concept of human rights puts peace and dignity above characteristics and color.

March 19, 2014

Nothing strikes me as more insane than a statist using "law" to validate government, as if a codex of pompous and incomprehensible legalese magically validates murder and robbery. Be gone with your self-important, megalomaniacal, and supercilious nonsense. It's not welcome here.

July 9, 2014

The term "livable wage" is meaningless. It's a tear-jerking term bereft of philosophical weight. When people use it, they're saying this: employers should pay individuals as high a wage as possible, even if they don't deserve it.

But this also means that the people pushing for a "livable wage" are saying it's okay to slam a gun in a business owner's face and tell him to raise his wages regardless of business costs. Therefore, if you're pushing for a "livable wage" don't pretend to care about people and say you want them to be better off when you're actively seeking to hurt them with violence. What you're doing is antithetical to humanitarian aims and decency.

March 10, 2015

The most asinine fear people have about voluntary anarchism is that in the absence of government, large monopolies and corporations would rise up and subjugate the population.

I have a couple of responses to these types of fear-loaded arguments.

One: I take it at face value that people who argue against monopolies genuinely hate them and believe they will wreak havoc on society if government does not regulate them.

The problem with this argument is that it is disingenuous and fallacious. How can an individual say with a straight face that they want to keep monopolies at bay while advocating for the world's most destructive and heinous monopoly—government—to control and regulate monopolies?

How can one's "genuine" hatred of business be taken seriously when they advocate violent tyrants controlling those "violent" businesses? The fallacy is clear: It makes no sense. It is hypocritical to hate monopolies but demand that the largest monopoly control the others.

This type of thinking arises because people fear government, so they use businesses as scapegoats; it takes less courage to publicly denounce and decry business. It is more psychologically challenging to denounce and decry the State because one risks ostracism and possible punishment if they do. Indeed, this also occurs because people are propagandized and conditioned to hate success and wealth. Not to mention, people grow up with the idea of the State as a paternalistic figure, so criticizing and condemning it would be akin to criticizing and condemning their own parents. The reasons why people buckle at the thought of criticizing government are legion.

Two: Why is there fear that anything will dominate the population? Where is the fear for what everyone is suffering right now? Where is the fear of the evil everyone lives under? The people who harbor fears about a business takeover are living in a delusion. They should simply look around. The government has already taken over and claimed the right to rule everyone. People are being killed in droves by uncontrolled police forces; a vast, imperialistic American military has been deployed around the globe at the behest of politicians, a multitude of laws to undermine the rights of the people has been enacted, and vast spying programs like PRISM have been imposed on the people. This insanity goes on and on ad nauseam. Wake up and smell the bloodshed.

I am just mind-blown that people can be so terrified of business when governments have always been the most horrific, atrocious entities. Governments alone have been the cause of most murders of innocent people. The statistics for government murders number in the billions throughout history. Nothing market-based or private can touch that number. It is just embarrassing that people still have such anti-industry biases with all the historical evidence at their fingertips. But alas, government propaganda and control are in full swing, not to mention the psychological resistances to questioning Big Brother, which I already mentioned.

February 7, 2016

Many people believe if someone "follows orders" they are exonerated from committing morally repugnant acts. If they wear a badge or don battle gear, they can carry out orders to assault and murder people with impunity.

This fallacious line of thinking is the sole reason why so many people have viewed different kinds of killing as acceptable and sometimes even noble. It is because of this contaminated view of morality—with its exceptions and caveats—that soldiers and cops have murdered people and rarely faced any consequences.

As a group of cooperative social animals with higher reasoning faculties, the human race has to move beyond this madness. As long as people hallucinate that certain groups have special moral privileges and can kill people in instances where others would be condemned, humanity will remain trapped in a Pandora's box of moral confusion.

There is no reason why murder should be condoned simply because a person has a particular job or function in society. Until the cognitive dissonance and groupthink dissolve, soldiers and cops will continue to destroy innocent lives, and many will continue to cheer them on as they do.

Let's work to change this ghastly and bizarre world. People are not helpless. The more everyone talks about deranged beliefs and the backward nature of authority, the quicker people can work to abolish institutions that allow unjustified killing.

April 23, 2016

How people use the term "human nature" as a scapegoat for acts of violence would be humorous if it weren't so damned heartbreaking. So long as people cite "human nature" as the cause of all the world's woes, they will also continue to support murderous governments and pretend to have no responsibility or control.

In this sense, they are victims of the "human nature" they cite. They are erroneously insinuating that they have no control over their own thoughts or actions. They are self-robotizing into conformity.

The great tragedy of the "all humans are bad" bromide is that it makes people forget that they can be good. It makes them forget their own heart and purposive behavior. It is their justification to be exonerated from responsibility or to care about future problems.

July 20, 2016

Just a few hours ago, a behavioral therapist in Florida was shot by cops while he tended to his autistic client. He had his hands up the whole time.

Luckily, he survived the attack. But when he asked the cop why he was shot, the cop said, "I don't know." This answer blew my mind. It's like they are programmed to shoot anyone.

The idea that you can "obey cop orders" and not get shot is one of the biggest lies spewed in society. Hopefully, these incidents will continue to wake people up to the inherent brutality of the system.

It makes me sad that this is the world we live in, but it makes me happy that we may finally have the power to change it for the better.

September 21, 2016

An ongoing, erroneous societal discussion concludes that there must be a balance between security and liberty.

This implies that some liberty should be sacrificed for everyone to have security.

But this idea is preposterous from the start.

If your civil liberties and freedoms are impinged on, do you have security? Wouldn't your security be undermined by the people who are spying on you, watching you, and creating laws meant to tame you and make you docile?

Considering this, we can now see clearly that security is a myth. No one is ever guaranteed security, and they certainly aren't being secured by the people making those claims. In fact, the people who are supposed to do the protecting are some of the vilest people on this planet.

In this sense, I would prefer to have *no security* because that seems a hell of a lot more secure than having violent and power-hungry individuals create laws under the delusional notion of providing me with safety.

I think I am better equipped to handle my own safety than a small group of government functionaries with the ultimate power and tools to oversee my life. All of this seems obvious. When will people realize the irony of believing that security can be granted in this manner?

"Security" is just a mealy-mouthed bit of rhetoric intended to subdue people and persuade them into giving up their freedoms without a fight.

"Security" is just a synonym for "servitude." If you claim government should provide security at the expense of liberty, you are saying you are okay with having a slavemaster who pretends to protect you.

If anything represents the height of Stockholm syndrome, it's this conversation about security versus liberty. It's nonsense.

September 30, 2016

When a politician claims they are committed to "fighting terrorism," what that means in straightforward English is they plan on being a warmonger.

They plan on committing terrorist acts themselves. The phrase "fighting terrorism" is just a piece of rhetoric meant to make people feel safe and secure and manipulate them into blindly following politicians.

We must remember not to believe in the myth of the politician as social savior, hero, public servant, or good parent. Politicians mainly do what they must to consolidate their power, by telling people what they want to hear. The truth is they are mostly violent sociopaths bent on gaining more power.

Quit selling your soul and sacrificing self-responsibility to kowtow to these megalomaniacs. As humans, we must have some gumption. We must focus on our own lives, friends, and families. We must quit deferring to people who claim to be "leaders of the free world."

The more we continue to bend the knee to these monsters, the worse off the world will be.

October 5, 2016

One of the most dangerous things anyone can say in society is "follow police commands at all costs."

Some people believe the best course of action when dealing with police is to obey and use the system to change things after the fact.

It is surprising that people still tout this way of doing things. We have history books that provide us with ample evidence of why this mentality is incoherent.

In a corrupt system, is it smart to preach blind obedience to the enforcement class? If anyone were in Nazi Germany, would they be telling the Jews that if they just obeyed the SS everything would be fine? What about Stalinist Russia or myriad other autocratic empires?

The logic of "just obey" does not compute. It does not necessarily create positive outcomes or prevent people from being beaten or killed.

In this regard, blindly obeying authority and not questioning the cops or politicians, whether it is in the moment or after an encounter, is the height of social suicide.

It is absurd.

As people who live in a world bloated with authoritarian violence, we should always be prepared to question, disobey, and fight back against anyone attempting to rule over us.

These people are not our masters, and we are not their slaves.

November 22, 2016

"Civilian" is the politically correct term for serf or slave.

December 13, 2016

It's sad when people conflate taxation with civilization. The fact that people see extortion as civilized means the propaganda machine has been manufacturing consent as planned. But this ruse must be unveiled for all to see. The truth must be known.

In reality, taxation is barbarism. It is the rhetorical method that rulers use to trick their serfs into servitude. Taxation is not civilized. Taxation is widespread violence. It is the antithesis of civilization. It is predatory. It is utilitarian philosophy taken to its logical end.

To destroy the very idea of taxation is to start civilizing society. It is to humanize humankind, bringing the apes down from the canopies and finally stuffing a soul into their meaty bodies.

The end of taxation means the beginning of a civilized society.

December 15, 2016

Want to know what my pet peeve is?

I am miffed when people erroneously use the pronoun "we" in a political context. For instance, people tend to refer to some atrocity the government committed or politicians passing "laws" as acts they were present for and participated in.

They say "we" dropped the atomic bomb on Hiroshima. "We" are fighting in Syria. "We" made a law to ban this or that drug.

No, no, no.

There was no "we." Some ruler, politician, bureaucrat, or other government functionary made that decision. It had nothing to do with you or me.

This tribal mentality is partly why people suffer from the delusion of democracy and end up believing in myths like the social contract, voting, and collectivism.

December 28, 2016

The scariest thing men do is beg people to follow the law when the law constantly condemns innocent and decent people to prison, servitude, or death.

History has shown that the concept of "law" is generally flawed, even when intended to protect people or property.

Law usually becomes the rhetorical device politicians employ to commit crimes. Seldom is the law used to protect anyone. Seldom is it upheld for the good of society.

If you want to see a saner society, try working from compassion, communication, self-ownership, and self-responsibility.

Relying on laws to solve all manner of evil only perpetuates evil.

March 11, 2017

Respect for authority is one of the most detrimental problems in society. It is this unthinkable drive to respect figures in positions of power that has led to the nastiest and bloodiest events in history.

There is nothing noble about falling in line and groveling before an alleged master. If anything is indicative of psychological impairment, it is the notion that some people should be worshiped simply because they are believed to have the power to hurt or control others.

For a truly civilized society to blossom, the world must be populated by individuals who harbor skepticism and disgust toward anyone who claims to have the right to tell people how to behave under threat of violence.

Authority has been the ideological disease of humankind. And finally, a mass of anarchists has been injected into the artery of society as antibodies geared to combat this illness.

With any hope, they will be able to neutralize the threat of belief in authority and start healing all the mental and emotional wounds from this awful affliction, which has caused the hurt and death of too many people for far too long.

An Open Letter to the Military Veterans

11/11/2015

Dear brothers and sisters,

I am writing to you on Veterans Day not as a foe but as a friend. I am penning these words with a heart toward convincing you that the commands you obeyed and the services you rendered were a detriment to you, your brothers and sisters, and all the people of the world. It is not my intent to be ugly, to shame, to condescend, or to incite you to anger or the desire to hurt me. I only wish to connect with you on a humanitarian level. Thus, I humbly request your attention to my perspective, to my truth.

Some of you will be reading this note from the confines of a wheelchair, from the safety and antiseptic bed of the hospital ward where you may be recovering from an explosion, from the shrapnel that pierced your flesh. Some of you may be processing tumultuous memories and nightmarish flashbacks with a therapist as you are forced to relive the death of your comrades or the enemy insurgents you slew heroically in combat.

Just thinking about how you may have to receive this letter, about what you went through, and what you may have done causes me anguish and anger. It causes me to recoil in terror. I can scantly imagine the inconceivable horrors of your experiences. It sends chills down my spine to envision the bombs, blood, guts, sweat, tears, dust, smoke, and bodies. The knowledge that you had to murder people or that people tried to murder you evokes a sadness in my being that I cannot find the words to describe. Perhaps I do not understand the nature of warfare, and so the language eludes me.

There is something I do perceive, however. I now realize a tragic fact. I understand what caused you to experience such grotesque madness, what compelled you to travel thousands of miles away at the behest of a politician to fight and die for America. I realize what put you in that wheelchair, what brought you to the shrink, and what still troubles your war-torn heart and ravaged spirit. It is a difficult truth, but not one I suspect you were conscious of or that you had the ability or permission to even consider.

The politicians who sent you to strange and foreign lands to kill did not have your interests at heart. They manipulated you and looked down on you. They did not have freedom in mind. They did not harbor love or appreciation for the people of the world. The politicians and special interests sent you to kill or die to further their ambitions and line their pockets with money crafted at the altar of destruction. They did it despite your goodwill and love of country. They did it out of hate.

This, my brothers and sisters, is a grievance I cannot stand to tolerate. It is a heinous crime against everything good. It is something that brings such a nervous trembling to my soul that I can hardly type the words without weeping. So, I implore you to consider that the damage done to your body and mind was not the fault of people living far away. The blame lies squarely on those who whisked you away to the killing fields. They are murderous, anti-freedom demagogues. They would rather watch everything burn than promote and maintain liberty. It is time for you to stand tall and realize that you wreaked havoc on countries for the ploys of cowards who played on your desire for freedom and peace. But sadly, what they wanted instead was suffering and death—and you were their plaything, their pawn.

I respect you, anyway. But I want you on the side of good now. I want you to realize what you have done, the cost of the orders you obeyed, and what you can do to heal. You can recover a smidgen of what has been lost by joining the ranks of good, by shunning the devils who call themselves leaders of the world. You can send the pain below and open your eyes to a whole new vista of freedom and truth. Now, reject the American government. Reject political hierarchy. Reject the insanity that comes with the idea that it is acceptable to murder other people by "following orders."

You may never recover from all the physical and emotional wounds you incurred in the wars, but you can recover a sense of dignity and decency. You can put one step forward and say proudly and honestly that you will vie for real freedom and shun the warfare state at every step with every fiber of your being.

Thank you for reading. It was tough to write, but I hope that you will respond with positivity and acceptance. I hope you can see things from my perspective and that you can fully empathize with my concerns and compassion.

Sincerely,

Sterlin Lujan

The Rituals and Delusions of Statism

October 11, 2012

As we move into election time, we need to remember one thing: We are free, self-governing agents. We don't need anyone dictating our lives to us. We should live unfettered, ruled only by the stirrings of our own conscience. To vote is to beg for freedom and to surrender our lives to the mercy and discretion of another.

October 18, 2012

The presidential elections and debates are just reindeer games for your amusement and temporary satisfaction that something is going to change, but you will never actually be part of it or have any real say in political comings and goings. No one can truly represent you as an individual. It is a slap in the face, an insult, to think another person can represent who you are.

April 9, 2014

I love how tax companies, friends, family, and everyone else make paying thousands of dollars in taxes seem voluntary and acceptable and a humdrum part of daily life. As an "ode" to tax season and the government: Fuck taxation. It's robbery. Always and forever. Period. Yes, I will pay this extortion. But it is not voluntary. I am doing it because you have a gun to my head—because you will find a way to extract the money from me, hold me upside down, dangle me, and snatch the loose change. In no way do I give my voluntary consent to pay because I drive on your shitty pothole-laden roads, because you send people in costumes to murder other people, or because some kleptocratic politician decided to fund his own pork barrel bullshit project. No, thank you. This is not me consenting. This me under duress and force of will. This is me picking your goddamned cotton—and loathing every moment of it.

July 4, 2014

Independence Day has nothing to do with the independence of individuals. It deals with the independence of a floating abstraction known as "America." What we need is a real independence day that celebrates the freedom of the individual from tyranny and institutionalized violence. But for this to happen, people must realize the importance of the individual over the tribe.

I yearn for this day. It may be just a pipe dream, but maybe down the road it will surface. I am weary of the tired fantasy that freedom and human decency exist under statism and that this day somehow glorifies it and celebrates them. It's just a fabrication, wishful thinking for what should have been—and celebrants cheer it on like they would a *Hunger Games* arena deathmatch. This makes me terribly sad, but I will maintain hope and optimism. I will cheer in my own way for the prospects of freedom.

Peace be with you all.

November 4, 2014

Get into that ballot box and vote, by golly!

But let us ponder a few important questions first.

Do you believe that forcing other people to live how you want them to is logical or humane? Indeed, picking a person to forcibly do your bidding is exactly what voting accomplishes.

Considering the wars, recessions, police brutality, drug war, hatemongering, and government corruption, will voting in another guy who is using the same system make any fundamental changes? Probably not. It's time for a new strategy.

If we're really free, why isn't there a vote for no government and absolute freedom? Wouldn't a free country give you the ability to make it a free country? It seems kind of fishy that this is not an option.

Needless to say, you will not see the likes of me at the polls.

Happy hunting.

July 3, 2015

Tomorrow there is a holiday about how the abstract entity called America gained freedom from another abstract entity called Great Britain, which involved a coup d'état, mass destruction, and murder all to perpetuate the same things. Sounds legit.

October 26, 2015

I never stand up for the national anthem, much less cover my heart. I let the plebs stand and worship their murderous, tyrannical government. If patriotic music is played in my presence it will be ignored, and I will solemnly shake my head at those who are too blind to consider what they are doing. They are literally pledging allegiance to their own slavery. Through the pledge, they are congratulating the drone-bombing of children. I couldn't care less about this grotesque religious ritual, and I mourn for all those who have lost their conscience at the altar of State propaganda. I can never condone sending troops to die overseas. I cannot support locking up thousands for smoking a plant or cheering on sociopaths who kill for entertainment. I will not stand and cross my heart for heartless insanity. Yet, I still harbor the conviction that more of you will awaken from these dangerous delusions. I believe that one day people will not so easily succumb to celebratory barbarism. I have hope for all of you, and that is why I do what I do and say the things I say. It is why I try to live a life of virtue and dignity, of self-ownership and voluntary peacefulness.

April 22, 2016

A recent video shows a group of men trampling the American flag, and the comment section is replete with people calling for their murder. Of course, this comes as no surprise for most people in our community.

But this kind of stuff makes my points that much more salient. People have to internalize the importance of emotional intelligence and self-awareness. Those who possess these traits are less likely to erupt with the urge to kill because someone is stomping on a piece of cloth. Furthermore, it would help all parties involved to demonstrate empathy through dialogue and come to an understanding. If no communication exists, all parties might as well be living in alien worlds apart from each other.

And for the record, a person has some deep-seated issues if they believe that people deserve to die because they place a piece of cloth underfoot. I realize these flag-lovers have their reasons why they cherish this symbol, but I doubt their ego and religious love of country would move them to turn their murderous words into murderous deeds (in terms of killing people who stand on flags in this "country").

A little introspection, consideration, and connective attunement go a long way.

October 8, 2016

Facebook is peddling advertisements to vote. I am truly fed up with these unapologetic solicitations to support the murderous and violent system. I never intend to vote for anything. Ever.

I also don't even believe in the concept of the "defensive vote." How can a vote be defensive when you are still bolstering the system by playing into it? I just don't buy that malarkey.

I understand that some people have to do things within the system to live, but voting is not something we have to do to survive or undermine the system. Matter of fact, voting often has the opposite effect by empowering politicians and bureaucrats with more arbitrary power.

Forget about it.

The age of voting has come to an end. It should be clear that the democratic process in politics has utterly and predictably failed. Voting is for those people who are holding onto the dream of a system that has already begun its descent into mayhem and absurdity.

In this sense, voting is like practicing phrenology in the age of neurological medicine. It is simply time to wake up to the truth and knowledge in front of us and start living without this belief that scribbling a name on a piece of paper or keying it into a computer is going to bring us individual happiness or a freer society.

Voting is a delusion. It is damnation. It is dead.

November 8, 2016

It doesn't matter who I vote for "for president." Here is why.

Best-case scenario:

Candidate 1: I continue to live and ignore the State as much as possible.

Candidate 2: I continue to live and ignore the State as much as possible.

Worst-case scenario:

Candidate 1: I take a helicopter ride.

Candidate 2: I perish in World War 3 with Russia.

November 8, 2016

"Make sure you go out and vote today! It doesn't matter who you vote for. Just vote."

In reality, It doesn't matter who you vote for at all. All voting selections involve more police violence, drone-bombing campaigns, political corruption, corporatism, and servitude of the masses. The only way voting would matter is if we could vote for zero government. But that is not an option.

If you want something done, don't vote. Instead, teach peace, freedom, and love. Live by the virtues of counter-economics and subvert the State. Live as a proud individual. Make anarchism a reality by living it and spreading the good word. That is our only savior. No warmongering sociopath elected to a violent government is going to help us. We can only help each other by practicing the virtues of liberty and compassion.

Voting is the Great Illusion. It is a pompous religious ritual that keeps this machinery of evil well lubricated and running. Quit feeding it. Stop believing in nonsense.

Another "brave leader of the new world" is not going to set us free. We cannot be unchained by cheering for and drooling over the tyrant who bonds us in chains. The emperor has no clothes; the system is naked in its malice.

And if we look closely enough and shine a strong enough light, the truth is easy to behold.

Save yourself some dignity. Don't give the system relevance or your imagined consent.

November 9, 2016

As I have mentioned many times, I did not prefer who became "president." I had no emotional stake in the game. My contention has always been that people do not need tyrants and rulers to run their lives, but many people have either ignored the anarchist message or been too hypnotized by politics to absorb the philosophy of liberty.

With that said, I am extremely happy with the outcome—but not for the same reasons as other anarchists. I don't gain joy or satisfaction from watching social justice warriors wallow in depression and despair at a Trump victory. I am not a sadist or a seeker of cheap thrills. I share many of the leftist ideas about this president. Trump is insane. He is dense, unsophisticated, unprincipled, alarmist, and childish. This is not a person I would want to rule me even if I had Stockholm syndrome.

I am extremely happy for another reason. I am happy because this election represents a lesson. It is a teachable moment. I have debated many left-leaning democracy lovers who supported Sanders and then switched to Clinton after he failed. Some of these people are my friends. However, throughout the election, they maintained a haughty and blind devotion to the system. They believed democracy was fair, that votes matter, and that the system is important. A few of them even argued with me directly, dismissing the philosophy of anarchism as too ideological or a pipe dream. They blindly swept anarchism under the rug while unknowingly cheering for their folly.

So yes. I feel vindicated. I am rife with pride. There is now a man at the top of their cherished system who is a burning symbol for the comical stupidity of it. He is a living mockery of democracy. He is the trickster who will open people's eyes to freedom. He is representative of everything that is wrong with voting, "participatory government," and politicking. He is a deep irony injected into the very heart of political life.

With this lesson given in such a timely manner, I want all my friends and acquaintances who have defended the system to reconsider the alternative—to consider anarchism and to understand why I slept so soundly last night. There is a reason I unflinchingly and repeatedly sing the praises of freedom, and if I could point to a single moment in history that justifies anarchism versus statism, it was this circus, this mad joke of an election.

I just hope my friends and acquaintances take some time to consider this information and start thinking about accepting other philosophies, which are less violent, less utopian, less insane, and more moral and logical.

Just look at what this system has wrought. Look at its logical conclusion. Look what voting has accomplished.

November 10, 2016

How many elections is it going to take to convince people that freedom is better than a ruling elite? Do people have to be disappointed, enraged, bamboozled, and made distraught over and over before they realize that government is garbage? Do the sheep need to be resurrected and led yet again to the slaughter? I have the utmost faith that people are smart enough to swallow their pride and admit their god has failed them. It is time to come to terms with other methods of cooperating socially. Obviously, a group of nincompoops charged with free reign to coerce people into living contrary to their natural inclinations is a hideously silly, dangerous, and lazy idea.

November 10, 2016

"Democracy is a fair system. Go out and vote! Voting works! This is the system we have, better love it or leave!"

"My president didn't win so I am going on an emotional rampage and protesting in the streets. The system sucks. Burn the system."

Pick one.

If you love your participatory government so much and believe the system is fair, why are you protesting and throwing a tantrum? Perhaps it is time to consider the idea that *no* system is the best system instead of pleading on the streets for a different master.

November 24, 2016

I am not an official celebrant of Thanksgiving. The holiday fails to resonate with me on a fundamental level, especially because of the arguably brutal nature that surrounds it. Nonetheless, I do not begrudge people who enjoy the festivities. I don't believe people want to focus on the perceived negatives, anyway.

So, I say revel in it. Connect with friends and family. Make good use of the fleeting time here. Demonstrate deep emotion. Radiate love. Share a union with fellow humans.

But these messages of goodwill and love are nothing new or novel for me to share.

I try to spread connection and compassion as often as possible. I don't hold this message tightly like a favorite teddy bear, and I utter it only on the singular day where it's fashionable to speak of thanks and companionship.

I embrace this message as if it were part of me, and I try to represent it wherever I go, even if I am imperfect and do not practice what I always preach.

Still, human connection is what moves our world. We are creatures of deep attunement with those who are closest to us. Attachment bonds are imprinted into our DNA. This is the essential element of our existence. Whenever possible, we should embrace this desire to connect and constantly touch the hearts of those around us—friends and foes alike.

But, like me, not everyone will be able to perfectly connect with and understand all humans. That's not even expected.

Yet, if we can muster the courage to comprehend this truth about human nature, it will allow us to widen our appreciation of being here. It will provide us with the tools to dissolve the boundaries between us. It will inevitably turn us into beings of love, even if we struggle with the ability to unerringly share that love with others.

So for me, for all of us, I hope we can be thankful every day for the fullness of our hearts and the indescribable joy we feel for living in this world near those who love us without conditions. And I hope we can allow this love to flourish so we can make the world whole.

Happy Thanksgiving.

Happy life.

November 30, 2016

"Make America great again. Drain the swamp." -Donald Trump

Kidnap and pillage private weed dealers. Kidnap and cage those who burn pieces of cloth. Posture on building border walls like North Korea. Continue to rule with an iron fist. More nationalism!

When will people learn that presidential candidates never keep their promises? This is the billionth time we have done this baloney.

Democracy does, indeed, feel like the worship of jackals by jackasses.

That was Mencken, right?

December 16, 2016

I am reading this *Washington Post* article from last week, and they said Russian propagandists helped sow distrust of democracy and its "leaders."

I find this hilariously asinine.

Is it not possible that these US leaders and their democratic process are what sowed distrust among the people?

When you extort the population, drone-bomb children in their cribs, lock up millions of people for consensual "crimes," and have a farcical election with two clowns as candidates, won't most people start to become distrustful of you? Won't most people start to hate you?

In my view, this displacement of blame onto various scapegoats is just a tell that peace lovers and advocates of freedom are winning the war on information sharing.

People are starting to realize that their political overlords are not only untrustworthy but also wholly violent and incompetent.

They are so incompetent as to pretend that it took Russian hackers to convince people they are bad.

You can't make any of this up.

January 11, 2017

I have not sacrificed my original principles or thought processes as an anarchist (although I have diversified my views and discovered a personal niche). Nonetheless, my underlying devotion to freedom has remained steadfast.

Neither presidential candidates were fit to rule me or anyone else. Clinton and Trump are doppelgängers of every other ruler that has ever existed. All presidents steal, lie, kill, manipulate, and pander to sycophants—albeit to differing degrees. A ruler being part of a different party or possessing different personality characteristics has had no bearing on my footing as an anarchist.

I was not happy or angry that Trump won the presidency. I had no emotional attachment to the specific outcome other than disgust for *all* outcomes. Trump is the mirror image of Clinton: Both are a representation of servitude via a kleptocratic, murderous system. Both tyrants would have been placed atop the same mafia, would have had to appeal to the same special interests, and would have ruled everyone within their territory. Both would have made promises. Both would have lied.

Indeed, Trump will lie. He will steal, commit drone murder, and cause undue harm to millions. He will do all the things Clinton would have done, but he will flavor it with right-wing rhetoric and right-wing fibs.

My preference has always been for no president, and I have never been a fan of incrementalism for anarchism because governments rarely, if ever, incrementally relinquish power. Certainly, having a president with a different skin color or genitalia type would not have made any difference. Having a president that is from the business sector versus being a career politician also makes no difference. A mafia don is still a mafia don if he has accepted that position.

My mission has been trained on changing society from beneath the floorboards—coming up from the bottom, educating people away from statism, and creating a critical mass of people to sway culture. This includes practicing apolitical compassion, preaching civility to children, engaging in civil disobedience, and living outside the scope of the system as much as humanly possible.

It is true, though—I have not been a perfect anarchist. But I have done everything within my grasp to help free as many people as possible and work toward making this world a better, more loving place.

Everyday Statism

January 20, 2011

Michelle Obama has teamed up with Walmart to reduce the amount of salt in food and promote healthier eating to put a stop to "child obesity." I thought it was the parents' job to make sure their children understand what a good diet consists of—not Walmart, and especially not Michelle Obama.

It's shit like this that can snowball into the creation of laws that ban cupcakes and potato chips.

March 10, 2011

So, the Federal Reserve Bank lent out nine trillion dollars during the financial crisis, several trillion of which went to overseas banks...All this money printed out of thin air or taken from our pockets.

Can someone explain to me how this is okay?

April 13, 2011

My fear of air travel does not lie in a fear of heights, fear of crashing, or fear of terrorists. My fear of flying hinges on dealing with the invasive TSA.

September 22, 2011

Do you know what gets old? The love-it-or-leave-it argument. In response to my position about the problems with government, most people say that if I don't like certain rules or laws I can flee America and move to another country. But this argument is nonsense because it assumes that the government owns America and that dictators rule absolute. Is it a civilized society where people tell others to leave if they don't like tyranny or if they don't like to be threatened with violence? Do you like the force and violence of society so much yourself as to tell others to leave? Why not just stop promoting violence?

December 28, 2012

Does anyone sincerely believe agencies like the TSA protect people? Are freedom and protection now secured by pornography scanners and blue-gloved fondling? How does the government protect us at airports when they first steal money from us to fund the porno-scanners and fondling? Someone make sense of this for me.

August 3, 2013

Tax-free weekend = theft-free weekend.

Look at all these people enjoying the benefits of not having to pay the "invisible sales taxes." Imagine the economy and personal elation if this theft were removed permanently.

That's the kind of world I want to live in. I am disgusted at the one we do live in, where every now and then our rulers give us a break and allow us to not pay tribute to them.

November 2, 2013

There were pseudo-protesters on the side of the road holding signs that read: "Impeach Obama."

Sweet plan, but I am assuming you merely want to replace him with another ruler in the dim hope that shit will change.

You might get away with not having a fascist health care plan, but ultimately, swapping rulers will not make you any less enslaved.

Your unborn will still be sold off into tax servitude, drug witch hunts will still ensue, children will still be murdered overseas, regulations and laws will still blossom, and on and on.

Stop believing that government will solve your problems.

December 7, 2013

I am infuriated. There's a social standard that when people are "irresponsible" and get arrested for possessing drugs, the family should not pay the bail to "teach them a lesson."

Well, you know what: Fuck that. If you think someone deserves to be tossed in a rape cage and made to stay for not paying a citation for a non-crime, you are no better than the sociopaths who decreed it.

Do you really believe such so-called "irresponsibility" merits punishment by kidnapping, ransom, extortion, and possible murder if this irresponsible person decides to defend himself against these costumed monsters?

Whose side are you on? Your friends' and family's? Or some asshole who lives a world away, calls himself a ruler, and believes his pen stroke to be the magical dictator of morality?

Wake up.

December 22, 2013

Before changing my thinking and becoming an anarchist, I never paid attention to police on the roads. There would just be a blur of passing cars. After coming into anarchism and learning to see detail, the blur turned to code, like in *The Matrix*. Now I see at least three cops a day with a peak of up to ten, granted I commute an hour to work.

They say these cops work to protect freedom and safety, but they are always stopping, accosting, harassing, and caging people. How does this protect freedom and provide safety? I suppose before I came to pay attention, I never thought about these cops because I assumed they were beneficial. That's why I never asked these tough questions. Now I know why: it's scary knowing that we live and work in a fascist police state where our every move is monitored, and we are controlled and allowed the minutest amount of liberty.

You can see this if you pay attention to all the enforcers around you.

January 21, 2014

It doesn't matter if people die from smoking pot. This is false, obviously, but who should care even if it were true? It is irrelevant. If people want to ingest either poison or ambrosia into their bodies, it's their decision. Let it be.

The idea that plants and chemicals should be banned is insidious and cowardly: it states that you're too dumb and irresponsible to make your own choices, so the rulers, who are supposedly smarter than you, are going to decide for you what goes into your body.

This mentality must end. People exercise control over their minds and bod-ies, and they are going to do this forever. People own themselves. They'll suffer consequences on their own.

People will do as they please, even if they are idiots. Therefore, people do not require assistance from a group of sociopaths to make choices, and coercing people to abstain from these things just adds an element of unnecessary vio-lence into the mix. Seriously, the blood spilled from trying to control people's desires is not logical, nor is it the moral high ground. Quit defending the so-ciopaths and psychopaths who do this.

February 5, 2014

It takes a special kind of ignorance to support the drug war. Anyone who goes against a person's natural right to put what they want in their body is worse than a tyrant. The body is the domain and hub of the individual. Nothing strikes me as sillier and more shit-brained than someone who sees the need to control people's choice to take substances. Get over yourself.

April 25, 2014

There's this Facebook page called the Officer Down Memorial, and they post situations where people who have purposely or inadvertently killed cops go up for parole, and all the fans on the page try to petition and raise money to fight that parole.

Well, I find this obsequious bootlicking pitiful and cowardly. Here's one situation why: A drunk driver accidentally swerved into a cop and flung her off a bridge while she was accosting someone on the streets. They gave this driver 11 years in prison for vehicular manslaughter. Fine. Good. Whatever.

Now, said drunk driver goes up for parole after seven years, over half his sentence, and these bootlicking uniformophiles are trying to squash the possibility of parole. I explained to them that it was vehicular manslaughter, and just because the victim was a cop changes nothing. She does not shit golden nuggets, and her uniform was not imbued with magical powers; she is the same as everyone else. There's no special or defining difference between "them" and "us." Quit elevating people to this godlike standard because of the bullshit superstitious notion called "authority." This kind of stuff turns my stomach.

May 1, 2014

Feminism is not a movement rooted in gender equality. It is a movement based on distraction from real problems. It is rooted in a government power grab that takes advantage of overly emotional and insecure women. Feminism is then drowned in the blood and screams of the many victims of the State's newfound power; hence no equality is granted. Meanwhile, women are made into dupes for the games people of power play.

Women! If you seek equality and individual strength, turn away from the real subjugator: government.

May 19, 2014

If you believe the criminal justice system dispenses justice, you might need to check your facts. How come people who possess drugs often get more time than those who kill people? How come a "fair and speedy trial" is neither fair nor speedy? In most cases, people won't go to trial for many months, up to a year. As for fairness, how is being forced into plea bargains fair? Many times, both defense attorneys and prosecutors will wrangle a defendant into accepting a plea deal not because it will be better for him but because they threaten him not to go to trial, citing potentially dire consequences.

The reality is that if everyone went to trial, this diabolical, unfair system would crumble to pieces. How come all the attorneys—the defense and prosecutors—are butt-buddies and work together to decide criminals' fates? It's almost like the trial by jury is unheard of, and people who commit nonviolent crimes are seen as the evilest of evil assholes when the reality is that they are regular, decent people.

This system must come to its much-needed conclusion, as our forebears made a huge mistake. The system is corrupt, broken, caters to the political elite, and is an all-around mockery of civility.

May 29, 2014

People react negatively when they hear about drugs like meth and heroin. They lose rationality and seek to punish anyone who uses these drugs. I see the reasoning. I get it. These drugs destroy the body and mind like rotting cancer. But our heavy-handed reactions have caused severe collateral consequences. Instead of trying to empathize, we demonize; instead of helping, we jail and shoot, and instead of searching for a remedy, we exacerbate the problem. We cannot answer the problem of drugs with violence. This is not the moral high ground. The drug users are simply making personal choices regarding their minds and bodies, and using force against them is a fascist, Stone Age cure— a cure that doesn't work.

Instead of violence, let us negotiate. Instead of demonization, let us strive for peace. Let us end these witch hunts. Let us treat all humans as humans. The drug war is not a war on drugs. It is a war on people, a war on our friends and families. Though their behavior may be self-destructive, our use of violence only mirrors the violence they use against themselves. This is not logical or appropriate.

The goal should be to aid, empathize, and care. So why haven't we? Why pile destruction atop destruction? Is it necessary to cage and shoot friends and family who use drugs? This must stop, friends. This is insane and barbaric. We don't live in the Stone Age anymore. We must stop. Now.

September 24, 2014

A Letter to Those Who Believe in the Legal System

If you believe that the criminal justice system is even remotely fair, you may want to take a second look.

It is not a justice system. It is an injustice system.

It favors the State in most cases and automatically works against the accused whether they are guilty or innocent.

It's the only legalized and acceptable form of discrimination in society, and some of the nastiest things have happened as a result of it.

A close, unbiased look at how hypocritical and insidious the system is should be enough to make you question your most fundamental beliefs about democratic law. Indeed, even without principle and philosophy, it is enough to dismantle old and tired worldviews.

Consider these reasons why:

1) Most offenders are wrangled into accepting a plea deal, which generally isn't a deal at all. They are merely harassed and browbeaten because both the defense and prosecutor aren't interested in going to trial, even if the trial would be better off for the defendant.

2) In some states, offenders are offered what is called deferred adjudication, which for all intents and purposes is supposed to be a legal second chance because no criminal conviction is given. However, in almost all situations, private and public, deferred adjudication is still viewed as a criminal conviction with the added evil of having no way to expunge it.

3) Most of the laws on the books don't address moral issues. They exist as revenue generators for the State. Any honest and logical person knows the war on drugs is bullshit and that the consequences of it take a far greater toll on human life than drugs themselves. Just look at the violence, especially enforced by police, that has occurred as a direct result of the laws against drug use. The same barbarism occurred during the prohibition era, which came to a grinding halt when those laws were lifted. These pseudo-moralistic laws are simply ways to make money. They have nothing to do with whether a person is committing a right or wrong act.

4) Once offenders have the stigma of a conviction on their record, they stand very little chance of obtaining respectable employment. Due to the rampant corporatism in place, most major employers do thorough background checks and do not make the decisions to hire or not hire themselves. They relegate the decision-making process to third parties who know jack shit about the person to be hired—except that they did wrong in the eyes of the government overlords.

Tragically, there are too many problems to list.

Either way, I beg you, suspend judgment of the accused, especially concerning the bullshit war on drugs, and let the enormity of the truth marinate in your brain. Let the enormity of the great fiasco that is the criminal justice system settle. Then you will see the truth.

You'll inevitably see that you're surrounded by a bunch of deranged fucks who masquerade as enforcers of justice while committing some of the most horrendous, inhumane acts known to us and are only interested in their own moral smugness and continuous climb to the upper echelons of greed and power. They have no true concern about punishing the wicked. They only care about themselves, as each of us does...except that they use this to hurt people. They use this facade to veil their wickedness, and they delight in punishing and fucking over good people for their own feels and reputations. It's a sick and disgusting menagerie of laughable so-called "justice."

And now it is time for you to see and for all of us to become aware.

It's time to think about doing things differently.

March 29, 2015

A discussion cropped up in class the other day about police officers dealing with the mentally ill. The professor asked, "What do you all think about police officers doing crisis intervention?"

Of course, I was the maverick. Most everyone agreed that police should play a role in helping the mentally ill and uttered various justifications in their defense. I was the only one who pointed out that police have an atrocious track record with the mentally ill. I used examples to buttress my arguments, including the recent incident in Dallas where the "schizophrenic" man was shot to death by cops. I don't think I mentioned the Kelly Thomas tragedy, but that is another example. As soon as I made my comments, everyone argued for making sure police are trained, adding that some police forces are better than others (yadda yadda).

At that point, I sat silent because I knew that if I spoke again, I was going to have to go into detail about the idea of policing and what police "do." I would have had to explain that from the ground up, the institution of policing has a vested interest in using violence and that police do not have an incentive to protect or help people with psychological issues. Police can receive all the training in the world, but at the end of the day, if they "feel like their life is in danger," they are going to shoot first and ask questions later. Police do not care about people, much less those with problems. Their job is to generate revenue for the State and lock people up, not assess mental states or "mental health."

June 27, 2015

This is rich. A bunch of people in robes and fancy suits decided that same-sex marriage is "legal" nationwide. But tell me: since when do another bunch of nobodies get to make relationship decisions for other people or otherwise involve themselves in the contractual sexual interactions of others? Why should any of these individuals have the right to declare it unacceptable or acceptable? Are people not responsible for making decisions about their relationships themselves? Are people perpetual children who need everything approved for them by daddy government? The very idea of this would be hilarious if it weren't so damned tragic.

August 27, 2015

Another shooting occurs, and the gun grabbers are out spewing their poisonous and nonsensical rhetoric. They are claiming that "America" needs sensible gun laws. In other words, they want to make it difficult for people to access and keep guns by calling on men with guns to disarm good people. This argument is not only based on circular reasoning but also lined with blatant hypocrisy. These disarmament apologists are disingenuous. They simply want to centralize gun ownership into circles of authority whether they realize it or not.

The anti-gun crowd also has zero understanding of recent history and examples. Places like Chicago already have hamstringing gun laws. And guess what? Violence has not declined. It has escalated. Whenever guns are banned and gun-free zones are erected, target-rich environments are created—environments perfectly suited to criminal actors. When good people are prevented from acquiring or wielding firearms, they become targets for those who don't mind using black markets to buy guns to hurt others. Gun laws do not stop psychopaths. They encourage violence, both from government and private goons. It is a zero-sum game.

Keep the government away from all matters, especially gun rights issues. Entrusting psychopaths to choose who gets guns and who does not is utterly batshit crazy. Could you imagine letting John Gotti or Al Capone decide who is armed and who is not? Yeah, it is the same scenario when people relinquish choice to the sociopaths in power.

October 1, 2015

A couple of months back, a Texas cop pulled over a black woman suspected of possessing marijuana. The deputy alleged that he smelled it. After he searched her and could not find it, he radioed for a female cop to find the evil plant in the suspect's body. The "suspect" apparently denied having any, so the female cop proceeded to finger-rape the woman in a public parking lot. From the sources I read, no plant was discovered.

I need everyone to think hard about this, especially the statists and bootlickers on my feed. How psychotic is the society we live in that street-side rape is permitted to locate a dried, smelly herb? Are people so deluded and cruel as to think that rape, possible kidnapping, and murder constitute justice and decency? You are one sick, twisted individual if you believe this is how people should be treated and dealt with for carrying around stems and flower particles.

And don't give me that "it's the law" bullshit. It's blind obedience like this that leads to the Hitlers and Hiroshimas of the world.

November 15, 2015

I am saddened to the core about how people are reacting to the Paris massacre. Everywhere, people are calling for the random and arbitrary murder of

Middle Eastern people regardless of whether they are terrorists. People are even cheering France's recent bombings against alleged ISIS units.

For the sake of argument, even if the dead Muslims were all evil (which they likely were not), answering senseless violence with senseless violence is not a solution to the problem.

Defending and applauding the idea of genocide is even worse. It sickens me that people can harbor so much hate as to condemn a group of people to death even if the individuals do not wish to hurt anyone.

This tribal mentality and barbaric mindset have many of you advocating for despicable violence you would normally shun. Yet, when the violence is advocated under the aegis of government and patriotism, it is considered moral and justified. This is just tragic. It horrifies me to live alongside people who want to promote death so readily and ravenously.

Have you no compassion? Have you no heart? Have you no soul? What must it take to sate your desire for blood?

Perpetual war does not end in peace. Warfare continues in the future, a mound of corpses piling up in its wake.

Stop this madness and chaos.

November 18, 2015

Everyone who follows my feed and material need not worry about me regressing back to statism by claiming that borders should be closed. In my mind, the whole concept of "borders" is wholly statist and nonsensical. Anyone who argues for closing or manipulating borders under anarchist pretenses is playing into statist politics, and this is something I will never adopt or accept.

Over the years, alarmists have argued from practicality at the expense of morality and decency. Slavers used to argue about the inefficiency of freeing the slaves and about how it would exacerbate problems at home. This argument rejects the ethics of freeing the slaves on principle. The same problem vexes the "anarcho-statists." Under the fear and delusion that "immigrants" will make the welfare state worse, they are calling for the use of violence to prevent people from traveling freely across geographies.

This mentality is an insult to anarchistic philosophies, and I will never play into it. Borders are fictitious lines drawn on maps by assholes with God complexes, and no alarmist non-argument will sway me from principle.

January 22, 2016

I do not harbor ill-will toward people who adopt the ideology of feminism, but I think it is a toxic idea and corrupting influence. Most feminists claim to support the goal of creating equality between the sexes. Even though the sexes are naturally, biologically unequal, I have seen very few, if any, feminists who seek to end male oppression, and I certainly have not seen any evidence that they have accomplished any goals for the sake of men.

These folks are mostly stuck fixating on what they believe are gender-focused attacks on females, yet males still suffer greatly. Males are the sacrificial animals of society. They are the first to be sent off to war to die, and prisons are overwhelmingly populated by men. Men are more likely to be victims of assault, robbery, and murder. Men are more often targets of genital mutilation. And yet, as free and "equal" as women are, some feminists are concerned with accumulating more power, and a growing number of them also want to make life more difficult and deleterious for males. Some, like the Femtheist, want to see males castrated, segregated, and controlled like cattle.

Thus, after sifting through the evidence and watching the frightening saga of feminism unfold before my eyes, it appears many feminists desire gender supremacy. Even the women who do not publicly support gender supremacy struggle to save and defend their ideology. They work to explain why they adopt an ambiguous philosophy brimming with bigots, control freaks, and a slew of misandrists with penis envy.

With that said, I fully support anyone with humanitarian aims of ending all oppression, especially the oppression caused by government and afflicted on all races, creeds, and genders. I am proud to join anyone who does not attempt to divide people for the sake of their feelings and those who are trying to target and undermine evil. But sadly, most feminists have taken the path of socialism and have fallen victim to arguments from emotion rather than examining the situation with a rational mixture of reason and feeling. I hope that many of them will defect over to the side of truth and accept empathy and compassion for all sexes and all forms of oppression.

That is my desire.

February 25, 2016

Social justice warriors believe they are fighting against the status quo. This is a tragic and erroneous notion. In reality, they are playing into the divide-and-conquer games of politicians and overlords. They are engaging in run-of-the-mill political correctness and sampling the social flavor of the day. They are not engaging in iconoclastic behavior nor upsetting the powers that be in any way. They are actually helping consolidate the power of the ruling class because social justice warrior "activism" splits people into various camps and directly or indirectly gives more legislative control to government criminals.

If social justice warriors genuinely wanted to combat the status quo, they would need to stop focusing on what hurts their feelings and look at who is pointing the guns and killing people. In their egocentric desire to stop people from being mean to them, they have unwittingly aided evil men in accomplishing their murderous and sociopathic aims.

Essentially, the ruling classes have taken advantage of SJWs' volatile sensitivity and desire to be part of the collective and used it to establish more dominance. Thus, social justice warriors need to start examining the situation outside of their teary-eyed perspective and start looking at where real injustice lies. They need to acknowledge the epicenter of evil and start outright combating government and actual authoritarian elements within society. Merely focusing on who is being mean, saying ugly things, or has sexist, racist, or other monomaniac beliefs has the opposite effect of their intended goals.

February 29, 2016

I want to clarify my position on the "open" versus "closed" border dispute so there is no confusion about where I stand. I also want to address some arguments surrounding this fiasco and bring a fresh perspective to bear.

I am for "open borders" in the sense that free people have the inherent right to travel unforced and unrestricted wherever they go so long as individual property rights are respected. But by the same token, I am against any State-mandated importation or care of immigrants. In my mind, this position should be self-evident and obvious since State borders do not suddenly materialize when alarm bells go off.

With that said, there are pockets of anarchists—some of whom are my friends—who believe (for purposes of pragmatism) that political borders should be manipulated to prevent more statism from erupting. The problem is that "border control" requires the use and escalation of State violence against innocent travelers.

This agenda is a devolution in principle and an insinuation of typical utilitarian thought—that the ends (border control) justify the means (sacrificing freedom). If my characterization of this situation is accurate, it would make anarchists guilty of succumbing to the same central planning statists recommend.

If I am missing a piece of this argument or lacking intimate details, I am open to counterfactual information and good-hearted attempts to convince me otherwise. But what I have witnessed so far are attempts to slyly justify violence under various alarmist cries, including fear of "invasion" from brown people who are overburdened by bombs and governments' global war on drugs.

March 8, 2016

For police to do their jobs, they must sacrifice their humanness. No person who uses evasive phrases like "I was just doing my job" or "I was just following orders" after assaulting or murdering another person can maintain respectability and integrity regardless of how much their badge may shimmer in the light. The conscience of the cop has been darkened and corrupted by social engineering. These husks of men now crawl around in the mud like lower creatures because they have sacrificed dignity and decency in exchange for barbaric insanity.

Indeed, the height of incivility is the sacrifice of people to the altar of culturally sanctioned brutality, and the police officer acts as a constant reminder and symbol of how societies destroy the souls of men.

In the police officer, we find all the repressions and homicidal impulses of people played out on the stage of life. The badge and costume have bestowed upon these men a "legitimate" outlet for their psychopathy, and in horror, we witness the ruination of everything good in the wake of their vindictive purging, of their cathartic bloodletting. Therefore, we must put an end to this blood magic. It is as unacceptable as any other form of violence. Badges, uniforms, and political rituals do not negate morality. We must stop providing power to cultural artifacts that bankrupt humanness. We must stop intensifying the urge to kill through hallucinated legitimacy.

April 4, 2016

I do not support the troops.

Not because I hate them. Not because I think all the people involved are vile scum. Not because of any latent teenage angst. Not for any of these reasons.

I do not support the troops because I cherish life, relationships, humanity, peace, and progress—and I cannot condone the murder squadrons that destroy all these precious things.

For the record, my sentiment does not just apply to the US military. It goes for all goddamned government-created war platoons on this planet. I cannot give my personal sanction to any person who chooses to blow away people at the behest of politicians or a mystical object known as the nation-state.

However, if a soldier realizes what he has done and comes back contrite and sorrowful, without the "Rah-rah-rah, kill-em-all" mentality, I can see room for forgiveness, especially if that individual can convince his brothers and sisters to disband and condemn the war machine.

There is nothing acceptable and honorable about promoting bloodshed, even if it is touted under the myopic and absurd plea of defending freedom, which is probably the most obvious lie regurgitated throughout the short annals of human history.

May 2, 2016

I am dumbstruck that individuals go so easily overseas to kill and die. There is nothing stranger and more terrible than knowing soldiers willingly travel to murder foreign, unknown people, all for the pomp and circumstance of nationalistic mythology.

It is hard to empathize with acts as confounding and brutal as this, but I see that these kids are duped and hoodwinked. I just hope they can see through the lies foisted on them by the sycophants and sociopaths. I hope they can disenchant the magic of the stars and stripes so they can turn and walk away.

War is sickening. Killing for the sake of a flag and following orders is downright unnerving. It makes me distraught and fills me with unending sadness. For the sake of peace and goodwill, I hope they lay down their arms and choose life over death. Brown people are not their enemies. They are human, and all are deceived by the cultural toxin of warmongering.

June 12, 2016

What happened in Orlando on June 12, 2016, is a terrible tragedy. My heart goes out to all of those murdered or wounded in the incident. In this time of grave need, I believe anarchists should be willing to provide as much compassion and condolences as possible, regardless of all the smarmy political baiting that is happening as part of the fallout.

Speaking of which, many anarchists tend to characterize what happened as a psyop or false flag campaign—as either a government conspiracy or clever deception.

I am a skeptical person, but I do not take my skepticism so far as to believe every mass shooting has some secret agenda behind it or was somehow faked.

The logistics that would have to go into constantly faking mass shootings would be tremendously difficult. Could you imagine having to plan and execute them and keep everyone in the know? It would be just as exhausting to fraudulently paint even minor details in a different light than the truth.

The government is already evil. We have enough evidence to condemn it without having to imagine that every mass shooting, military move, counterattack, bombing, or other nefarious deed is a de facto false flag or complex conspiracy meant to sway the public.

The public is already easily swayed without having to go through a bunch of rigmarole.

June 19, 2016

A video with two men kissing was recently posted, and there were a lot of negative and homophobic reactions.

I have two thoughts here.

One: If you have an emotional reaction of disgust when you see men kissing, that stems from your own emotional and psychological problems. Kissing is not a harmful act; it does not hurt other people. If you feel loathing or hatred, I encourage you to seek help. Something might be the matter with you, not these men.

Two: I make these comments not as a social justice warrior or in an attempt to defend entitlement mentalities. I only mention this because kissing is an act of love and compassion. Two people engaging in intimacy is non-problematic from a voluntaryist perspective.

Nonetheless, I strongly disagree with using government to silence people who have issues with homosexuality. Employing government violence and coercion to stop haters will not work. It will have the opposite effect and rigidify their hate.

Hatred is a tragic thing, but it is not a moral issue. It is a psychological issue. Therefore, I promote communication and therapy to help people with hatred deal with their internal issues.

If two people's consensual actions disturb a person, that person has a lot of self-healing and internal work to do.

June 28, 2016

The draft is a terrible, disgusting ritual. There is nothing decent about pridefully sending innocent young adults off to die for the nefarious interests of sociopaths. I do not understand how some people can live with the idea that the youth should be sacrificed for the occasion of war. Is there any humanity left in humanity?

The fact that forced warfare is still on the table as a possibility speaks volumes about the brutal nature of this society.

November 8, 2016

One can learn a lot about how people view government and other tyrants by studying the life and psychology of drug baron Pablo Escobar.

Escobar was a duplicitous person brimming with contradictions. On one hand, he saw himself as the noble, benevolent savior of Colombia and a protector of the poor and downtrodden. He wanted to become a leader within the political class in Colombia, as well.

On the other hand, he saw himself as the powerful cartel leader Don Pablo or El Patron, and he nonchalantly ordered bombings and murders without any regard for life.

Because of how he viewed himself and the way he developed and tended to his public image, the working people of Colombia fell in love with him.

Many people, especially in the city of Medellín in Colombia, saw him in the same light as he saw himself: as a protector and saint-like figure. They saw him as an embodiment of good. However, the same people maintained this vision of Escobar while he murdered thousands of people in bombings, shootings, and assassinations. Although many of his targets were either Colombian police officers or politicians (he claimed self-defense), children and other noncombatants were murdered in his campaign against the State.

The important thing to notice about Escobar here is that he is the "civilian" reflection or version of the politician. He cultivated his desire to be loved by the common people and leveraged his charisma to make it a truth. In this regard, many overlooked his immoral acts.

The others who acknowledged his immoral acts could never recognize the same actions in political figures. Politicians regularly order murders and bombings, yet the people cheer for them and love them because they provide handouts and sate the psychological needs of the slobbering masses.

In my opinion, Pablo Escobar and other cartel or mob leaders represent perfect character studies on how people fall in love with evil. They demonstrate why people easily dismiss reprehensible acts for the allure of powerful men, and I think this is part of the truth about why anarchists are oftentimes fascinated by mafia dons and cartel bosses. They provide us with insights into how power corrupts the hearts of unprincipled, desperate people.

December 29, 2016

In the hypothetical event of an all-out war with Russia, I will not be drafted. I will not be coerced into joining the military. I will not spill blood because of the petty disputes of politicians. I will not be a pawn in a game of thrones. The men of always are free to murder each other in cold blood for all I care, but I will not kill others at their behest nor attempt to win their war.

I would rather be called a coward, traitor, or scum. I would rather languish in a cage. The only cowardly move would be to unquestioningly join the killing squads.

But doing that would make me a real traitor—a traitor to my principles, values, and everything I hold sacred. I would be a traitor to peace.

Never will I be forced into a blood feud with people I don't know. Never will

I part with my beloved wife to take on other men's burdens. In this regard, I will be a hero. I will be a hero for the unending battle to abolish governments and rally for global peace.

January 6, 2017

The guy who allegedly shot up the airport was an ex-army soldier. In one of the articles I read, a relative said he went "crazy" because of being in the military.

This does not surprise me.

Members of the military are trained to kill, and those violent tendencies don't vanish after they finish their tour. They come back to the US with all that pain built up, and if they are unable to seek help, their pain can grow into an uncontrollable rage that will explode into violence.

Their pain could be the result of many issues, but moral injury and being brainwashed in boot camp sets the stage for those individuals to lash out with violence more easily.

Generally, if those people have already committed murder overseas, moral injury can cause them to undergo significant stress—enough to alter their thinking and feeling. This combination of agony and the urgency to kill is what allows these people to turn anyone into enemies. That is precisely what the military does: It manufactures killers, and these killers aren't always going to train their focus on who their boss says to kill. They may snap and harm someone else.

In my mind, this is more of a reason to abolish the military and warfare state. The whole process of brainwashing and tricking young people into murdering others is disgusting and tragic. It darkens their souls and causes vast suffering. And if these warriors become unhinged, there is no telling how their rage will be unleashed on society.

The business of the military is a nasty business. It is something we could all do without, lest more innocents die as they did in the airport incident—lest there is more indiscriminate killing overseas.

January 9, 2017

The "United States" has a history of supporting terrorism, not countering it.

February 20, 2017

There are protests galore with people saying, "not my president."

This is confusing to an ungodly degree.

Why is any president "yours"?

Why is there this kinky and filthy attachment to certain rulers? Is there a way to escape the Stockholm syndrome and urge to mollycoddle murderers and maniacs?

There is no need for these tyrants to act as surrogate abusive parents to you. It's time to grow beyond this disturbing need to claim that any president is "yours." It is time for the paradigm of self-respect and self-love.

No president is "yours." You own yourself. You are a champion of yourself. You have dignity and decency. You are civilized. You are an amazing human being. I implore you to move beyond this mentality for all presidents—for all people who would encourage you to kiss the ring and lick the boot.

The coming of anarchism is now; the self-respecting individual is emerging.

March 8, 2017

I am glad WikiLeaks is releasing information about CIA hacking for one particular reason: The hacked companies now have some incentive to repair or service hacked products. However, if they refuse to repair their hacked devices or encryption protocols, then shame on them. I hope they lose business and fail.

None of us wants or needs government in our lives, especially not to spy on us while we privately communicate with our loved ones and business partners.

All hacked companies: I implore you to do the right thing!

Get your shit together. Keep the government out of our business.

March 12, 2017

"ISIS is the most dangerous terror group."

No.

The United States government is.

April 11, 2017

If you dehumanize a person or culture, you are mentally preparing to spill blood.

The Psychopathology of Statism

5/25/2016

The stars and stripes are ablaze and burning bright. The hiss and crackle of the flame can be heard as charred and half-smoldering bits of cloth float away on an uncaring wind. The odor of the smoldering fabric can be smelled in the air by pedestrians as the remaining scraps spread across the land.

This scene portrays the desecration of the American flag. It is an idea and action that throws millions of people into the bloodlust haze of illogical, frenzied anger. These people discard sanity upon seeing or thinking about flag desecration because the flag represents the magical artifact of a beloved nation.

Tragically, this latent rage also highlights an underlying condition. When someone purposely destroys the flag, people rally to condemn and shame the person who did it. Some of them take their anger further. They intimidate or threaten the flag destroyer. But individuals who want to hurt the flag burner are not upset about damaged property. They are distressed because they worship the symbolism behind the flag. They are enraged because of their blind obedience to nationalism. It has nothing to do with any rational moral ethic.

This nationalism that leads people to coerce or hurt others over colored tendrils of cloth is part of a contagious, pathological condition also known as "statism."

An Ideological Disorder

"Statism" is the ideological disorder that claims an abstract entity known as the nation-state must exist and that it bestows upon some humans the right to rule others and punish them for transgressions against authority. It also suggests that certain geographical regions, like "America," have special meaning insofar that shaming them is considered disrespectful and disloyal, even though "nations" are merely masses of land.

Every facet of statism is psychologically problematic. Flag worship, patriotic obedience to authority, politicking, and love of landmasses all verge on insanity, but people living in this matrix of delusion do not recognize it. For them, it is a fixture of their lives. It is a silent cult. This manifestation of ritual statism is so deeply embedded in people's minds that they do not suspect anything is wrong. They are "clinically ill" but do not recognize it because they have adopted the shared madness of patriotic fervor.

People who are violent or who do not experience empathy and concern for their fellow humans are usually labeled as psychopaths by psychiatry. In his fascinating book *The Science of Evil*, psychologist Simon Baron-Cohen lists the traits psychopaths possess. They include an inability to experience the emotions of others, purposeful manipulation of people, and the desire to hurt or harm others. Interestingly, statists often fit the criteria for mental illness, but psychiatrists are too blinded by culture to see the bias in their diagnostic procedures. According to the *Diagnostic and Statistical Manual for Mental Disorders* (DSM), "There is a pervasive pattern of disregard for and violation of the rights of others occurring since age 15 years, as indicated by three (or more) of the following: having hurt, mistreated, or stolen from another."

The characteristics listed above classify the perfect diagnosis for people suffering from statism, which could be called a personality disorder. The *DSM* goes on to explain that hostility, callousness, and manipulativeness are primary qualities of personality disorders.

If psychiatrists were honest about the logical application of mental illness, people who worship the State would be the first to be diagnosed with antisocial personality disorder and perhaps schizophrenia (when people use terms like sociopathy and sometimes psychopathy, they are ultimately referring to antisocial personality disorder). These are the kinds of people who want to harm or hurt those who do not follow their ideology. They are people who believe flags talk to them, who see the nation as a real object, who will trick children into joining their cult, and who will arbitrarily kill for government.

Consensus Delusion

The most tragic aspect of this specific psychopathy is that it is a form of consensus delusion. It is shared by most of the tribe, and its members see their behavior as normal and acceptable. It has been ingrained in the culture and is immune from psychiatric scrutiny. As a result, most people believe the State has the right to rule and that everything related to it is holy and sacred. If anyone transgresses, they should be adequately harassed, scapegoated, punished, and bullied.

Statists initiate aggression and immorality, but oddly, they are considered mentally healthy. For much of American society and mainstream psychiatry, disobeying State authority and trespassing on collective values are terrible wrongs, while obeying the status quo is an absolute right.

All of the aforesaid tribalism is kept in vogue by politicians and judges in robes who act as the voice of their god, the State. They even speak for this god as if they were its priests, and they discipline wrongdoers as if they were subjects. It is a nonsensical and anti-humanitarian sickness.

Terence Mckenna summed up this culture of psychosis: "We are caged by our cultural programming. Culture is a mass hallucination, and when you step out of the mass hallucination you can see it for what it is worth."

The Saving Grace

McKenna was right. People currently under the enchantment of statism are not damned to an eternity of believing in violent ideology. Like most "mental illnesses," their behavior and thoughts are not symptoms of a permanent disease. Mental illness does not exist in this sense. It is only a descriptive label of certain behaviors. Contrarian therapists only use it to understand thinking and behavior from a context of human action and choice, not as a physical ailment.

That said, the label of psychopathology in statism has categorical merit. People are troubled in their deranged views. They are "crazy" to think that burning a bit of cloth is evil, that politicians have authority, and that geographical regions contain magical power. Luckily, it is not beyond their ability to snap out of their confusion and behavior.

Instead of choosing statism, they can choose the power of the individual. They can set their eyes to notions of freedom and peace. They can forget their desire to harm others and realize they have been duped by a culture-bound religious movement. They can lift their eyes to the heavens of truth and dispense with old dogmas. They can behold the greater truths of goodwill, love, and anarchism. All it takes is for them to examine all prior assumptions and worldviews. All it takes is one Zen moment of clarity and insight. That could be their saving grace.

The Moral Virtue of Anarchism

February 7, 2011

The strength of a person lies in his or her virtue.

February 8, 2011

The non-aggression principle should be the central virtue for any self-loving, world-loving person.

December 11, 2011

What is the ultimate source of morality? Is it merely a human construct for living in society? Is it evolutionary? Or is it an edict from God? Where do we derive our concept of morality?

January 13, 2012

Morality is not merely a guideline for the treatment of others or a proclamation for good behavior; it is more so a reaffirmation of the golden rule. Morality is really about reciprocation and the sharing of civility.

August 21, 2013

You don't need to consult a history text, wonder what some historical figure thought, or do rigorous research to realize that murder, theft, and rape are wrong. This is the kind of thinking that ivory tower intellectuals want you to embrace; that way, you can remain in a state of confusion regarding every obvious moral problem.

January 24, 2014

I feel sorry for anyone who adopts Nietzsche's philosophy. He reveled in contradictions and a disdain for morality. Some people might not know this, but in the early 1900s, Clarence Darrow defended two boys, Leopold and Loeb, on murder charges. Their defense revolved around the idea that due to their lack of free will and their belief in the Nietzschean Übermench, or Superman, the boys were not responsible for their crimes. This philosophy comes from Nietzsche's idea of being "beyond good and evil." This is also why Hitler supposedly endorsed the same ideas. Indeed, some people might point out that these people misinterpreted Nietzsche. But I reject that idea. If someone reads your work, somehow misinterprets you, and believes what you said validates murder, you were not clear or coherent in what you were saying. You probably weren't in your right mind when you were trying to convey your message. I've never burned a book before, but I am tempted to use *The Will to Power* as kindling.

March 14, 2014

People wrangle over the idea of government being too intrusive or too overbearing, but very few address the central issue: that government is control and violence. No one admits the nature of government is always to become intrusive because the sociopaths that cling to power want to intrude and act like overbearing father figures. They want to control you and hurt you if you do not comply with their demands. So instead, more people need to wrangle over whether government should exist at all and whether people should be legally allowed to beat and shoot people if they feel like it.

March 15, 2014

I spent some time reading Nietzsche's *On the Genealogy of Morality*. His idea was that morality sprung out of the slave's desire to cope with and hide his envy for the master. Over time, this envy altered the good-bad distinction into the good-evil division of morality. Nietzsche claimed morality originated from the ruling class telling the slaves what the difference between good and bad was: that "bad" was poor, slavish, downtrodden, ugly, etc., while "good" was wealthy, successful, intelligent, beautiful, etc. But as Judaism and Christianity grew and the ascetic mentality developed, so did this envy or "ressentiment" for the rulers. The religious person would then use his asceticism, self-denial, and piety as a cover for his envy and hatred. Nietzsche referred to this change as the "slave revolt in morality" and religious morality as "herd morality."

This idea triggered Nietzsche's most telling position on morality: that morality was only useful for slaves, peasants, and the masses. He said morality could be useful for the master or strong person per se, but that he should develop his own ideas and morality and move beyond good and evil. This is also why Nietzsche saw such vast nihilism among Europeans.

Nietzsche was a brilliant wordsmith and was witty and ironic, but logic, reason, or a systemization of philosophy never crept into his work. He never considered first principles, universal morality, or reasoning from evidence, and therefore psychopaths and murderers have confused his writing with "moral" elitism and allowed his work to give them justification for evil. Leopold and Loeb and Hitler all stand as examples of evil people who studied Nietzschean philosophy, though Leopold and Loeb murdered one boy, and Hitler committed genocide. Leopold and Loeb truly believed they could commit the perfect crime, and Hitler saw Jews as subhuman (and even though Nietzsche criticized Judaism, he was apparently not anti-Semitic).

April 15, 2014

Anarchists are simple creatures.

We shun the initiation of violence. We love self-defense but do not chastise pacifism.

This is why government cannot be part of our philosophy: governments use violence to enforce laws.

Anarchism literally means no rulers, no kings, Rulers, kings, or wiseguys. all use violence to enforce their leadership. This is a no-no.

Now, you will undoubtedly ask if anarchism is possible. Just remember one thing:

Do you ever personally intend to use violence to force your will on others? Are you okay with caging and killing people who do not obey you?

If you are not okay with these things and find them revolting, you might be an anarchist.

You see, anarchy is not scary or crazy. We just want to be left alone to live without the omnipresent threat of violence against us for living how we wish.

Being an anarchist is the mature way of being. Government decision-making is not—despite what we have been taught.

Remember that when you feel the emotions that might crop up from listening to an anarchist, the anarchist is not trying to hurt you or scare you away. The anarchist just wants to be your friend.

It is just that people have been engineered to react emotionally against certain ideas. Plus, we all suffer from problems of ego and want to be right all the time.

But remember: Anarchism is an evolving philosophy that is finally starting to draw interest for its practical implications. Just let it embrace you as you mull it over.

Anarchy is about peace, freedom, and truth. It is about having true civilization, and really, truly being a good neighbor, Samaritan, husband, wife, brother, sister, and individual. This is what everyone strives for but what the anarchist actually lives.

April 26, 2014

Some people are too sycophantic and fearful to change their views, so they'd rather kiss the ring of their masters than betray the evil they condone. This upsets me. I understand that brainwashing is involved, but let us be real. We do not need to devote much mental energy to the fact that taxation is theft and governments are based on hurting people. These are self-evident facts.

What will it take to wake you up, to see that all the kleptocratic politicians are naked and wearing no clothes? What will it take to free you from the mental shackles of government and dissuade you from the belief that using violence to get results is a net good? Are you really willing to be fodder for these assholes? Are you that weak? See yourself for who you are, come alive, be alert and awake, and inspire others to break their chains.

I see decent people out there who know something is wrong, and now anarchists are bringing the truth after thousands of years of human arrogance and stupidity. See this truth. Show others this truth. Protect our loved ones, our children. Put an end to these vampires, these megalomaniacal buffoons. They are eating our souls, and one day we will pay for our indifference and false security if we do not work against it. The time to ripen and see ourselves as complete and knowledgeable is now. Don't let it all slip away. Start brandishing our words like firebrands against evil. Our words will invoke change. I am sure of it.

May 17, 2014

Politicians are not your friends. These thugs are not your servants. They are not here to protect you and take care of you or build the roads. They are sadistic individuals with a penchant for violence. They just give lip service to all these feel-good, fluffy bunny plans, which in reality are hollow and superficial. They are playing with your emotions, pretending. They are worse than crooks, as so many realize. These people would see you die and go about laughing at your corpse. These are twisted people, yet you remain eager to perpetuate government knowing that pricks like this will clamor to hold official positions. How long will you play into their silly, contrived game? How long will you vie for your own slavery? How long before you stop playing pretend with them?

April 26, 2016

Anarchism is without a doubt one of the most psychologically functional philosophies.

If one chooses any other political arrangement or violence-laden doctrine, that individual is expressing a latent desire to punish and harm others as an act of vengeance for what has been done to them in the past.

Conversely, the person who selects anarchism as their compass has come to terms with aspects of their emotionally chaotic world. They have confronted the juggernaut of the inner self and dispensed with the petty urge to forcibly control and manhandle others.

If you feel the urge to hurt people or the desire to have the government manipulate and coerce individuals into adopting a specific idea or behavior, it might be smart to introspect and delve deeply into your soul to exorcise the demons. Trying to micromanage various aspects of reality is stressful.

If the above does not work—they call it psilocybin. It will help you start that process.

July 11, 2016

Anarchism is the apex of social evolution. If anything represents a shift in thought or consciousness, it is this gathering fellowship of freedom lovers. Denouncing murder, theft, assault, and abuse from all segments of society— especially government—is a sign of growth. It is change and maturation. The coming-of-age story or rite of passage in this historical context is humanity's ascendance to global anti-statism and people's awakening to the depredations of authority. Therefore, I say welcome to the future.

November 6, 2016

Government is not healthy. If an individual or group employs violence as its means to accomplish goals, that individual or group is compromised. There can be no healthy person or organization that resorts to childish aggression under the aegis of the noble cause. This behavior is simply fallout from ages of coercive parenting, authoritarian education, and the pseudo-philosophy of "might makes right." We must encourage everyone within society to deprogram and unplug. What has not worked and what has caused mass harm and genocide must be recanted and retooled in favor of something more peaceful, alluring, and innovative.

November 25, 2016

Anarchists don't accept bloodshed and chaos.

Government rulers accept those things.

April 21, 2017

I am not a moral nihilist. However, I am a moral inconsequentialist. This is the philosophical position that moralizing, regardless of whether it's an objective fact, doesn't necessarily sway people to that position.

Moral inconsequentialists believe communication efforts and relationships trump the need for hard moral positions. If people have strong relationships and open communication, they can practically and interactively solve their problems without needing to invoke right or wrong.

In the case of aggression or harm, it is up to the individual to make decisions about what their morally defined position suggests in terms of action.

Nonetheless, if we can create and build strong relational bonds, moral positions become irrelevant to the way people develop and build communities.

This is especially true in cases where we are constructing freedom cells or octalogues, where individuals' philosophical positions may vary drastically.

Note: A freedom cell is a small group of people who come together to build communities based on the principles of anarchism and liberty. The group is usually made up of at least eight members, and they engage in skill sharing, agorism, self-defense training, and growing food. They try their best to live off the grid or without having to accept State-based handouts or support. These folks have come together to create freedom-based communities because they hope to craft a better world without leveraging coercion or violence. Derrick Broze has developed the idea substantially and given people the means to create freedom cells via his online network at https://freedomcells.org/.

Anarchism Takes Courage:
Helping People Escape the Cult of Normalcy

03/02/2016

Anarchism is about courage. It takes poise to help people escape the cult of normalcy where they revel in a haze of disinterest, violence, and depravity. But when anarchists attempt to persuade people to discard love of their culture coma, blood, and carnage, they usually receive a reprisal in the form of dismissive slander and appeals to State piety.

It goes without saying that the aforesaid defensiveness will crop up. Anarchism is not a philosophy one can peddle without expecting a backlash. Anarchists require gumption to spread their ideas. They need not hide in the basement and avoid attacks; anarchists must eventually emerge from the basement and lay siege to the idea of statism. They must not be too fearful to communicate lest they become miserly in their attempts to liberate the downtrodden.

However, the person who adopts anarchism must also consider the threats and challenges. They must fully comprehend what they are getting into. There will be pushback from all social segments, and much of the resistance will be vicious, childish, and sometimes violent.

Thus, anarchists must try to convince everyone of their servitude and begin moving in the direction of sovereignty, especially with friends and family.

Courage in the Family Unit

As soon as anarchists utter one word about the liberation of mind and body, friends and family will likely alienate them, ostracize them, and turn them into social pariahs. They will talk about them behind their backs and perhaps excommunicate them from the clan.

When anarchists make a stand for truth and liberty, they are de facto removing themselves from the cult of familial normalcy. Out of necessity, they are taking a stand against violent relationships and the bad ideas that circulate within family systems. They are focusing on a wholly positive and moral set of principles, whereas friends and family are entrenched in the banality of evil.

Yet this is also a good step toward infecting the family with enthusiasm for freedom, and it should not be taken for granted. Writer J.K. Rowling summed up this ability to question friends and family. "It takes a great deal of bravery to stand up to our enemies, but just as much to stand up to our friends," she said.

If anarchists do not understand this sacrifice or they buckle under pressure from friends and family, they may not be ideal candidates for the job. However, it is okay to remain silent in some instances and shoulder the burden of anarchism in secret. The anarchist family member must pick and choose their battles.

However, if anarchists never chat about freedom and never put themselves on the line, they will wither away, and their families may never know the truth. This would be a tragedy, which is why courage is the epicenter of anarchistic action. It is the melody that freedom lovers play to the hymn of bravery. Ultimately, if anarchists can get in touch with their families on this issue, the world will be better for it. When the family culture changes, global culture likewise changes. It just takes that one impulse to act without fear.

But there is an equally dire problem. Dealing with the family is not the most dangerous area where the anarchist must use courage.

The Looming Threat of Government

Anarchists must eventually challenge government sociopaths. This particular battle could give rise to violent reprisal, though. As soon as anarchists start talking negatively about the State or challenging government agents, they may become targets. Government entities may try to use the chilling effect to quell dissent. The chilling effect refers to legal threats that cause fear and alarm, effectively silencing dissenters. Finally, governments may resort to violence. It is nothing new for an agent of the State to harm, cage, or harass an anarchist.

Cop Block activist Ademo Freeman can attest to this. He has been trailed to court and other places by government goons. One can also ask Come and Take it Texas founder Murdoch Pizgatti about his interactions with the State, as well as his friends who have been locked up for trivial "offenses."

Many anarchists have had run-ins with cops, and few of these interactions ended peaceably. However, notice that these anarchists continue to do what they do. They continue to manifest courage in all of their exploits.

The Anarchist as a Prey Species: Evolving Uses of Nonviolence and Communication

Anarchists have historically been a prey species for bureaucrats. They are the hunted because they are the ones trying to overturn the aggressive hierarchy and create stability among the people. Thus, the courage of an anarchist equates to absolute fearlessness. The anarchist could die in the process of being disobedient.

Therefore, some anarchists and libertarians have invoked the porcupine as the image of ceaseless defense. Its spines represent pinpoint protection against its natural predators, though anarchists have not yet needed to unleash a barrage of spines. They have tried to employ less lethal or painful tactics.

Modern anarchists are using peaceful interaction, nonviolent resistance, and nonviolent communication to spread truth, which involves tremendous bravery because nonviolent resistance can also get bloody.

However, it is more difficult for governments to react to this kind of dissent with violence. Historically, when a government tries to squash nonviolent protesters and revolutionaries, that government ends up damaging their already questionable reputation. Once that happens, other regimes target that government out of an attempt to save the idea of statism as a representative symbol of the people. Thus, the ability to be steadfast and exemplary may pay off for anarchists.

Escaping the Cult of Normalcy, Creating a Culture of Courageousness

Anarchists must maintain testicular fortitude. When they get the ball of dissent rolling, they will likely undergo assaults from all of those they engage, including friends, family, society, and government thugs. But if they remain vigilant, people will start to see them as role models, and consequently, they will help people escape the cult of normalcy.

The cult of normalcy relies on passive acceptance of the status quo, which is why unflinching courage is so important for anarchists. If anarchists employ tenacity when they spread ideas, those ideas might be more easily entertained by members of the citizenry who are entrenched in the matrix of everyday statism. In this sense, courage represents the cure for the various authoritarian memes being injected into society.

No doubt, when people realize the strength of their soul, they will eventually spit in the face of those who claim to be their masters—they will rebel not physically but culturally, mentally, and emotionally. They will reject the notion that they must be meek and docile before those who insinuate themselves as parasitic entities bent on feeding off of them forever.

Therefore, this new direction of freedom through courage represents the birthright of humanity, and it may eventually spur a paradigm shift, changing a culture of conformity into one of courage.

"I wanted you to see what real courage is, instead of getting the idea that courage is a man with a gun in his hand. It's when you know you're licked before you begin, but you begin anyway and see it through no matter what.

—Harper Lee, *To Kill a Mockingbird*

PART 2: RELATIONAL ANARCHISM AND THERAPEUTIC LIBERATION

Anarchy and Emotion:
Toward a Softer Aesthetic for Freedom

03/31/2016

> "The world will not know peace until we learn to understand each other's emotions."
>
> —Bangambiki Habyarimana, *The Great Pearl of Wisdom*

I made an unconscious, unwritten vow when I turned into an anarchist. I swore to sacrifice emotion and discard weakness and frailty. I would stop being soft, reactionary, and volatile. I would champion reason and brush aside feelings. I would be unflinching in my resolve to argue truths, and I would not allow emotions to spoil my articulation of them.

If there was one thing I internalized, it was that emotions were less than desirable. They were yucky and unacceptable. They represented human folly, and they needed to be more than just controlled. They needed to be squelched. Emotions were the lifeblood of statists, of sheep who could not think and who could be easily herded. Reason, on the other hand, was the domain of the übermensch—of the anarchist.

In this way, anarchists stood above the common person. They were immortal in their technique. They were like the Greek gods atop Olympus, looking down smugly on the unwashed masses.

An Introduction to Anarchist Types

It is true: Most anarchists shun emotion. They pretend they do not possess it or imagine it as dichotomous to thinking. They infuse their rhetoric with straightforward, clear-headed logic. If too much emotion seeps into their philosophizing, they are no better than the voting cattle. This remains the bedrock of anarcho-capitalist and voluntaryist thinking.

Ayn Rand's views on emotions are shared by most voluntaryists, as well. "An emotion that clashes with your reason, an emotion that you cannot explain or control, is only the carcass of that stale thinking which you forbade your mind to revise," she said.

In Rand's view, emotions that "clash" with reason are mostly problematic and useless. However, sometimes it may be important for the heart to override reason because reason does not account for closeness and empathy. It also denies our innate urge to connect deeply with other humans. Rand clearly placed thinking above emotion.

The anarchists who share the objectivist view of reason, with their disdain for emotions and sentiment, are called "hard" anarchists, whereas emotionally intelligent anarchists are called "soft." These are called the "anarchist types."

"Hard" anarchists wrap their emotional lives in a straitjacket and imagine they can help change society through raw argumentation and brainpower. "Soft" anarchists, on the other hand, believe community and love can foster change for freedom. They rely less on proving anarchism can work by constantly articulating formulaic plans.

Soft anarchism is the new aesthetic I am advocating. It is a unique stratagem, a different vision for creating change and building communities. It appeals to human psychology rather than logical proofs.

The Hard versus Soft Continuum: 'Feeling' Our Way into Freedom

Hard and soft anarchists are not terms that speak to political leanings like left-right or libertarian-socialist. Hard and soft refer to the emotional availability of the anarchists within each category. Further, hard and soft are not necessarily binary constructs.

The hard-soft designation can be seen on a continuum where middle- to soft-range is more acceptable for balance and healthy psychological functioning. But as I stated, most anarchists sit on the hard end of the spectrum.

Softer anarchists do not denounce reason or interact with their fellow humans in a volatile or illogical way. They simply reach out with their hearts to make contact with others. They practice what psychologist Daniel Goleman referred to as "emotional intelligence."

Speaking about emotional intelligence, Goleman said, "If your emotional abilities aren't in hand, if you don't have self-awareness, if you are not able to manage your distressing emotions, if you can't have empathy and have effective relationships, then no matter how smart you are, you are not going to get very far."

Goleman's ideas eloquently illustrate why emotion trumps reason and why soft anarchists may have a better chance of helping shift the dominant culture toward a more emotional-anarchic expression.

Soft anarchists have a sense of other people's inner worlds. They grasp emotional content. They attempt to empathize and relate through compassion.

This is how they spread anarchism. They wish to "feel" their way into a free society rather than beat people over the head with dry, syllogistic wordplay.

The Culture of Anarchism

I originally adopted the idea that I had to promote anarchism from the pulpit of reason. I was a "hard" anarchist. I thought I had to do everything to emit an aura of tough and unflinching confidence. Emotions were not part of the equation.

This anti-emotion stance was not explicit, though. It was embedded in the culture of anarchism. It had a life of its own throbbing beneath the surface. I remember witnessing it, but it was only a speck. It barely penetrated the edges of my psyche. But when I consider everything in retrospect, the truth struck me.

As I recall the anarchist books, videos, blogs, essays, podcasts, and other content I trudged through, the anarchist attack on emotion seemed clear. These anarchists wanted to be as rational as possible, to obliterate government along with everything soft and sensitive.

If these hard freedom lovers were not writing about Aristotle, Rothbard, or Rand and their logical and economic rationales, they were invoking their style and mentality. For them, empathy, compassion, connection, and love were banned from the anarchist lexicon. In their hunger for truth, they forgot about humanness.

Evidence of 'Hard' Anarchism and Its 'Logical' Consequences

The Case of Molyneux

(Note: After this article was written, Molyneux eventually disavowed anarchism entirely and became popular in the alt-right and neo-fascist movement. In my mind, this occurred because of his lack of emotional literacy. In a way, this article foresaw his shift in thinking and philosophy.)

An example of a hard anarchist is Stefan Molyneux. He actively promotes the concept of defooing, which means shunning one's family of origin over logical, ideological, and principled differences.

Molyneux advocates the practice for those who have been hurt by their families or spanked as young children. I agree that abuse and spanking are horrible practices, but almost all families are corrupted by dysfunction in the current culture. Thus, blindly advocating for people to cut ties with their families is simply not realistic and does not solve interpersonal problems. Instead, it ignores emotional realities and creates further trauma.

Many people have complicated attachments to their families, and defooing means sacrificing any chance of reconciliation or shared understanding. It also means that the opportunity for the family to comprehend anarchism is stymied and undermined.

The damage that could result from this, both emotionally and culturally, seems lost on Molyneux. His concerns have only congealed around an ego-centric drive to free anarchism of statism, which underlies an extreme form of logical thought that destroys the possibility of helping some populations understand freedom. It is my opinion that Molyneux's "reasoning" may have the opposite effect on some groups.

A Libertarian Gamer article (site now defunct) put it this way: "Defooing is an over-glorified act of cowardice and running away from opposition through not being able to persuade the statist that their statism is violent. If anyone wants liberty to grow, there are many people who need convincing."

Molyneux allegedly caters to a train of thought in line with psychological reasoning, but in practice, he muddles psychological principles with personal ideology, corrupting the heart of interpersonal wisdom.

With that said, this is not a personal attack. I aim to highlight the consequences of hard anarchism and shine a little light on the rigid mentality that permeates anarchist circles, as well as how reason can bump heads with emotion, leading to disastrous outcomes for the cultivation of freedom.

A Few Thoughts on Brutalism

Economist and anarcho-capitalist Jeffrey Tucker has also pointed out another possible manifestation of the hard anarchist mentality: the brutalist.

In an essay called "Against Libertarian Brutalism," he condemned some libertarian segments for their malice, indiscretion with certain issues, and their desire to apply anarchist logic to the extreme. Even though Tucker pointed out that brutalism involves racism, sexism, and other divisive politics, I saw his underlying point to be that brutalists are utterly devoid of empathy and compassion for various groups.

Tucker said:

> In the libertarian world, however, brutalism is rooted in the pure theory of the rights of individuals to live their values whatever they may be. The core truth is there and indisputable, but the application is made raw to push a point. Thus do the brutalists assert the right to be racist, the right to be a misogynist, the right to hate Jews or foreigners, the right to ignore civil standards of social engagement, the right to be uncivilized, to be rude and crude.

At one time, former anarchist activist Christopher Cantwell acted as the perfect representative of brutalism. He took his position so far as to throw around dehumanizing insults at anyone who believed or behaved differently from him, especially if they mildly appeared to be on the "left" in terms of various proclivities.

But fortunately for many, instead of consolidating his position within anarchism, Cantwell only alienated himself, made enemies, and was actively blacklisted from various conferences and meetups. It turns out that taking anarchism to this kind of extreme does not pay in dividends, and he unsurprisingly devolved back into aggressive statism.

(Note: Cantwell eventually ended up in prison and was dubbed "the crying Nazi.")

Women and Anarchism

It is possible that this brutalist behavior also pushes women away from freedom communities. Anarchists have constant trouble appealing to women. Based on page statistics from The Art of Not Being Governed page, women represent a minority of followers.

There are several theories as to why this is the case, but I believe it is because women are more naturally inclined to be emotive and empathetic. All the hard-hitting argumentation devoid of emotion turns them off. In this regard, they may view anarchist circles as men's-only clubs.

This is not to imply that women do not think or exercise rational thought. It is only to say that women want more emotional variety and subtlety. They want their hearts to be stimulated along with their minds, and it is my impression that a movement toward softer anarchism could raise appeal levels for women.

After I started focusing more on the gut than the brain, I saw increases in female followers on Psychologic-Anarchist. I expect that this increase will continue as I flesh out the ideas and continue to build emotive communities, allowing everyone to move toward a more relational and caring version of anarchism.

(Note: My Facebook page Psychologic-Anarchist was eventually censored and shut down by Facebook in October of 2018 after amassing 50,000 followers)

Toward the Doctrine of Relationalism

As I have attempted to demonstrate, anarchist groups have mostly been comprised of people uttering the same "logical" truths in a kind of echo chamber. They are stuck on the economic, logical, and moral (LEM) vectors of thought. They have not considered tackling the issue of anarchism and combating statism from other angles. My goal is to observe the situation from an emotional, dialogic, holistic, and visceral perspective.

I think some people have been so swept away by the ongoing uproar of voluntaryist groupthink that they have not independently contemplated the current situation. I just hear a lot of people parroting Molyneux, invoking Mises, or regurgitating Rothbard over and over ad nauseam.

As an aside, that is not to say that these philosophies are bad or wrong. It is only to say that they appeal to specific groups, and anarchists have not moved far from them in their annunciations of truth.

But now, I feel like the community is maturing and branching out; more people are becoming interested in psychological expressions of freedom. The community is growing based on spirit, depth of character, human acceptance, and kindness.

It is this intelligent yet sensitive group that relates to others in a nonviolent and caring fashion without necessarily needing to invoke the NAP at every turn. It is the beginning of an anarchist culture that accepts the tenets of relational anarchism and can communicate without needing to invoke morality at every turn. This, I believe, heralds the next school of thought within the philosophy of anarchism.

Relationalism

February 2, 2011

I think the best kind of political action is talking to each other. Active dialogue on anything works wonders, but honesty is always the best policy, as they say.

July 28, 2012

Being a good leader is not about forcing people to follow you, nor is it about being charismatic enough. Good leadership is about developing relationships with people and caring enough about them to earn their trust. Good leadership hinges on how well you allow people to commit to you and your vision.

October 21, 2013

There have been more and more people getting upset at my message, deleting me as a friend, or otherwise threatening me and telling me to shut up.

This is my message to those folks:

I love you. Each of you, especially if we are close. So, hear me out. My message is one of peace and hope and truth. If I say offensive things and you become angry, it's because my words echo a truth that contradicts everything you have known. But this is not because what I say is wrong. It's because you're mentally latched onto what society tells you is moral and good. But listen to your heart and hear me out...I speak truth while bearing a white flag. I only yearn for freedom, nonviolence, and mutual appreciation.

March 8, 2014

Anarchy is simple: I should be able to live my life without having to worry about someone "legally" caging or shooting me for making a decision. I should be able to succeed or fail on my own. To wit, anarchy is about engaging in voluntary relationships. On the other hand, violence against peaceful people is unacceptable. Some people see this as a radical idea, but it is natural to live without being violated and harmed by State-sanctioned goons. Just let organic and relational anarchy happen.

May 27, 2014

Anarchists often devalue emotions or push them aside and pretend they are Vulcan. They pretend that they have perfect logical thought, that they are infallible. I am guilty of this hubris, too.

This is often a good thing because emotions have led us astray and caused us to believe in and follow things that are dangerous or destructive. Religious persecution, warfare, Nazism, racism, sexism, and all forms of hate have stemmed from the pit of the lizard brain and led to some of the worst and most pervasive chaos and strife society has had the displeasure of suffering.

But anarchists have pushed emotion so far to the side that they have forgotten empathy and the power it has for changing hearts. If anarchists worked on the heart rather than the mind, more people would be eager to change their attitudes. Of course, this is not to say that anarchists are a bunch of brutalist assholes or that this even matters or is relevant. It's just to say that pontificating from the altar of pure reason is failing. It has failed. People recoil at the suggestion that they are aiding and defending murderers and psychopaths; they become defensive at the suggestion that they are interested or complicit in robbing others, and now they wholly strike out at the anarchist with contempt and hatred. Their minds and hearts have shut down, and they shun the anarchist.

They see the anarchist as a spiteful creature, spitting hate and venom. Their perception of the anarchist hearkens back to the myth that anarchists are just a bunch of edgy teenagers. Anarchists must see this mistake and awaken to the power of empathy and compassion. Simply telling people how violent and nasty they are has had a minimal effect. I do see where it has worked in some situations, especially with younger, more malleable crowds, but now we need another path that can help guide the more deeply indoctrinated and older generations into the light.

I recently tried this method on people, and I received positive feedback. Now, it *has* felt counterintuitive. Maybe it gives too much leeway to outright evil, but I am convinced that most of the evil in people is impure. They are just misled and abused souls who believe they are in the right and that anarchists are the bad people, but this idea of the anarchist can be changed by portraying the movement in the light of love. I believe this because the goals of statelessness focus on erasing violence, which starts by showing how peaceful in mind and heart anarchists really are.

This does not mean we should mind our manners to the point of walking on eggshells or that we should refrain from creating Facebook pages called "Libertarian Brutalism." It just means we should understand psychology and practice empathy. We should share what we have in common with others and where we would like to be in terms of living in our community. It's a kind of emotional anarchism that naturally precedes non-aggression and nonviolence.

These are just some of the ideas that have welled up within me over the last few years of being a voluntaryist and observing the climate of the community and movement. It is where I feel more of us should be headed. It's all about the heart. The logic comes after, oddly enough.

June 6, 2015

It is difficult to talk to people about freedom. Most of them have not considered it. They have not thought beyond what public education has taught them, so they regurgitate the same claptrap they have been spoon-fed their whole lives. Thus, it takes a lot of patience to explain and express the precepts of liberty and to respectfully challenge dangerous and distorted worldviews.

Part of being able to calmly express these ideas means not only bombarding people with reason and logic but also empathizing with their plight and leveling with their humanity. People cling tightly to their views as a result of ego psychology and the complexities of nature and nurture. They build resistance to other ideas over time, and this allows culture to take advantage of the malleability of the human brain.

But that is also the psychological edge anarchists have. They can turn the tides with the proper approach and use the malleability of the brain to introduce better ideas.

Anarchists must be gentle and ease people into learning. For example, virgins may be hesitant about sexual intercourse. They might be nervous and afraid. This virginal anxiety compares to the philosophical virgin. When it comes to certain ideas, they must be introduced to them with trust and respect, slowly. If the experienced anarchist tries to insert and inject the ideas of anarchism too quickly, the intellectual virgin's defense systems activate, and they never return to consider the ideas. This is why the anarchist should remember that intellectual foreplay is a good method of greasing the brain and preparing it for the orgasmic beauty of philosophical truth.

I apologize for the graphic nature of the metaphor, but in all seriousness, expertly using psychology and neuroscience will be a key factor in helping people grasp anarchism, and it won't be considered brainwashing because anarchists will not have to coerce or use forcible pressure to alter them. Anarchists will simply use voluntary, consensual, and natural methods, which will in turn help heal the brain from the toxins of a vicious culture.

October 13, 2015

Dear statists,

I write this letter in peace. I want you as a friend. I want you to be an anarchist's friend and ally. Here I will express how I think and feel, which is how many voluntaryists think and feel. Hopefully, you will be able to empathize with us, and we will be able to communicate on the same wavelength. Bear with me, for the things I say may be uncomfortable and jarring.

Using government to control people is soul-murder. It is carnage and chaos. Just live your life. You can solve problems in accordance with your will. There is no need for a system that monitors and polices everyone, stamps papers and records, spies on and scans its people, and employs drone bombs against children.

Why do you believe men must initiate violence against other men for optimal social cohesion? Belief in government is merely a personification of latent mommy and daddy issues. Discontinue this fantasy. Separate. Detach the umbilical cord. Refocus. It is time for you to move beyond repressed adolescence. It is time to stop appealing to authority only to sate your utopian and morbid desires. It's time to shake yourself into clarity, to realize you are not as dependent and pitiful as you think. You are strong, intelligent, and noble. I am only here to help, to tell people they can choose, that they can acknowledge that they are not serfs—and neither are the people they wish to subjugate by proxy.

It is time for you to move forward, to allow humanity to embrace its urge for freedom and decency. If you do not, you are helping extinguish truth. Like a wind-swept candle, everything loved and cherished will be snuffed out forever.

That is not your goal, is it? Is it not your motivation to keep the peace, to allow others to subsist and thrive? Stop pretending safety can be granted by the monument makers and war brokers. It cannot. The only thing blind obedience achieves is annihilation, oblivion, and darkness. Do not succumb to the ghost manufacturers, the life rapists, the murderers and henchmen of the State apparatus.

Succumb only to the dignity of your own conscience and consciousness. That is what Mother Earth bestowed on you. It is your birthright. Do not allow it to wither away in the decadence of illusion and under the guillotine of government. Do not consent to the politician-kings. Speak out against their evil and corruption, and eventually, they will no longer prey upon the flesh and fortune of the weak. Seek only the pleasure and logic of nonviolence, of zero institutional coercion. Seek freedom and love. You are stronger than ever, and the time is ripe. Break your shackles. Spread your wings and look to the heavens. Peace is beckoning, and the light of truth will embrace you. The State will finally break into pieces and become the ashes of a misguided past.

Sincerely,
Sterlin Lujan

November 2, 2015

For many anarchists, anarchism is about reasoning from first principles and making strong arguments. I concede this is an important aspect of convincing people of the beauty behind freedom; however, our communication should not just contain arguments from dry reason. It should also contain rich emotions. It should contain our feelings regarding this urge for sovereignty in all of its kaleidoscopic expressions.

The anger, hurt, pain, and contempt from being subjugated and enslaved should be brought to the surface in a tidal wave of brutal honesty. I believe this because most of us, as a result of the abuse we have suffered, have lost our ability to put feelings into language. But if people can know our anguish and anger, they may regain some comprehension and conscience.

Argumentation alone is not enough. We must compel people to empathize with our struggle, to stand in our shoes so they may awaken to their servitude and feel and experience truth.

We must grasp our feelings and let those around us know them intimately and deeply. As social creatures, this is how we touch the hearts and minds of those who cannot see their fetters and feel the cuts from the lash. Thus, I beckon us all to feel—to feel so strongly and emphatically that it brings people to tears. I believe universal freedom depends on it.

November 7, 2015

I am trying to be more active in my use of nonviolent communication, or compassionate communication. I think if we can remain calm and dignified when we talk to others, especially about difficult topics, we can help change the way we *both* think. We can connect on a similar wavelength and find common ground. In the past, I used to get angry or defensive too quickly. I let my lizard brain take over. The fight-or-flight response ruled me.

However, I've noticed that when I focus on the other person and use compassion, I can usually make more inroads in the conversation, as well as remain calm. I can let the other person know I understand their plight, that I empathize with their predicament. Nonetheless, I still have a lot of work to do on myself. But if I am trying to convince people that my attitude and ideas are important, then that person must know that I want the discussion to be about us, to be about the *we* rather than just pure logic or cold truth. The connection and establishment of an equitable partnership is more than half the battle.

January 21, 2016

Anarchy is not a philosophy that condones destruction and death. It is a philosophy of communication and connection. As an anarchist, I am like any other human. I want to harmonize with you in such a way that we both fully understand each other. I do not want to be hidden in black robes, deep in some hermit cave with my nose in the air. I want you with me as an anarchist, to appreciate the philosophy not only as an expression of how we can live together but also as an aesthetic for how we can exist and experience each other. As an anarchist, I am still a social animal, a human being that longs for love and relationships. I just want to show you that we can work together, and you can be an anarchist with me. My goal is not to divide and conquer or foment strife. My goal is to bring us together so we can live without others lording over us. I just want to work in tandem with you, to live in lockstep by solving our problems and pursuing love as we see fit. I do not want to hurt you, and I do not want you to hurt me. I want us to get along as adults. And that, my friend, is what an anarchist desire. An anarchist is about peace and love. And this is one anarchist who wants you to share my experience. Will you join me?

March 11, 2016

I urge all of you who accept government as a necessary evil to consider the psychological ramifications.

You are saying to yourself, "I am subservient. My own life has so little value that I need others to control it. I don't need freedom because I cannot trust my instincts and problem-solving abilities."

You are thus sacrificing self-esteem for the esteem of mortals who believe they possess the divine right of kings. You are bending the knee with the belief that others should hold your hand from cradle to grave as if you were a perpetual child.

Your belief in rulers has kept you stuck in an earlier developmental stage. You have not come to terms with childhood impulses and the shock of authority on the system. Thus, you remain hitched to the notion that violent parents are always needed. You have not overcome the essential crisis of trust versus mistrust. Paradoxically, your heart tells you to mistrust all authority, but in a confused act of desperation, you continue to trust all people who represent authority. And you battle this trauma throughout life.

It is a tragic scenario based on the dysfunctional abuse we have all suffered; but if you consider this truth, it may allow you to break free and grow into the adulthood of anarchism.

I realize this is painful and humiliating to hear because I, too, suffered this psychological battle of anarchism versus familial servitude. I am not trying to be ugly. I just want to help everyone overcome the immaturity and cultural dogmas about authority. For humanity to progress, we must all grow. We must all change.

March 16, 2016

To my fellow human,

For our relationship to be as healthy and fruitful as possible, I simply ask that you respect my rights and not violate me with aggression or ask a government to violate me. If you can accept my truce, it is possible you and I will relate to each other and empathize more easily. It is possible we will come to terms with each other's humanity and that our closeness will create a truly civilized society. Right now, government thwarts our connection because it intrudes on our interpersonal space with violence. It cuts off our ability to understand each other, and that is not what I want. I want to embrace the light of your soul, but when you adopt the darkness of government, it makes it difficult for me to be near you. It creates disharmony in our interaction and divides us along lines of violence. So, in a message of peace and goodwill, I hope you will choose our friendship or acquaintanceship over political hegemony. The community of the human world is grown from the topsoil of our social relationships, and when they are thrown into dire straits, we suffer stress and anguish as a result. We suffer the wrath of our ugliest impulses. Let us please move beyond that. I love you.

—Sterlin

March 25, 2016

Anarchism is not just about its logical underpinnings, moral positioning, or economic truths. It is also about raw emotion and the psychology of the self.

Even if everyone assumes that anarchism is wrong on logical or empirical grounds, rejecting it has dire consequences for individual functioning.

In other words, there are relational and psychological consequences of denouncing freedom.

When a person rejects anarchism, that person is saying his life is unimportant and meaningless. He is saying he must have a sociopath threaten him and control his life and choices. He is dispensing with self-esteem, self-concern, and self-love. He is saying relationships with certain people should de facto involve force and authority.

Lack of the anarchistic philosophy, therefore, brings about dysfunctional interactions with those who deem themselves "rulers," "politicians," or "kings." It creates an emotionally bankrupt and unstable social environment, which the individual helps maintain through statist relationships.

This is the psychological problem of statism, or the self-acceptance and relational principle of anarchism.

March 26, 2016

The problem with statism is it intervenes in our interpersonal affairs and emotional worlds. We cannot live and love without the imminent threat of government manipulating our ability to connect with each other.

But if we adhere to the relational principle of anarchism, we can begin building a community of empaths who accept each other's humanity and do not wish to control other humans with violence.

The relational principle is not an academic or cognitive exercise in logic but a psychological value that is at the root of our biological impulse to seek love and belonging. It is about building a community not on reasoning alone the understanding of our emotional needs, as well.

However, for clarification, it is also not about emotional volatility or anti-individualism, nor is it necessarily anti-reason. It is simply about attunement with other humans and understanding based on dialogue and communication.

March 27, 2016

Anarchists want to communicate their ideas to you in a nonviolent manner, without Molotov cocktails, in the hopes you will reciprocate. If you are willing to listen, anarchists will listen in return. The anarchist intent is never to hate. Some mild confrontations may occur, but this is sometimes necessary for growth. Without a bit of stress regarding a hot topic, no one would learn or appreciate the material. Anarchists are not here to act like teenagers living in their mother's basement, either. Anarchists are here as mature representatives of a relational and love-based philosophy that happens to be growing extensively. Anarchism is dialogue. It is not destruction or immaturity.

Won't you involve yourself in the conversation? Times are changing, and anarchists want to bring you along for an amazing ride.

April 4, 2016

Anarchism is not just a political philosophy. It is a medium of exchange. It is a means of emotional transfer. If a person self-discloses that they accept anarchism, they are saying they want to have harmonious, authentic relationships. In other words, they have shunned force and fraud and have instead grasped intimate and personal attachment. They have given up on the social rules that impel people to control and coerce people. Anarchism is the ultimate conductor of emotional energy because it surpasses political philosophies, moving instead into a realm of love.

If a person identifies as an anarchist, they are taking an anti-political stance, which means they are ready to live as a true human being, devoid of the inclination to harm, manipulate, and control. It is the next step in human moral and logical development. If a person encounters an anarchist, they should hug them and surrender themselves to the purity of their soul. Anarchists are miles ahead of their time and culture. They will teach people what it means to truly care about humanity. They are the non-charlatan shamans, the neo-lovers. Modern-day Jesus without dogma and damnation.

April 13, 2016

Relationalism hinges on love and human attachment. As a philosophy, it is contingent on people's desire to be with other people and form relationships. In other words, healthy human connections necessitate absolute freedom.

In this light, relationalism is not a detached model for new sociopolitical arrangements nor a dry run of endless debates and objective presentations. It is not a strictly cognitive exercise. Instead, it is a psychological expression or aesthetic that implores people to create loving and harmonious relationships without the desire to undermine those relationships through coercion.

It is also not only a philosophy. It is a process and a dialogue. It was what philosopher Martin Buber called the "I-Thou" connection. It is a heart-level instinct based on human psychology. This acknowledgment of the feeling vectors of anarchism represents the relationalist mindset.

April 15, 2016

Planting seeds. Teaching empathy. Rocking the boat. Undermining authority. Spreading love. Endangering culture. Engendering peace. Living enthusiastically. Nurturing children. Not voting. Contemplating truth. Growing trees. Condemning psychiatry. Forming relationships. Leading by example. Sharing stories. Being vulnerable. Emphasizing change. Demonstrating courage. Undergoing hardship. Embracing differences. Deconditioning children. Filming cops.

We live and breathe all these things. We are anarchists. We are iconoclastic. We are everywhere. It is time to build a different culture, a better community, and a stronger world.

Be prepared.

April 21, 2016

Relationalism does not stand opposed to anarcho-capitalism or voluntaryism. The relationalist ethic decries coercion and initiatory violence, as well. But instead of being a logical, ethical, or moral consideration, it is a psychological and emotional principle.

It asserts that emotions and interpersonal connections are mental states that are naturally antithetical to violence. Thus, individuals wanting to reach people from a narrative or communicative stance have a framework to work from. The key is literally in the dissemination of compassion and love—and likewise, the production of these mental states in other people.

The problem therapeutic anarchism has with anarcho-capitalism or voluntaryism is just contextual or content-related. It regards perspective or strategy differences. Instead of appealing to logical, economic, and moral vectors, it appeals to heart- and gut-based factors. It is the emotional framework for freedom.

May 5, 2016

Many voluntaryists choose to appeal more to the mind.

As a relationalist, I choose to appeal more to the heart.

I have no problem with the intellect. I love it. But there is an abundance of brains in anarchist communities. Therefore, I have picked the heart as the focal point for my interactions with people.

No, I am not anti-logic. I am not anti-voluntaryist. I still use those methods of interpersonal contact. I just believe in the power of love. I believe in the power of true dialogue for helping expedite the transformative process.

Some people will indeed ignore this method—and perhaps even fear this type of communication—but I trust that employing the heart-based approach for freedom will convince more people of anarchism.

The aforesaid method feels most natural and authentic for me, anyway. I hope others feel the same.

May 8, 2016

I have learned a lot of patience over the years from speaking with people with authoritarian mindsets. I now understand that backing them into a corner with verbal jujitsu and trying to "win" the argument does not necessarily make them convert to freedom.

People are mentally free to pursue whatever philosophical or ideological paths they want regardless of the logical strength of a philosophy. There are many more variables that go into what ideas people accept, and these variables all have to be considered before one attempts to express the inherent beauty of anarchy.

Therefore, when communicating my thoughts to people, I try to enter their system and meet them where they are in life. Then I convey my connection to them and empathize with them on the points we agree on. I believe this method works to help people change more quickly than beating people over the head with strict argumentation.

I also feel better after the discussion knowing that they did not shut down or become so defensive that they thought I was an egocentric asshole. This perceived arrogance helps push people away from anarchists and makes them skeptical of the results of total freedom.

May 14, 2016

Voting for any politician is not in line with compassion or therapeutic anarchism. When people vote, they tear asunder social relationships by pitting themselves against their neighbors. How can anyone get along when they attempt to install a politician to hurt or coerce others? By its nature, electing an official into office is contrary to the development and growth of a culture of love. A softer society is created through nonviolent cooperation and spontaneous order. It is created through creative problem-solving and dialogue. Political interference undermines this and renders the heart obsolete.

May 14, 2016

Statism tends to exacerbate insanity.

Lately, people have been going bananas over this transgender bathroom controversy. This situation highlights how politicians manipulate the voting population into fighting for relatively trite issues. These kinds of issues are replete with social justice platitudes and insincere emotionality—thus, the multitudes are easily convinced to care about bathroom usage. This is because it is safe. It feels righteous. It is politically correct. And it covers up government atrocities.

While babies are killed in their cribs by drone bombs, millions of people are caged for possessing a pill, and billions of dollars are extorted from the population, people rally to grapple over who can pee in a bathroom stall.

For anyone viewing the situation from the outside, the whole fiasco comes across as a haunting, sickening, and ironic joke. It makes these alien observers feel like they are living in a strange purgatory where everything is comical and hellish at the same time.

As anarchists and relationalists, if we hope to reach many of our brethren—the authentic nature of our compassion must outstrip the inauthentic games the politicians are playing. We must win our fellow humans over with love because it might be the only thing that can save us from this carnival of horror and strangeness.

May 24, 2016

The ability to communicate compassionately with other people is a matter of emotional intelligence and conscious control of the fight-or-flight response.

Tragically, many anarchists are not any better at controlling their communication than any other person. They may claim rational calmness, but I rarely see this play out in discussions online. In reality, it takes practice and effort to quell emotional upsurges of volatile energy.

If this control is not practiced, the anarchist will become enraged and start shit-talking or shitposting, and this form of communication does not have the positive effect of allowing the recipient of the message to feel warmth and connection. And it is this connection that is a prerequisite for effective persuasion.

It is true that a lot of people online don't care about this, anyway. All they care about is trolling and trying to trigger people.

I think that is a waste of time and energy. Thus, I try to take all my communications seriously; I assume others want to have an authentic conversation with me. I approach the discussion with relationalism and nonviolent communication in mind.

When I do this, it allows me to fine-tune my emotional responses to their disagreements and also to get into their heads and feel out what their reality is like. It allows me to see what it is they need at that time, helping me to better articulate and express anarchist desires more accurately and beautifully.

It creates a true dialogue and makes their neurological functioning ripe for considering change.

June 11, 2016

When it comes to social relationships, we have to establish healthy interactions and boundaries. But for this to occur, we all have to overcome our childhood experiences. Most of what we endured was hellish and traumatic, even if what happened to us was considered culturally acceptable.

I say this because compassionate anarchy seeks to create positive and healthy relationships with all people. It seeks to establish a community of love and relational awareness. It is a format of interaction built on an edifice of cultural dignity and decency.

Compassionate anarchy renounces the logical, economic, and moral patterns of attempting to convince people of the virtues of anarchism.

Instead, relationalists look at the connections among people and try to help establish nonviolent communication, problem-solving, and understanding of needs, both psychological and physical.

It is in this approach that initiatory violence is whittled down and the urge for violence translated into a clearer communication of needs. It is in this atmosphere that the ideas and culture of statism start to decay.

The need to persuade and outthink everyone and convince them of logical, economic, or moral truths is a misrepresentation of needs. It is an ego-based desire that can be remedied by authentic, loving contact with other people.

June 13, 2016

What does it mean to humanize anarchy?

It means accepting and explaining anarchism as *not only* a philosophical doctrine, logical proposition, or economic theory but also a psychosocial model for the most optimal relationships in society. Anarchism is a catalyst for social intimacy and stronger, clearer communication among people.

For a stateless society to manifest, logical persuasion and grand economic theories may be necessary conditions to alter social makeup, but they are not sufficient.

The heart must be included in the equation. Love must be considered because it is through the conduit of care and compassion that different, more beautiful communities are erected.

Proclaiming "I am right" from purely cognitive vectors is not a guaranteed inroad to anarchism proper.

Authentic connections must be established, and people must be made whole.

June 29, 2016

The groundbreaking insight of relational anarchy is that it is based on forming relationship bonds with others. In this sense, it undergirds and strengthens voluntaryism.

It can even act as a bridge between all forms of anarchism to clarify communication and resolve seemingly intractable differences. When compassion and authenticity are shared between anarchists, we work toward creating a larger, unified group of cooperative freedom lovers.

Oftentimes, when we get lost in the content of our differences, we miss the underlying emotional resonance we have in common. If this connection can be brought to the surface, it is possible to find mutual acceptance.

Of course, this does not mean we will always agree on every issue. Differences in philosophical opinion are natural. However, when we are communicating and empathizing on a similar emotional wavelength, we can accomplish almost anything.

July 9, 2016

A new vision of anarchism without adjectives and based on human connection and relationship attachment is cropping up. It is a particular view of freedom that sees the shifting tides of society altering not because of brilliant arguments or economic schemes but because of a conscious realization that peace arises from shared empathic states and emotional ties.

In other words, psychological findings will finally be thrust into society-at-large via practical action that will greatly reduce the factors that lead to bureaucratic violence and social trauma.

Of course, I could be wrong. But I do see how modern psychological knowledge vindicates anarchism on many fronts.

It is a goal worth pursuing.

August 15, 2016

A lesson in debate etiquette:

Even if you have good points to make, if you cannot communicate them with decency or tact, your points are likely going to fall on deaf ears.

No one wants to sift through inflammatory expletives to find the meat of an argument.

Being hostile and verbally aggressive is usually an indicator that you are not willing to communicate or share dialogue in the first place.

I always hope I can be a model for treating others with kindness and compassion, even if I adamantly disagree with the other individual's position.

People are not cannon fodder for my ideas, and I am looking for connection as much as I am an intellectual duel.

November 1, 2016

Whenever I chat with people in person about anarchism, I try to connect with them on a fundamental level. If I don't build a rapport and share an understanding with a person, they will likely remain disinterested in the philosophy.

However, if I project the authenticity of my character, I believe the force of my genuineness and kindness gives them pause to consider what I am saying before reacting defensively. This is the compassionate method for steering people in the direction of anarchism without disabling their ability to consider the ideas or making them prone to leveling abusive counterattacks.

Remember, when we try to convince people of anarchism, they have a headful of propaganda and misunderstandings about our philosophy. It takes a kind heart, wise words, and empathetic understanding to truly come to terms with another person and show them the beauty of anarchism. If we can muster this level of interaction with others, we may be able to convince them to reconsider their notions about how society should be ordered.

With that said, we cannot expect to be perfectly compassionate all the time. After all, we are humans with flaws and triggers of our own. But more importantly, being compassionate and personable with people does not mean sacrificing logic or amending our philosophy for the sake of sparing them from dealing with difficult subject matter. As anarchists, it is a given that the information and truths we provide are not going to be instantly palatable. Nonetheless, I think compassionate communication and rapport-building should still take precedence over conveying the content of our philosophy.

November 21, 2016

One of the key insights I have tried to bring to anarchist philosophy is that it is more than a philosophy. It is even more than a way of life.

By denoting "no rulers," anarchism is indicative of a relationship status with other human beings.

When we proclaim ourselves anarchists, we are saying, "I want to have an authentic and purposeful relationship with you based on the principles of treating each other with dignity and without violent aggression."

In this regard, compassion and connection are inextricably woven into anarchist ideas. You cannot be an anarchist without suggesting you want peaceful cooperation and union with other human beings.

This places anarchism beyond just politics and directly into the realm of human interpersonal psychology. In this regard, anarchism is not just nonpolitical, but it is also relational.

Now, what fruit this idea will bear is still beyond me.

November 21, 2016

I try to rise above this divisive political notion of "left" and "right," even though I have been guilty of using the terms myself.

However, I don't think any person fits nicely into these ill-defined political spectrum labels. I understand that these terms are easy to apply and allow for a streamlined understanding of a person's political leanings, but they often deprive people of their individuality. It saps their uniqueness and undermines their ability to move beyond the confines of their label.

What makes the left-right tag situation worse is that some anarchists are starting to apply the term "leftist" to other anarchists in an arbitrary fashion, and yet the term doesn't necessarily encapsulate their specific viewpoints. In most cases, it misses the mark or just acts as a pejorative term based on disagreement rather than the truth about a person's flavor of politics.

That said, the compassionate anarchist seeks to bring people together, create connections, leverage empathy, and demonstrate that the State is bad no matter what specific inclinations one has. In a way, the compassionate anarchist represents a kind of nonpolitical or neutral form of anarchism. It is anarchism for the economically indifferent, based on the premise that these sociopolitical arrangements will be worked out cooperatively after the State has been dissolved.

The ultimate goal of this vector of anarchism is to help create the paradigm shift necessary for anarchism to crop up, and it relies chiefly on getting people to understand the basis of the philosophy through humanitarian love—not necessarily through political and economic considerations, be they "left" or "right."

This is the reason my (now-banned) Facebook page Psychologic-Anarchist did not always focus on economic differences and likely why many "communists" found a home there, as well. I just really hope that in the end, we can all solve our problems cooperatively and without violence.

November 24, 2016

Logic, economics, and morality are important vectors for persuading people to adopt anarchism.

However, we often forget about the heart.

To get people interested in anarchism, we have to show them compassion. We must share ourselves. We must use dialogue and narrative. We must present them with our authentic selves.

This is called relational communication.

It is always a prerequisite for helping people understand the philosophy. Without it, many emotionally aligned people will distance themselves from the philosophy and not consider it any further.

And while it is true that people ultimately have to decide on their own, our dignity and decency will seed themselves into their consciousness and hopefully burst into the fully-grown product of anarchism.

Let's not forget human psychology and our desire for connection when we share our beautiful philosophy.

November 29, 2016

There has been a lot of debate about what strategies are best for getting more people involved in anarchism, and one of the most recent ones has been to just reject "leftists" because of their philosophy, including their rejection of the private property ethic. This is partially where the joke about "physically removing them" or "tossing them out of helicopters" originates.

But I must air a grievance about this approach. I am vehemently opposed to this as a strategy for producing more freedom in our lifetime on a couple of grounds. My primary appeal is to human psychology, which I touch on here.

The politics of rejection is a strategy that dismisses diplomacy and undermines the fundamental truths about human connection and communication needs.

When we create divisiveness rather than brotherhood based on ideas, there can be no ability to work toward a solution. If people do not have a proper understanding of each other and their wants and needs, this could create a recipe for disaster in heated political climates.

It is no wonder there has been a constant war between "left" versus "right" throughout history. Few have come to the table to figure out how to work cooperatively and build communities in both parties' interests. Instead, they have gleefully spilled each other's blood for ideological purity.

It is true, of course, that some people will not want to work together. A small percentage of people are outright psychopaths who simply yearn for conflict. Therefore, for the sake of clarity, I am not suggesting we attempt to communicate with people who are already prepared to use violence. These men of always likely cannot be reasoned with. They can only be ostracized and dealt with in a physically defensive manner.

However, most of the population has not succumbed to the lust for violence. They are simply people who have been indoctrinated into their ways of life. They have been conditioned by the major institutions within their culture. It is unwise to "throw these people out of a helicopter" (not work with them) all because we have erroneously chosen not to understand their predicament and realize they can be reasoned with.

If we empathize with this population, make connections, and leverage our natural, genetic yearning for attachment and bonding, we can—and will—produce the necessary environment to live peaceably beyond the confines of government.

The human animal harbors a need for emotional connection. Modern attachment psychology has taught us this truth, and if we try to diverge from it, we will likely continue down the path of devastation. If we are to have peace and create a stateless society, we must all come to the table as adults ready to mutually work together to resolve economic and political differences.

We did not evolve into these large, cranium-bearing hominids only to destroy ourselves through the politics of rejection.

December 5, 2016

As a soft anarchist, when I talk about freedom and statelessness, I am not trying to make a logical case for it. I am not trying to woo you with my ability to call out a fallacy, break down your thought processes, and wax eloquent about how well I use syllogistic wordplay.

I am not interested in playing mind games or winning a debate. I couldn't care less about any of that.

As a soft anarchist, my goal is to find ways to connect with you—to discover our shared ground and make any interaction we have pleasurable and purposeful.

The underlying rationale for this perspective is that our relationship trends determine how anarchism manifests itself, how freedom based on relationship patterns grows.

Of course, this is not to say our communications will exist in some kind of relational utopia where we are all living in perfect harmony without ever offending each other.

Indeed, we may offend each other. We will not be politically correct. We may hurt each other's feelings. This is the way of things.

However, if we can come to understand one another through our communication differences, we may be able to spur anarchism via comprehension and diplomacy. Anarchism will likely not rise as a result of "who has the best argument." If that were the case, anarchism would probably already be in full swing. Instead, I think we need to work on how we relate to each other.

In my perspective, the existence of government is based on a fundamental flaw in society—the fact that we often unlearn how attached and connected to other humans we are.

Our childhoods were tumultuous because our primary caregivers undermined our relationships. Indeed, most cultures do not provide children with adequate emotional nurturance. It is through this dehumanizing and demeaning process that the desire to connect is replaced with a desire to inflate the ego and avenge our childlike selves by lambasting any proxy parent who tries to hurt us. As we grow up, we rebel against our desire to be with other humans because the pain of being hurt is too much to bear.

I believe that if we can start to process our relationship patterns—not just the physical abuse we may have endured but also the emotional injuries we received—we may be able to produce a kind of initial phase of anarchism. The more we can connect with ourselves and others, the less we will desire violence and proxy violence via the State.

December 12, 2016

I am tolerant of ideas and the people who espouse them. This is not because I accept any given idea or the woofuckery of blind "leftist tolerance." No. I'm tolerant because it is part of the character I have built. I rarely let ideas threaten me, and I do not get triggered easily. I have cultivated a personality that is geared to finding the middle way. I am looking for avenues of diplomacy and an opportunity to discover the middle ground. I have my principles and perspectives, but I don't want to fight, and I want to try to take the fight away from you. We do not have to devolve into mouth-breathing troglodytes. If we are truly rational and empathetic, we can learn to work together cooperatively and mutually. There are always solutions. Violence need never erupt if you are willing to do the hard work peace requires. I certainly am.

This is what it means to be a compassionate anarchist in practice.

December 18, 2016

Anarchism is straightforward.

I want to relate to you in a peaceful, non-coercive way. I don't want our relationship to be tinged with violence. And if you can adopt my way of relating, you will essentially be an anarchist.

However, bear in mind that for our relationship to function in a non-coercive and developmental manner, you cannot use other men to hurt me. You must drop the superstition that governments benefit us. In reality, they tear our relationship apart because they initiate proxy violence against me on your behalf.

Let our relationship be clean of that ugliness, nastiness, and violence. Let our relationship and our bond be strong.

December 20, 2016

10 things I do to promote the philosophy of relational anarchism:

1) Talk to people about the principles and ideas and act as an educator.

2) Never insult anyone.

3) Try to level with everyone even if I disagree, although I admit to imperfection in this category as I sometimes enjoy debating down the line.

4) Be psychologically minded and aware of my triggers.

5) Pay attention to context and process more than the content of a persuasion encounter with others. (Content refers to the actual arguments and debate language. The process is the emotions, body language, and human connection involved.)

6) Leverage empathy, primarily in meat space but even online.

7) Try to maintain healthy relationships online and off, although I cannot expect perfection here, either.

8) Always be mindful of the three axioms of communication: The message sent is not always the message received. One cannot *not* communicate. Nonverbal communication is more powerful than verbal communication.

9) Read constantly on psychology, counseling, and anarchy.

10) Love myself and those closest to me while establishing a secure enough bond from which to explore the world in a stress-free manner.

December 27, 2016

The greatest strength of relational anarchism is that it disarms critics and trolls and opens up many people to empathetic and authentic communication.

The effect is stronger if the anarchist is genuinely compassionate and has a desire to work with naysayers rather than browbeat them to satisfy their ego.

This more humanistic vector is the driving force for preparing the world to live in anarchistic communities. It is preparing people to understand that connecting with each other is a powerful tool to help prevent initiatory aggression—perhaps even stronger than bashing people over the head with moral dictums and axiomatic truths.

But providing people with a comfortable blend of all vectors can wash away the grime of statism and latent aggression. However, pure argumentation has a demoralizing effect without the proper use of communication tactics.

Communication ability is where relationalists shine.

January 2, 2017

The primary theme of holistic and relational anarchy is empowerment.

Softer anarchists are looking to empower individuals and everyone who associates with them. These anarchists are constantly trying to find ways to connect with people and create allies, friendships, camaraderie, and communities. Empowerment has its roots in strong social dynamics and compassion.

These anarchists are ultimately focused on relationships, communication, family, and friends. Without this vector of anarchism, anarchist communities would be lost focusing on only the logical, economic, and moral elements—and this aspect of anarchism only empowers people to a small degree. Sometimes it even disempowers people, especially when they forget to connect and let arguments deteriorate into ugliness.

Let us not forget the importance of compassion—of empowerment through human connection.

January 5, 2017

When people challenge me on my ideas or thoughts, oftentimes my knee-jerk reaction is to deconstruct their argument in the most logical way possible and leave the scraps of it for the vultures.

And in the past, that would have been my approach. I would have done it as aggressively and with as much vitriol as possible, and I would have felt little human connection or empathy in the process.

But as I have adopted the relational approach, my knee-jerk reactions have quickly changed to a mentality of observation and compassion.

I ponder the individual first. I ask myself what they want or need. Why are they threatened by this idea? In what way can I communicate my idea that is palatable to them? Do we share any common ground? Can we relate?

Instead of just considering the idea and who has the superior logic, I try to work with the individual. I blend logic with empathy. I weave together ideas with humanism. I actively consider the process of that exchange, as well as the content.

Granted, I may not succeed with this method or vector every time I engage with someone, but I at least know I am modeling a positive approach for helping get people involved in anarchism. I am being true to myself and how I authentically want to treat people. I am attempting to meet my basic psychological needs, as well as theirs.

I adore this paradigm for anarchism.

January 6, 2017

It's difficult for some people to internalize relational anarchism because they immediately want to understand it or deconstruct it logically. This is where things get tricky. Relational anarchism was never meant to be a strictly logical construct. It was supposed to be a psychological doctrine or vector for producing anarchism through relational tactics, empathy, compassion, and open communication. It was not intended to be something amenable to syllogistic deconstruction precisely because this type of deconstruction is antithetical to true human connection.

However, it is impossible to completely divorce our desire to reason from the process of analyzing relationalism, and I respect that. I just hope people understand that it is not really meant to be subject to that type of scrutiny, and this is also why I usually shy away from engaging in a "logical debate" about relational anarchism.

But honestly, I am getting way ahead of myself. I am still developing the ideas. It is still in its infancy. I am not sure how this will all come together in the end. I believe these are fascinating thoughts, though.

January 14, 2017

I am very open to criticism and alternative thoughts regarding my ideas, and I allow people from all walks of life to provide their input on my feed. I love taking in a multitude of ideas, and I especially love other conceptions of compassionate anarchism.

I don't believe I have a monopoly on this vector of thought. I prefer having a community of ideas where friendly competition and cooperation coalesce to develop the best version of them.

I also interact with as many people as I can. A big part of this philosophy is community-building through interaction, empathy, and mutuality.

And honestly, I don't care if your economic preference is communist or capitalist. If you are willing to cooperate and coexist so we can figure out how to live and thrive sans the State, we will get along perfectly. We may even come up with innovative new solutions to social problems and discover a new map for viewing the anarchistic, geographic landscape. I believe innovation is stifled in the absence of empathy, communication, and cooperation.

For all practical purposes, this is how my philosophical assumptions regarding relationalism play out. It's not all abstract, nor does it have its basis in abject woofuckery.

Relationalism is practical and feasible at its core.

January 14, 2017

I have offended, aggrieved, agitated, and pissed off more people talking about compassion than when I speak about property.

What does that tell you?

January 16, 2017

The difficulty of advocating compassionate/relational anarchism is that it's not a philosophy based purely on axiomatic principles.

It does have an emotional framework and loose set of principles, but the strength of the doctrine depends entirely on the people involved with it.

Compassionate anarchy is about recognizing the importance of communication and connection with others. Therefore, the strength of the idea is dependent on the character and goals of those who adopt it.

If people understand the psychological advantage of adopting relational anarchism, they will be able to put it to good use to build a stateless, loving society.

But in the long run, no logical argument will trump the power of violence-free human connection. No rational soliloquy will overcome the beauty and brilliance of the most compelling story. In the end, amplifying empathy and love to create freer societies will triumph.

And to this day, I don't know of many philosophies that believe anarchism can be created through interaction, process, and emotional education.

In the past, most have believed anarchism had to be spread through argumentation, condemnation, and violent revolution.

February 1, 2017

I am unnerved by identity politics, and I do not believe identity ideas are compatible with relational anarchism or other compassionate philosophies.

It is dangerous that identity apologists have adopted the idea that people should automatically accept gender, race, and other identity politics. It's dangerous that terms like "microaggressions," "whitesplaining," and "mansplaining" have entered into public discourse and have started to influence governmental policy and culture.

These ideas are dangerous because none of us can control what other people say or do. These ideas are dangerous because identity politicians want to charge a great number of people with thought crimes. These ideas are dangerous because they influence governments to write violent laws that are centered on reverse racism and hatred of Eurocentric populations. These ideas are dangerous because they perpetuate the idea of the "historical wound," of the notion that all people of a certain race or gender should be culpable for the suffering of other races or populations.

However, something more dangerous has cropped up because of these ideas.

In the mind of the identity apologist, being compassionate, empathetic, or a decent human being has become conflated with identity politics. These political groups have attempted to usurp compassionate philosophies and suggest that one cannot be compassionate or civil unless they speak the language of identity politics and talk incessantly about "oppressed peoples."

As a contributor to relational anarchy, I wholeheartedly reject these bromides and tangents of snafu.

An empathetic or compassionate person is going to relate to a person regardless of their suffering or background. The relational or compassionate person also realizes how demeaning, ostracizing, and politically dangerous it is to use the language of identity politics. The compassionate individual thus rejects the use of this language to be authentically compassionate and civil because the politics of identity is based on generalizations and stereotypes of certain classes of people that may not reflect reality and are certainly not rooted in compassion.

Therefore, a compassionate person will never accept identity politics: They understand that the identity apologists have an agenda. These apologists are dead set on achieving vengeance. They want to take their resentment out on a certain "class" of people who in their minds are responsible for committing past crimes. But tragically, their crusade against these classes is a recipe for brutal communism, totalitarianism, and rampant hatred. And all these goals are the opposite of being compassionate and dignified.

To possess true positive regard, empathy, and decency toward people, identity politics and the language of identity politics must be totally rejected.

Compassion is the absence of identity grudges.

February 2, 2017

What I am really challenging is the "fight mentality" that many people, especially anarchists of varying stripes, have adopted. I ask things like "Where do you disagree with me?" and "What can we do to find common ground?" I ask these questions in the hopes that I can mitigate their fight mentality and work toward more open communication and connection.

This is difficult, though, because people who harbor "political beliefs" have difficulties not seeing everything else as a "contradictory item" or other people as "enemies." Using relational psychology is an attempt to get underneath these views and discover new ways of working together and interacting to build the kind of communities anarchist societies need to thrive.

February 4, 2017

Relational anarchy is the new model for anarchism. Relational anarchists question the approaches of the economic schools of thought. The philosophy offers novel new ways to spread anarchism without exhausting everyone with controversial moral and economic invectives.

A key insight of relational anarchism is that a stateless society cannot be maintained or built without a relationship component. It cannot be created without acknowledging our human desire for connection with others.

As I have mentioned before, when someone says they are an anarchist, they are making a relationship statement. They are saying, "I want us to have cooperation and trust, and I don't want violence involved in the dynamic. I want us to be together peacefully."

In this regard, anarchists are always interpersonal psychologists looking for ways to rebuild society along the lines of relational principles.

Indeed, the presence of a ruler in society is always a sign that the society has deep-seated problems with defining and understanding the nature of healthy relationships...and so relational anarchists have emerged to right all these historical wrongs.

Can you grok me?

February 7, 2017

I believe anarchist counseling theory will be a real thing.

Anarchist ideas are coming into mainstream consciousness, and anarchist philosophy recognizes another group of subjugated people: the people downtrodden by politics and political rulers.

In this light, counselors will inevitably acknowledge the plight, trauma, and suffering of anarchists.

This new kind of academic integration into the helping professions is what anarchism needs to continue blossoming and flourishing. Anarchism should not be defined only in terms of political philosophy and economics.

Anarchism impacts many domains of life, and its effect on consciousnesses and human emotion is a glaring blip on the radar that needs close examination.

Things are changing for anarchism as a philosophy. Many more good things are coming.

The world is pregnant with freedom, and anarchists simply need to wet nurse it into the world.

February 10, 2017

Mirror neurons. Anarchists should learn to use them. They bring us together. They bring people to us. Mirror neurons are brain cells that naturally activate when we watch people and learn from them. They also activate in other people when they are watching us.

Mirror neurons are the biological proof that social modeling works on a neurological basis. If anarchists can model peaceful, loving, and empathetic behavior, people will naturally gravitate toward us and learn from this behavior. These specialized brain cells represent proof of how connected, interpersonal, and group-oriented human beings are. Anarchists should leverage their knowledge of biology to advance their philosophy.

This is partially why, in my mind, the way we communicate our ideas might be *more* important than the ideas themselves. When people are attuned to our behavior and our activities, they may naturally internalize the anarchist perspective. This is why I always say the process of our interaction is as important—if not more important—than the content of what we say.

February 14, 2017

Philosophical, political anarchism is about the macro level. It is about large-scale structural change. It is about deposing rulers. It is about moralizing and teaching. It is didactic, cold, and jarring. It can be rough around the edges, but it is certainly a no-nonsense approach to freedom.

All of that is good. I agree with it. Relational anarchism is different, though. It is more elegant and cleaner, like pure crystalline MDMA. However, its focus is slightly different and more subtle. It is more intimate and more experiential.

Relational, psychological anarchism is about the micro level. It is about individual interpersonal relationships. It is about employing empathy and compassion to instill anarchism through behavior, human connection, and direct relationships. Relational anarchism is about showing people how to connect to eliminate the State. It is about anarchism in the space between us.

That is why new groups like Compassionate Anarchy (Facebook group) are in the process of figuring out how apolitical connections can work to foster human connections sans rulers and tyrants. This is all novel. All new. All groundbreaking.

Anarchists have indeed talked about psychology and compassion in the past, but these new iterations of thought are finally starting to take shape as something formidable in the anarchist armamentarium of thought, and I welcome you to embrace this lovely approach with open arms.

We will have freedom sooner rather than later.

February 17, 2017

Telling people how they should feel is always a mistake. I am sometimes guilty of it. I think it's learned behavior from past issues.

Telling people how to feel borders on being tyrannical. It's an unwillingness to provide someone with the freedom to feel as they please.

It only inflames a situation and demonstrates a lack of empathy. If there is one thing I could improve about my communication skills, it would be to never tell another person how to feel.

Instead, I should attempt to relate to them and convey my empathy for their emotional state.

Sometimes this is hard, though, because in the past I used to see emotions as dirty and icky things.

I think many people are in the same boat. In childhood, if we had our emotions ridiculed or squelched, it probably led us to characterize emotions as bad. It has likely made us bottle things up.

In this sense, the cornerstone of personal growth is to demonstrate emotional openness and compassion. It's through this process that we gain awareness of the depth and beauty of other people.

Try not to berate other people's emotions, and instead try to understand them. There is great wisdom to be found here.

March 2, 2017

People are not "naturally" evil or corrupt.

People are products of their environments, decisions, and total behavior. Their brains are shaped by a multitude of forces, which are expressed through their dynamic personalities.

If people do not suffer attachment injuries when they are young and are taught the power of healthy relationships, they may develop more positive relationships and healthy morals as they age.

People who say human nature is naturally corrupt or broken are either unaware of the neurology behind human behavior or projecting their own inadequacies onto others.

The human animal has a huge capacity for change based on many variables. There is not one "warrior gene" that makes a human evil or corrupt. This gene certainly exists, but it's much more complex than that because early environmental triggers play a huge role in how humans mature and develop. They play a role in how the "warrior gene" is expressed. This manipulation of genes by the environment and environmental stimuli is referred to as the science of epigenetics.

It's not nature versus nurture or nature or nurture only.

It is nature via nurture.

March 4, 2017

If anarchists possess emotional intelligence, we will be even more influential.

March 7, 2017

I have taken a lot of criticism for daring to venture outside the logical, economic, and moral spectrum of anarchist theory.

I don't mind the criticism, though. I believe the anarchist philosophy is evolving beyond merely a political, legal, logical, and moral framework.

Anarchism is embracing apolitical, holistic, and psychological perspectives.

Anarchism as a movement and community orientation is concerned with relationships—with how human beings relate to each other. Suggesting that anarchism means without rulers is a de facto indication of a relationship scenario where violence is considered unhealthy and detrimental to human survival and our ability to thrive.

Taken into context, this position allows society to be examined from a psychologically oriented anarchist position and attempts to solve social problems with what we know about human behavior in terms of relationship strategies that mitigate violence and reduce harm.

I am super excited to be at the forefront of this new development in anarchist philosophies because I believe it will herald a new wave of individuals learning about anarchism from this perspective rather than the traditional logical, economic, and moral considerations. In the long run, I believe it will bring more people to the philosophy.

March 17, 2017

Compassion is the key to circumventing the banality of evil.

March 21, 2017

Some anarchists get so rabid about making arguments and proving other people wrong they forget about the human dimension of interaction. Some of them even appear to have lost their humanness along the way.

I admit I was the same for a long time. I was angry and bitter. All I wanted to do was rage. I used logic and morality as a coping mechanism for my anger.

However, that turned out to be bad because I pushed a lot of people away. I just attacked people. I ventilated and projected. I thought being human and trying to connect with others was fruitless and futile, and so I let my psyche run roughshod over everyone.

In my mind, anarchism had to be hard-won through logic, economics, and morality. In reality, this had a negative impact. It made people wall up. It fortified them against my views and empowered their statism. It made them say "fuck you" and go back to loving their roads.

Finally, I realized all I was doing was concealing my emotional world and that in the process, it made me seem inhuman—almost like a robot. Lifeless and dull.

When I came to terms with my anger, I began to remember that I am human. I remembered I was alive and throbbing with vitality. Then I started trying to connect with others, and I gained the insight that these human connections are more important than just being right. They are more important than raw logic and moral argumentation.

Ironically, even if anarchists are right in their objective analyses of society and morality, human connections outweigh being right in terms of helping people see the beauty and truth of anarchism.

Human emotional connections are the firmament from which we can build new worlds. These connections can help anarchists create communities without sacrificing humanness or pretending the best logical argument will help structure society.

Anarchists must remember one thing: Compassionate and empathetic connections are always antithetical to violence. They are antithetical to the cold, sterile, and detached order-giving that bureaucratic administrations always resort to.

Compassion is the way. It is the Tao of anarchism.

March 23, 2017

This is how some voluntaryists think about communists:

"The less communist a society is, the more productive it is. The less inclined to cooperate with communist nations those societies are, the more likely they are to be able to drive communist societies into economic collapse."

Unfortunately, that also means it becomes more likely that communist societies will initiate force against their neighbors in search of additional resources to stave off such collapse.

"It's safer simply to kill them all than to invite a protracted struggle that will kill people who haven't subscribed to the fallacy of communism."

This reasoning is an absolute shame because the types of individuals who espouse it are unwilling to even consider figuring out ways to coexist and create new societies. They have already prepared for bloodshed, and they are salivating and excited for it.

As a relational anarchist, I reject this view with all of my heart. There have been communists who are willing to work with my softer side and to try to resolve disputes in the absence of the State. There is no reason to imagine the need to murder people based on an ideological label and envision everything as a protracted struggle. What happened to communication? What happened to negotiation and dispute resolution? Can we not work things out? Should we just harbor a constant fight mentality for the sake of creating perpetual warfare?

This is horrific, and I am ashamed that this kind of thinking has infiltrated anarchism.

March 23, 2017

I don't find economics to be useless or bad. I think it's important. I just believe relationships and compassionate interaction will help us resolve disputes and build anarchistic societies more quickly than ramming the proper economic approach down people's throats.

Don't get me wrong, my economic vision for society is capitalism because it tends toward greater personal freedom. However, socialists and other traditionalist anarchist thinkers tend to believe supporters of capitalism are evil and bad in their own right because they support "labor slavery."

Therefore, we have to consider their positions and find ways to communicate that reduce the likelihood of bloodshed.

Generally speaking, we would agree that they are logically and morally incorrect, but one can't just tell a communist that and proceed to get into a logical tug-of-war. This usually ends badly, with each party talking past one another and getting triggered.

In my mind, relational anarchism bridges that communication divide and allows us to build societies from the ground up based on compassion. This implies that economic differences can be properly resolved in the process because we have dispensed with the "fight mentality." It might even mean we find new ways of approaching the problem of economic differences, which is not a perspective I have seen many anarchists adopt to approach this problem.

Economic theories should not be a barrier to building freer communities, but they can sometimes obstruct our goals as anarchists. Some even tend to get stuck in this enclosed way of thinking. This engenders binary, I-am-right-and-you-are-wrong ways of relating.

This is why I believe relationalism via compassionate interaction is the true crucible from which the new, freer world will be spun into existence.

March 29, 2017

Here's what relational anarchism does: It moves us from theorizing about systems to individualized communication. It takes the logical urgency to be right and replaces it with the humanitarian need to connect. When this type of connection takes place, any type of social, organizational, or economic problem can be solved. In this sense, relational anarchism moves outside the realm of traditional and conventional anarchist thought. It goes from political to apolitical. It goes from nonhuman to human. It goes from hate to love, and love solves all woes.

April 8, 2017

Relational anarchism is an interactive philosophy that musters guerrilla empathy.

April 9, 2017

This is how I imagine a lot of anarchists are in their personal and intimate relationships:

Anarchist's significant other: "I love you, baby."

Anarchist: "Define what you mean by 'love!'"

Anarchist's significant other: "I only care about you."

Anarchist: "That's a fallacy."

In my estimation, this type of communication is what creates problems in real-world scenarios where emotional valence is lost in the riptide of intellectualization of every discussion.

I encourage anarchists to also get in touch with their feelings, with the deep emotional states that make up their humanness.

There is poetry as well as freedom in the emotional perspective.

April 15, 2017

Very few anarchists have suggested other anarchists stop arguing the logical, economic, and moral positions and start finding common ground.

Why?

Why is the fight mentality so entrenched? Why do people love to pilot their economic theories like they are on a kamikaze mission?

Must these ideological differences cause such a rift between people? Must the nastiness and nonsense remain forged between camps forever?

I get that there *appear* to be irreconcilable differences between communism and capitalism but look at the logical consequence of taking either position to the extreme in terms of acceptance; it is perpetual hate. In the end, it is outright, bitter annihilation.

If people become so stuck in their ideologies that they come to embrace an evolving hatred of people who harbor antithetical views, can there ever be the creation and maintenance of freer societies?

I think we must start with communication, emotional connection, and shared empathy between people. Without this, all we will ever have is an ever-widening gyre of pitched verbal battles punctuated by apparent bouts of ideological insanity.

I believe that the use of relational anarchism and the creation of freedom cells can thwart the madness and create communities of people who are willing to find mutual solutions to their longstanding differences.

If I am wrong, fine, but at least we get a momentary reprieve from the tiresome, endless cascade of back-and-forth drama-mongering and hate-speaking.

Who is with me?

April 16, 2017

If you believe government is necessary, think about how you treat people. Do you actively want to lock them in a cage or kill them? Or do you tend to act more compassionately with those in your life? If the answer is that you treat them with love and dignity, you're probably not a true supporter of statism.

April 19, 2017

Sometimes the most hated people are those who promote compassion and connection.

April 27, 2017

Once people start communicating rather than dehumanizing each other, a magical thing happens.

They start negotiating solutions to resolve their disputes. But so long as competing factions rile each other up, hate-speak, and otherwise objectify each other, there can be no solution. There will only be distrust, misunderstanding, and inevitable bloodshed over the long term.

It's time to embrace relational anarchism and relational interaction. This is part of how freedom cells and agorist communities will proliferate to create a freer tomorrow—an anarchistic tomorrow.

April 28, 2017

If you accept government, think about the consequences of this decision. Your friends and family become susceptible to government violence. It's almost like you hurt them by proxy. Surely you don't want to align with a system that could hurt all those you love, including yourself.

If we all want to maintain strong relationships and connections with those close to us, we must reject government on relational grounds. We must reject it because it is the antithesis of dignity and decency. It is a monster that destroys lives and has zero compassion.

Disavow government. Explore relational anarchism.

Anarchy and Emotion:
A Heart-Based Philosophy for Transforming Society

4/13/2016

I study counseling psychology. I learn to use skills that help people deal with personal issues, trauma, mental issues, and stress. But saying I "help" someone is a misnomer.

In reality, I empathize with an individual. I leverage their desire to connect with another human. I do this to show a person they possess their own ability to cope with the stressors of life. In other words, I help them help themselves. My relationship with a client is what the counseling profession cleverly refers to as the "therapeutic alliance."

The therapeutic alliance states that a counselor joins with a client, and together they form a bond. They enter into an emotional rapport, which accounts for any healing that takes place. Current research in counseling suggests the client-therapist bond contributes to positive outcomes. This is the open secret of all therapy. Healing occurs because the client and counselor share an authentic connection.

In 2001, a comprehensive research summary published in the journal *Psychotherapy* found that a strong therapeutic alliance was more closely correlated with positive client outcomes than any specific treatment interventions.

This psychotherapeutic reality does not really come as a surprise considering 50 years of research have fleshed out the truth. Evidence shows the therapeutic alliance works.

I invoke this idea of the therapeutic relationship because I hope to reconcile counseling insights and psychotherapy with anarchist political philosophy. Counseling psychology, in my estimation, has unveiled what it is that humans seek most in life: emotionally fulfilling relationships and interactions free of coercion.

A Softer Interpretation of Anarchism

I believe the aforesaid truths of therapy and counseling can be applied to voluntaryist thinking for the creation of a new kind of anarchistic philosophy, as well as community.

I call it relationalism. It promotes the absence of rulers and total freedom through relationships and social healing rather than through the traditional routes of argumentation, persuasion, or economic theorizing (although the philosophy is not opposed to any of the traditional vectors of anarchism, as convincing people of this philosophy will likely also require argumentation).

I, along with others, have also referred to relationalism as "soft anarchism," "therapeutic voluntaryism," or "anarcho-relationalism." I am certain that more names for this particular philosophy will arise as others begin to discuss it and tease apart all the implications.

There are three primary thought processes or underlying assumptions behind relationalism as an emotional framework for freedom.

1. Current conceptions of anarchism have been hyper-focused on solving the logical, economic, and moral problems of society and government. They are embedded in an echo chamber where buzzwords like *non-aggression principle*, *property*, and *self-ownership* dominate cultural language. Thus, relationalist anarchism is a new formulation that looks at other, softer determinants for building an anarchist society, and it attempts to move beyond fashionable memes and tropes.

2. The soft interpretation of anarchism suggests that humanity's emotional and relational closeness acts as a prerequisite for voluntaryism, anarcho-capitalism, and many other non-coercive social arrangements. In other words, if people are attuned to each other's feelings, there is less of an opportunity for violence and aggression to erupt. This is the application of the therapeutic alliance to society-at-large for building a freer, more psychologically stable world.

3. To build a social order based on logical, moral, or economic truths, humans must first grapple with their emotional worlds and how they relate and interact with all people. They must learn to heal each other through being together and uniting, much in the same way a counselor helps a client get better through their mutually agreed upon alliance. In this sense, the philosophy of relationalism sees the anarchist as a social healer who creates communities and nurtures love.

In a way, the relationalist accepts and expands the common voluntaryist meme that "statism starts at home" and applies it universally across all cultures and all human interactions. It is true that the parent-child relationship is paramount to creating a healthy human, but the idea of relationalism must permeate all crevices of society-at-large and remain present throughout the human lifespan for full impact.

The Relationalist Ethic

Normally, people do not feel the same sense of empathy, connection, and closeness to people they do not know. Relationalists, however, see everyone as part of an ever-widening and interrelated socio-emotional system. Thus, therapeutic anarchists seek to treat everyone as if they can make authentic, loving contact.

In the spirit of the counselor or therapist, the relationalist wants to join with others and form an alliance. Relationalists see rapport as a mainstay of culture, and they attempt to apply it everywhere as they walk the world.

But for this to occur, relationalists must adopt a single and simple tenet that guides their interaction with others. This gut-level concept is called the relationalist ethic.

The ethic states that soft anarchists attempt to achieve a relationally focused community because shared feelings, empathetic connections, and closeness are always antithetical to violence. They are different neurological states. They are binary mental positions. They are opposites. Empathy and love cannot exist in the human mind at the same time as violence and aggression. Therefore, the stronger the culture of relationalism, the less violent and more anarchic it becomes. This assumption or theory is based on evidence gathered in psychotherapy research, and the hope is that it will remain intact on a socio-global scale.

I do not agree with everything Jiddu Krishnamurti said, but this quote sums up the relationalist ethic in terms of a softer attitude toward society: "Love is the missing factor; there is a lack of affection, of warmth in relationship; and because we lack that love, that tenderness, that generosity, that mercy in relationship, we escape into mass action, which produces further confusion, further misery."

This is not to say that every person wants to accept loving connections with strangers, but the relationalist contends that if relationalists do not try to connect with strangers, they may in turn jeopardize their own relationships. It means that entities like the government may crop up and hurt all relationships. Simply speaking, government is the result of people's lack of relational focus.

As an aside, this position is not intended to suggest that relationalism is a utopian agenda. It is just to say that if empathy is accepted as the cornerstone of a healthy and less violent society, it should also be a component of culture. Surely, violence will still manifest in society because people are imperfect, but this situation is worsened when governments destroy relationships.

But why exactly do relationalists need to worry about government? Krishnamurti disliked all politics and thought change could occur without looking at "political" cures. Why do relationalists claim to be anarchists? Can't they just promote empathy and love and be done with it?

The Psychological Problem of Statism and Relationship Desecration

To be sure, the relationalist aims to build an anarchist, emotionally-oriented society. As the relationalist ethic states, soft anarchism wants to achieve total freedom from rulers and authority because these ideas conflict with the concepts of love and sensual union.

A truly empathetic society cannot exist so long as authority and government loom over it and interfere with human interaction. It cannot happen because governments use violent aggression to sway the masses to behave in certain ways.

This mentality thwarts the possibility of having a truly love-based culture. Relationalism is thus expressed in anarchism because governments naturally destroy interpersonal connections.

Here are several examples of how government and the political classes prevent and dissuade people from forming social therapeutic alliances. I could provide hundreds of examples, but for this essay, four will suffice.

1. The governmental institution of police removes the possibility of empathic love from the whole population by providing society with aggressive force and hateful authoritarianism. The mere presence of police puts people in a state of fight-or-flight, which tends to erode the empathy circuitry in people's brains. This is especially true if it causes increased stress hormones to flood the body. Policing is likely another symptom of the poor relationship systems and interactions that exist in society-at-large.

2. The drug war is a political edict that, by its nature, tears apart families and ruins stable relationships. Whenever a loved one is kidnapped by police enforcers, it destroys the relationship between "government" and that person, and it also undermines that person's ability to take care of their family, which tarnishes the overall attachment bonds in that family. Additionally, if most family members agree with the State that their own loved one should be kidnapped, extorted, and caged, it further divides that family along ideological lines. This situation is wholly antithetical to the relationalist perspective, and it applies to all members of society, not just the family system.

3. One of the most hideous examples of government destroying relationships and undermining compassion is Child Protective Services. This institution thrives off of its ability to break up families and destroy close-

ness among family members. It is in this government-created anti-family atmosphere that truly stable and caring relationships cannot be nurtured and continued. As a disclaimer, it is certainly true that some children could actually need to be taken out of abusive families that already have horrible relational interactions, but the State and these kinds of institutions only exacerbate relational problems within the family environment.

4. The military is probably one of the most destructive institutions for the development of interpersonal and empathetic connections between people. Anyone who joins the military has their ability to feel the pain of another human systematically desensitized in boot camp. The only time a soldier's feelings return is when they come back from the war with emotional or moral injuries psychiatrists refer to as PTSD. To continuously heal social relations, the standing military in all of its manifestations must be abolished.

Essentially, governments are in the business of destroying relationships; they engage in what I call *relationship desecration*. Governments transform human emotional functioning into an enterprise of volatility and violence. When relationships are constantly torn asunder by the State, people become even more violent and volatile. They lose their sense of connectedness with other humans, and instead of being awash in empathy, they are ensnared by hate. Therefore, relationalists maintain a philosophy of emotive anarchism.

The evidence for relationship desecration is clear if one merely looks at the psychological research on what authority does to people's ability to connect with others. In other words, the belief in authority blocks people's feeling capabilities. Stanley Milgram, who conducted famous experiments on obedience to authority, elaborated on this concept.

> Ordinary people, simply doing their jobs, and without any particular hostility on their part, can become agents in a terrible destructive process. Moreover, even when the destructive effects of their work become patently clear, and they are asked to carry out actions incompatible with fundamental standards of morality, relatively few people have the resources needed to resist authority.

In relationalist terms, people can't feel for the person they are hurting; they cannot empathize and connect. These are the reasons why relationalists must promote not only love and interpersonal interaction in society but also the abolition of government and authority to heal society and create an environment that cultivates empathy rather than destruction.

Additional Thoughts on Relationalism

Relationalism hinges on love and human attachment. As a philosophy, it is contingent on people's desire to be with other people and form relationships. In other words, healthy human connections necessitate absolute freedom.

In this light, relationalism is not a detached model for new sociopolitical arrangements nor a dry run of endless debates and objective presentations. It is not a strictly cognitive exercise. Instead, it is a psychological expression or aesthetic that implores people to create loving and harmonious relationships without the desire to employ coercion to undermine those relationships.

It is not only a philosophy but also a process and a dialogue. It was what philosopher Martin Buber called the "I-Thou" connection. It is a heart-level instinct based on human psychology. This acknowledgment of the feeling vectors of anarchism underscores the relationalist perspective.

In addition, relationalism is not an appeal to emotion from a logically fallacious sense, nor is it a suggestion that people should get carried away with their emotions and forget higher brain functioning. It is only to say that the focus of anarchistic interactions should hinge on dialogue and rapport. It is the idea that we can exercise rational faculties but also stay in sync with our emotions.

This philosophy is something totally novel, and this is just the first of many articulations. It is a fertile field for developing a host of interesting and helpful ideas, which ultimately are a psychological technology everyone can employ.

As of now, to my knowledge, the therapeutic findings of psychotherapy have not been applied to anarchist political philosophy nor integrated with any accuracy. Therefore, I hope this articulation will help others in the relationalist community continue to build these ideas so we may eventually dissolve the State apparatus and learn to love each other with full integrity and the whole strength of our humanity.

A friend and fellow relationalist of mine, Gordon Peters, expressed what soft anarchism for the community could look like in these beautiful words.

> The community facilitates a healthy physical, spiritual, and mental climate for all. The community is open to all services, as individuals are led to provide them. The community understands that coercing an Individual into unnatural service will harm the health of that individual and the health of the entire community. The community arcs towards simplicity and common sense. The rest is celebration.

Psychology and Its Implications for Freedom

October 23, 2014

Older psychological theories emphasize the idea that our past experiences color our emotions, thoughts, and behaviors in the present. I don't buy into this model anymore. I mean, I understand that the past certainly affects us in many ways, but we all can work on our thinking in the now and alter our feelings and behavior. We're not hamstrung by the abuses we suffered in the past, and as rational creatures with individual wills, we have the power to take control of our minds and push ourselves squarely in the direction we want to go. We are not slaves to our past selves. We are heroic creatures with the ability to forge new identities and become as stoic and resilient as we need to be to survive and love ourselves. Never give in to the idea that our past colors us so much that we have to be paralyzed by it. The future holds much more than we can ever even begin to see if we allow mistakes of the past to drag us down.

October 31, 2014

Many people dismiss psychology on the grounds that it is not scientific. Now, I agree with the previous statement. Psychology is not a hard science; it is science lite. But this is also a misunderstanding of the value of psychology. Regardless of the discipline's scientific efficacy, it has humanistic value.

Indeed, we cannot predict human behavior with accuracy, and correlation doesn't equal causation. But this is the result of free will and the non-deterministic nature of man. Thus, psychology must work with imperfect models to understand the desires and drives of man to help alleviate his suffering and problems. If psychology were a science and we could accurately predict the behavior of man, life would become very boring and robotic. Understanding people would be complete and therefore silly. Life would amount to a bland and lackluster repetition of the mundane with no surprises or spontaneity.

That said, psychological experiments and theories, while still using the scientific method, can give us a nice lens to peer through when it comes to human behavior, and this can aid us in creating frameworks for grasping how men feel, think, and behave. In other words, it can give us insights into the human condition.

But what truly makes psychological ideas so great is that we can bring these ideas down to the therapeutic (clinical) environment and use them to help people who are struggling with the problems of everyday living. This is where the gold lies, especially considering that counseling is statistically equivalent to the efficacy of psychiatric drugs. I believe counseling has more value in the long run because it allows the person to explore themselves and uncover their problems' root causes, whereas most drugs only sedate the individual and mask their underlying issues. This should give people more drive to promote psychological awareness so we can put a stop to chemically lobotomizing people because they "suffer from" what others find odd or morally questionable.

Thus, I will be extremely happy to enter the field. I just wish psychologists and counselors could compete freely in the market for their services without the State controlling who can practice what essentially amounts to talking to people. But we all know the truth of why this is. The State must have the aid of psychiatry to control people and to formally label behaviors both the State and psychiatry deem evil and wrong. This is a bastardization of a very wholesome field that is based in the heart and rooted in empathy.

I just hope I can influence change in the field. That will be my goal.

November 12, 2014

I am passionate about one area of counseling: the ability to work with people, help them see new choices, and assist them in finding their own solutions. A lot of the time, due to many factors, people miss opportunities for growth and change. Instead, they feel lost, stuck, or immobilized, and seeing new opportunities can help empower them. It lets them know they have more control over their lives than they previously thought. They can author their unique destinies. They can take control of their actions and thinking and move in whatever direction they like. Life may be a maze, but it's a maze that individuals help construct as they seek the final destination. It's a splendid idea that we're not total slaves to our environment. Instead, we are masters of our own miniature universes.

May 31, 2015

I do not believe there has been a proper integration of anarchism and psychology, especially with the psychology behind why people want total freedom and what drives them to secure it. Thus, we find ourselves at the dawn of an anarcho-therapeutic revolution where a new theoretical approach to psychotherapy will be born out of the principles of the anti-ruler philosophy.

This approach will draw from existential theory, choice theory, and modern neuroscience. I believe it will help influence more people to consider the importance of anarchism in our relationships with those close to us, as well as society-at-large. I believe this with all my heart.

July 13, 2015

Anarchism and psychotherapy are natural allies. When anarchists deal with problems, they attempt to tackle them from a rational standpoint rather than a purely emotional one. If anarchists can take this mentality into the counseling chair and help people see their conundrums from this vantage point, they can not only change society from a structural standpoint but also help people who are hurting.

Of course, in the counselor's chair, things get more complicated. Anarchists will have to learn to empathize with their clients, which isn't always easy. However, if a balance can be struck between empathy and rational decision-making, well, then, the anarchist can help heal broken people, and these people will naturally disavow authority and embrace self-responsibility.

Anarchists must also consider ethics. They cannot—and should not—just preach anarchism to the client. Luckily, the deep truths of anarchism hinge on voluntary decision-making and conscious understanding of problems. These ideas need only be watered, and they will blossom. If feminists can bring their flimsy ideology into the counseling chair, it should be a cakewalk for anarchists to do the same.

I have a few ideas for a much better theoretical and practical approach to get anarchists involved in professional psychotherapy. This is another idea that anarchists can implement now and that gets us more involved in the world. It is a livable goal.

May 19, 2016

When I question the legitimacy of mental illness, I am not saying you don't suffer. I am not saying you don't hurt or that you have not endured traumatic experiences. I am not trying to dismiss years of personal difficulty or life hardship. I can see the pain and experience mirrored in your eyes. I have suffered my own misfortunes, anxieties, and soul sickness.

Trust me, I know how you feel.

When I question the legitimacy and validity of mental illness, I am only promoting the beauty and strength of your spirit. I am providing hope. I am saying your brain is not diseased or broken. It has only adapted to survive against the hardness of your reality. But you can rebuild it. You can recover. You can grow from all the trauma and fear. You can control your stress expressions and learn to cope with your woes.

I am saying this because I believe in self-responsibility, and I know there are those out there who would have you imagine that you are damaged, helpless, and in need of dangerous psychiatric drugs. Some would laugh at your pain and would love to see you on your knees. But I am here to offer compassion and truth. I believe you can stand up to these pharmacrats who revel in your darkness and rage. I am here to see you swell in strength and love.

Therefore, I believe you are not diseased and broken. It is why I believe you are just haunted by the ghosts of a decadent culture. It is why we all must shed the destructive notion that we are mentally ill and why we must use our pain and suffering to find meaning and fight back. We must leverage our anger and undermine this system that wants us to commit self-sabotage.

Are you with me?

Anarchy Is Not Just a Childish "Phase"

5/5/2016

There are people who thought anarchism was just a "phase" I would grow out of. They saw my "beliefs" as a way to lash out. They thought I was being juvenile, and they did not take me or my ideas seriously. But I am still here, advocating freedom seven years later.

These long years consisted of long days spent thinking about and meditating on liberty, contradicting various ideas, and rebutting the contradictions until I discovered a synthesis—until I finally hit on the fabled a-ha moment.

Now I know I will always be an anarchist. Some aspects of my philosophy have undergone restructuring and change, but my desire for unadulterated freedom has grown stronger.

Anyone who believes anarchy is just a "phase" or an aspect of adolescent turmoil has failed to grasp the spirit of the age.

Things are changing; times are different. Many people of all ages and backgrounds finally realize the philosophical maturity of anarchy. They no longer want to be straitjacketed by violent laws and poisonous cultures. They want to live in actual freedom, not this pseudo-freedom peddled by parasitical politicians.

Only one less mature "phase" exists.

It is the phase of humanity's dark past, which consists of the belief that ruling people is necessary. People are stuck in this ugly, brutish era. It is the idea that violence must be used to organize society, make it function, and create prosperity. It is the phase of government. It is what people must grow beyond. It is why anarchists have cropped up in multitudes.

The anarchists have risen from the ashes of humanity's decadent past to contradict the darkness of the old regime. They are here to turn consensus culture on its head. They seek to reverse the trend of authority-worship and expose people to a beautiful truth.

As a result, government apologists are starting to shed their shackles and confront freedom without fear. They are leaving the childish phase behind and breaking through the cocoon of statism.

They are metamorphosing into the butterfly—changing from a lower form to a higher one, from unconscious violence to conscious love, and from statism to a state of anarchy. This is the most beautiful and powerful transformation a human individual can undergo.

I am glad I made this transition. I hope all anarchists can help carry more over. The world on this side is much more beautiful, emotionally relevant, and peaceful.

If you are not an anarchist, would you be willing to take a peek at this more wholesome world? The beyond is beautiful, and anarchists can tell you all about it.

> "Where love rules, there is no will to power; and where power predominates, there love is lacking. The one is the shadow of the other."
>
> —Carl Jung

The Predation of Children

April 17, 2011

C hild abuse of any kind is the absolute most destructive thing. I shun everything from punching and slapping to verbal abuse and even spanking. Aggression used against children damages their ability to grow and change and develop virtue. Part of the problem with aggression in society relates directly to our treatment of children. Love your kids with peace and kindness, and the world will grow peacefully and kindly.

August 17, 2011

What Burns Me Up: Hitting Children.

A lot of people think it's acceptable and amusing, but I think hitting children in any manner is cruel, including spanking. At my job, people constantly spank their children. Today, two ladies came through my line at work while I was working the register. One taller, dark-haired, slightly chubby lady moved past her buggy toward the register, presumably to pay. In the buggy sat two children, probably not a day older than two. Another woman, about the same build, stood behind the buggy.

From observation, I gathered that one child belonged to each woman. As the dark-haired woman began to slide her card at the debit machine, a child tried to lean forward in the buggy and press a button on the debit reader. The woman standing behind the buggy saw it and immediately reared back to strike the child. As she lunged forward with the hit, she seemed to sink back at the last moment, landing an awkward half-slap on the child's back. In horror, she realized that she had hit the other mother's child and started to apologize profusely. The other woman didn't even seem to notice the mishap and continued to pay. The child seemed more confused than hurt because the full force of the swing was obstructed by the woman's sudden thought that this child was not hers to strike.

The situation was absurd. The woman felt bad for hitting her friend's child, but if it had been her child, she probably would have kept hitting him. Apparently, in our society, it's okay to beat the shit out of your kids when you're out shopping or getting ice cream or whatever. However, don't you dare hit another person's child. That is a major grievance. Every time I see someone strike a child, it takes every inch of my person not to yell at them from the top of my lungs and ask them how they would like it if I reared back and slugged them for doing something so trivial and minuscule. It boggles the mind that people don't have more patience with their children. I mean, that woman didn't even form half a thought. She reacted unthinkingly to a child's presumed "disobedience." She reacted how she always does, I'm sure—without any patience or a single thought about how else the situation might have been handled. If she would have thought about it, she would not have hit someone else's kid.

Word to the wise: Hitting children is not the only way to discipline a child or help them understand what is or is not appropriate. Children are curious, intelligent, and eager by nature. Asserting your size over them because they "step out of line" goes against the very things we teach children about life and growing up: that hitting and bullying are not okay.

However, in most cases, we teach them that self-defense from attackers is okay. So what would it mean to you if your two-year-old reared back in response and slapped you in the face? I recommend trying to accommodate our children's sense of wonder and awe about the world instead of reacting with knee-jerk malice whenever they do something we perceive as insolent.

Children are miracles. Our future. Let's stop and think about what we're doing in terms of taking care of them. It's this kind of anti-parenting that makes the world the violent and aggressive place we live in.

On most issues, I don't give a shit what people do, but striking children... that just gets to me.

August 15, 2013

It is not necessary nor logical to instill fear in your child to control him or her. As counterintuitive as it sounds, instilling fear in your child only creates resentment and causes the problems or behavior you dislike.

February 6, 2014

This may sound like either a giant leap or merely common sense, but it has profound implications: You do not own your children. They are not your property.

April 17, 2014

I believe when parents tell their children they "brought them into this world and they can take them out," the parents are being unbelievably selfish and treating their children like slaves.

When parents have this mentality, they believe their children should be beholden to them to the point of the child sacrificing himself, his desires, and his autonomy.

Now, I am not saying it's necessarily morally wrong for parents to strongarm and guilt-trip their children in this manner (kids have their own ideas and thoughts), but if you are a parent and you see your child retaliate or shun you, don't be surprised. Your efforts to extort their autonomy have driven them to rebel and disassociate from you.

So this status is more of a cautionary meme warning parents about psychological reactance, which just means that people will react in seemingly contradictory ways to authoritarian demands: authoritarian parenting can actually lead to less respectful children who do hazardous, idiotic, or taboo things to spite their parents as a form of lashing out.

Treat children decently and with the same respect you require of them, and they will see you for the decent and responsible parent you are.

May 7, 2015

In modern parenting memes, allowing children to just be children is a great sin. If children run around, make a lot of noise, and disturb the adults, they are considered misbehaved and in need of corrective discipline. People who witness this, especially relatives, tell the parents to control their children and make them fall in line.

Psychologist Jean Piaget said children are little scientists; they are exploring and fact-checking the world. But they are also little artists; they are exercising their wonder and creativity.

Remember, their little brains are still developing. Being authoritarian and trying to control their every move, including normal developmental outbursts, can potentially have very negative consequences. Great caution must be taken here. Parents often say they are "disciplining" their children when they are really just acting impatiently and emotionally against them.

Tantrums are not signs of problem kids or developmental issues. They seem more like coping mechanisms and side effects of learning about a strange new world.

When children are allowed more freedom to be children, they are less likely to develop problematic attachment styles and experience mental and social problems later, especially regarding moms and dads who use negative punishers as placeholders for authentic parenting.

Remember, children did not consent to being brought into this world. Treat them with the respect they deserve. They are new to everything.

July 16, 2015

The greatest practical contribution anarchists have brought to the world is peaceful parenting. This is not to say they invented or thought of the idea. It is just to say they are the most assertive conveyors of it, which is not surprising since they are devoted to the consistent application of the non-aggression principle.

Anarchists hope the outcome of peaceful parenting is also a more peaceful world. The studies show that spanking and harming children is godawful and causes nothing but a vicious cycle of trauma and problem behavior. If parents can wake up from their authoritarian impulse to batter children, all people might be more likely to see the novelty, beauty, and ease of a voluntary society. Right now, because people have been taught that might makes right, they wear blinders that darken the world and impel them to believe that only strong-arm tactics and the bloody end of the switch bestow discipline and peace upon humanity.

One day, anarchists will be eternally thanked by posterity for freeing the world from the inhumane treatment done to little ones for far too long. This new view and treatment of children will ring out far and wide, and people will finally unleash a great sigh of relief.

August 26, 2015

Children are not property—what a ghastly idea. If a person owns another person, that is slavery. That person is chattel. If children are considered chattel, they become vulnerable to abuse, manipulation, neglect, and maltreatment. Thus, seeing the child as a slave imbues people with disdain and negativity toward them.

As a matter of fact, in today's current culture, children are generally considered property. They have few rights. They have little freedom. Parents feel authorized to hit and beat them when they "step out of line." People ought to be ashamed of the state of life for children. If children aren't treated as humans—with dignity and decency—no one can expect to have a dignified and decent world. People can expect mass bloodshed and violence because they taught their children that abusing, enslaving, and harming others is the norm.

Tragically, everyone pretends and hallucinates that all the violence and debauchery are just facets of "human nature." In truth, this is a collective delusion wielded to brush off responsibility. Things have to change. A world built on the edifice of harming children is a world no one really wants to live in.

I am just glad that more people are starting to value safety and affection for kids. They are starting to see that treating children with love and as individuals is the only way to raise them with respect and appreciation for others. Harming and enslaving children is a recipe for planetary disaster. It is the formulation for life that will make ghosts of everyone sooner rather than later.

September 12, 2015

A lot of times, children tell their parents that they hate them in fits of rage and fury. A parent should not confuse this with a tantrum. This critique toward a parent is genuine. It is the result of pent-up and repressed emotions from earlier traumas and the fact that parents mostly control and manipulate their children.

If you are a parent who believes your child utters these things often, you might reexamine your parenting style. These types of attacks often come from teenagers but sometimes much younger children. During puberty, children are hormonal and are finally able to feel their emotions under the onslaught of all their bodily changes.

If parents have used violence and various forms of control on their children, intense resentment may crop up, and the child will let the parent know in spurts. Do not dismiss this as a "kid just being a kid" or a side effect of adolescence.

There is a chance that the child does actually hate you but will later tell you how much they love you. They only do this because the hate is repressed, and they still rely on your guidance. Instances of children saying things like this to parents can be diminished if Mom and Dad practice peaceful parenting and treat their children with the respect they also expect from their children.

A lot of times, later in life when children grow up, they will not tell their parents they hate them anymore because they have been reared to love their parents regardless, often through subtle forms of coercion. But the pent-up resentment and anger can remain seething below the surface only to show up in other forms, including the child taking revenge on the next generation for the way they were treated, perpetuating the cycle of punitive parenting and abuse.

September 30, 2015

Parents often do the wrong things when their teenagers start experimenting with drugs. They catch them and impose strict rules and harsh punishments. Such draconian disciplinarian techniques intensify problematic behavior rather than prevent it, and this makes teenagers loathe their parents.

In social psychology, this issue is known as reactance theory and is based on how individuals behave when their freedom to choose is restricted. To stop a teen from resenting and disobeying, parents must be less controlling and forceful.

Oftentimes, a light touch can produce the desired effects. It seems like a paradox, but studies in interpersonal neurobiology also seem to support this technique. The more nurturing and open parents are in allowing their kids to choose, the more positive neural connections teenagers build, which manifests as parental love and respect.

October 6, 2015

When I was a youngster, I was diagnosed with ADD. They said I could not pay attention to the teacher and that I often got lost in my own world. I would not read what they wanted me to, and I resorted to reading my own material, usually fantasy sagas and other unpopular fiction. They constantly had to discipline me and complain to my mother about my attention span. As a result, they believed I needed to take speed to correct this "mental illness."

The Ritalin they gave me addled my nervous system. It made my little mind race to where I could only sit and nervously look outward, like a statue, eyes plastered in confusion and fear. I had a superabundance of emotions overload my still-maturing brain. The meth was too intense for me at such a tender age, and so I fought back. I pretended to take the medication but spit it out because it was hurting me, turning me off to learning and education and preparing me for a life of brainlessness.

It was not what I needed. It was unhealthy. The adults were wrong. Drugging a preteen was not the answer. It is still not appropriate. It is psychologically damaging and possibly bad for the brain. In reality, I was a sensitive and intelligent youngster, but I did not easily obey authority.

I viewed learning and education through my own lens, and I needed someone to nurture and tend to that, not force-feed me their pedagogy and indoctrination. I needed support and someone to teach me how to be an autodidact, to pull myself up by my bootstraps. I did not need consensus education and mainstream "child-rearing." It was a burden to my soul, and I had to compensate for all that trauma by checking out further from reality to survive as one of humanity's most hated things: a boy child.

Today, I feel the same way. Kids, especially young boys, should not be chemically lobotomized with meth. They should not be labeled "learning disabled" when they are actually advanced and anti-authoritarian. These traits should be celebrated, not punished. Being smart and emotionally sensitive is not a disease or defect. It is the trait of a leader and thinker. It should be commended and praised.

October 17, 2015

Public schooling is one of the most heinous institutions in existence. There is nothing positive about it. It is the meat grinder that processes children's brains into mush. There is nothing in the psychological literature about childhood development that lends acceptability to the idea of a standardized, one-size-fits-all educational system. Each child is unique and views the world differently, so assigning them lemming-like roles and rules to follow is short-sighted and cruel. Most kids are curious and have idiosyncrasies that are ignored or subdued by educators. Kids are not all built for a world of sameness and grayness. No wonder people grow up with so many psychological issues and a broken fight-or-flight response.

The most creative, innovative, and unique children suffer the most. If they display their individuality and desire for specialized learning and advanced knowledge, the system moves to sedate and hamstring them. They are put into remedial classes, drugged, and manipulated. Their parents are lied to and manipulated, as well. It is as if the system administrators subconsciously know these children have a penchant for revolutionary ideas that fall outside the norm, and that is too scary and unpredictable for the cultural engineers. They must put a stop to this blooming disobedience and strength of will. These kids must follow suit and fall in line. They need to be adequately retrofitted for society, so they don't make waves and undermine good pedagogy and the order and chemistry of culture. The secret is that education shuns novelty unless it is manufactured within the status quo. Anything outside the scope of mainline thought, especially if it is illegal or taboo, is quickly squashed, and the child is punished. This is not education for the sake of learning. It is obedience school. This is adult culture systematically taking vengeance on the younger generations for the abuse they suffered as youngsters.

Do you remember your youth? Was this your experience? Something has to be done about this. Our children are not cattle to be led to psychological slaughter. It is time to overhaul the whole system. It is worse than broken. It is an institution of insanity, a vice grip clamping down on the brains of our future, and it is wholly unacceptable and unforgivable.

October 26, 2015

If there is anything true about "human nature," it is the importance of mother-child attachment from birth and during the formative years. In an environment of deprivation and stress, a child could be significantly impaired psychologically. It is this early atmosphere that helps determine the course of the individual human being, and without secure attachments and 'good enough' parenting, the child may not grow up with strong neural integration, which could lead to fits of violence, authoritarianism, or social withdrawal.

It is possible to reverse this trauma with therapy and diverse experiences, but not without a lot of legwork on the part of the trauma survivor. This highlights the importance of empathetic and positive parenting as soon as the baby leaves the birth canal. Without early bonding, the child starts life with a handicap that could lead to disaster.

I fear that too many children are ushered into this world with some of their first experiences being hellish, violent, and depraved. Hopefully, we will all get to the point where people understand the importance of early attachment and love. I will preach this truth until my death.

March 18, 2016

Most of us have lingering resentment and anger from being exploited and hurt as children. Trust me, I have gone through my own personal hell. But that's not to say my experiences have been any worse or more traumatic than anyone else's. It's just to say that unleashing anger and raging in vengeance has not helped make the world a better place. Indeed, it has only fanned the flames of brutality.

This is why I constantly try to exercise unswerving patience when dealing with people, which includes treating them like humans and being fully present for them regardless of their history. Life is a rough place, and it's unfair to all of us. But we all must start the process of empathizing and being there for others if we are to heal the world for our children.

If we can't stop the cycle of abuse and viciousness that occurs as a result of abuse and viciousness, we're doomed. I am just glad the problems can be answered early in life by showing children peace and beauty so they can grow up to show their children kindness, as well.

This prospect greatly improves my desire to help the world become better and for individuals to heal and become whole. Human genetics do not determine that an individual will inevitably become a dick. This is a choice. It is based on the elbow room to choose and make decisions about how to interact with the world at large.

April 15, 2016

Hitting children is an unacceptable and disgusting practice, even if it is justified as "spanking." Besides the fact that spanking is a morally questionable issue, the psychological evidence that hitting children causes lasting harm is legion.

When children grow up in a hostile environment where their parents "spank" them for whatever reason, the child learns that they cannot establish their parents as secure bases for exploration. Their sense of attachment deteriorates. Their fight-or-flight response is damaged through over-activation, and then it malfunctions throughout life. This malfunction is what leads that child to likely suffer from substance abuse issues, enter violent relationships, commit self-injurious behavior, become plagued by depression, and ultimately victimize their own children in desperate acts of unconscious revenge.

Tragically, the only way to help children heal many of these wounds is for that child to seek counseling services or manage to find a nonviolent relationship as an adult, where proper healing can take place. If not, the individual is likely to suffer the slings and arrows of that abuse for years to come.

If you were hit as a child, you must realize that what was done to you did not make you a better person. You did not turn out okay. That is a social myth. It is only used to justify future attacks on children. Take this into consideration and stop hitting. Stop perpetuating the vicious cycle. The ignorance and violence must end. You do not want blood on your hands, do you?

May 13, 2016

I cannot emphasize how important it is for parents to provide limitless care and love to their children. Without proper attachments at a young age, children can grow up with all types of emotional problems that can translate into aggression, substance abuse, and other forms of everyday malfunction.

Studies suggest that early emotional deprivation in children can have devastating long-term consequences, which, without counseling or concentrated and willful efforts, can be extremely difficult to overcome.

As humans, our brains are very plastic and malleable to environmental cues. That means they are amenable to change and healing regardless of how rutted in a behavioral repertoire we have become.

However, as adults, once we get stuck in habits, routines, and ruts, it is very difficult for us to break our old behavior or thinking patterns. All of us probably understand this; dieting is a perfect example. Anyone who has tried to eat healthier knows how difficult it can be to alter old dietary habits forcefully and willfully.

This is identical to what happens to adult children of parents who neglected, spanked, and abused them. They get stuck in a lifelong dance of negative reactions, addiction patterns, and violent outbursts that they may never grow out of without being placed in an enriched and curative environment.

Therefore, I am currently advocating that we build cultures and communities that are naturally positive and loving, especially toward children: we have a scientific understanding that strong brain growth and overall good development occur because of the nurturing quality of our environments.

These emotionally functional relationship patterns create less violent and more loving civilizations.

May 20, 2016

Parents: When your children question authority and break arbitrary rules, they are not bad, and you did not fail them. Many naysayers will condemn you for being too "permissive," but that is only because they are petty tyrants and control freaks.

The ability to challenge people with power is a sign of independence and intelligence. It is a trait parents should nurture. It means the child does not want to be another obedient drone. Instead, they want to be a freethinker. A maverick. An anarchist. That child has a sense of freedom and courage this world desperately needs.

If your child follows this path, you should praise them and celebrate your parenting. If you would have shit out a lemming, the world would just have another carbon copy of a drooling automaton running around.

Tragically, most kids grow up to fit this programmed mold. They will want easy, simple lives as adults. They will want things to be superficial. They will silently obey and submit their soul to their masters. They will feign freedom. They will be pleasant serfs who fake happiness to get along. They will be alive but walking comatose.

I salute you if you brought a freethinking, anti-authoritarian child into the world.

Rejoice for birthing and training a child with a yearning for liberty and peace, and laugh at those Neanderthals who compel you to micromanage your child and hit them when they "step out of line." Love the fact that you put another decent human being into this sickening world of statist mayhem.

June 15, 2016

When I think about children, I don't think of them as little hellions who need to be commanded, forced, or bent to the whim of authority.

I think of children as inexperienced reflections of our future selves who need cooperation, respect, guidance, trust, and a real sense of love...a love not warped by the violence of spanking and coercion.

We should treat them with great compassion and as if all of them comprise the crucible from which our world was spun into existence.

We should not treat them like wretched little things that are beneath us. We should not imagine them as shame-bearers, as evil creatures in need of a good throttling.

No!

The young ones are the flames of life; their flicker keeps the decency in this world burning bright.

To sacrifice the children at the altar of autocratic, harsh discipline and other abuses is to harm our bloodlines, sacrifice ourselves, and unmake the whole species. Our progeny and their psychological health are what will inevitably help heal this broken world.

June 27, 2016

Government is the cultural manifestation of early attachment trauma and dysfunction in the family unit.

Statism really does start at home.

December 8, 2016

If anything runs contrary to compassion, it is the maltreatment of children.

In the soft anarchist perspective, children are human. They are not defined as wretched burdens. They possess the same dignity as everyone.

Anarchists are correct when they say children have not received true social acceptance. For most of history, children have been unimportant others. It has been acceptable to harm them—even brutalize them—so long as this brutality falls within the scope of customary standards.

For instance, hitting and emotional abuse toward children have been culturally sacred rituals that were not fully criticized until the modern age. But even this criticism did not take its final shape until the rise of compassionate anarchism.

These anarchists not only recognize that spanking and hitting children is bad but also that emotionally tormenting them and preventing them from sharing their feelings can be damaging.

That is why anarchists educate people about the harm emotional maltreatment can cause and seek to show parents that repressing children's inner worlds can cause psychological disruptions that lead to many problems. But this emotional abuse is obviously compounded by physical abuse such as spanking.

Children are precious and beautiful. And I hope we can all respect and appreciate them with the utmost compassion. If anyone deserves it, it is the children.

May they retain their innocence and love.

December 31, 2016

Children should be treated with utmost dignity and love.

When children are harmed and caregivers relate to them negatively or violently, it destroys their ability to form bonds or empathize freely with others.

When parents spank, scream and yell, or otherwise torment their growing young, those children start to view their caregivers differently.

They may see their caregivers as their protectors and primary sources of love, but they may also see them as monsters.

This paradoxical shift is an inevitable result of caregiver betrayal. It makes children conflicted, confused, and distraught.

Now the children only attempt to cater to the whims and needs of that parent with the hope that they will receive the love they so desperately yearn for, though they are now on high alert for impending threats from the person or people who are supposed to love them.

In practice, this paradoxical situation has been referred to as an attachment injury. It is biological and considered to be a result of trauma. The child's brain both recognizes the caregiver as good and bad simultaneously, and thus their fight or flight emotional mechanism trips regularly likely faulty wiring, causing fear, panic, anger, and anxiety to overwhelm them too often and exacerbate the possibility of substance abuse, self-harm, and other problems as they grow up.

For caregivers to prevent this from happening, they must nurture the children. They must bond strongly with them and try to meet those needs. This does not mean caregivers must be perfect. It just means they should treat their children with dignity because neglecting or abusing them can cause irreparable damage.

Children must be protected at all costs, and that is why a compassionate and relational perspective toward children is vital for their development and the development of love everywhere.

January 10, 2017

Schooling is one of the worst things a child can undergo. The school is a mechanistic institution that dehumanizes the child. It is psychological barbarism. It is a terror campaign aimed against the youth.

A child is forced to sit for hours at a time, follow a rigidly authoritarian structure, and become conditioned to bells that signal when to move and act. All the child's energy, passion, and enthusiasm are reduced to numbed inactivity and cold lethargy. All of the child's desires and youthful exuberance are repressed as the child is prepared to live in a society of control, a culture that is based on the constant fear of being watched—like that of a menacing panopticon. Schooling is the nastiest example of cultural abuse that people have sleepily ignored or passively accepted. It is a modern malady shamefully etched on the heart of humanity.

The public school system must be totally abolished and replaced with organizations or setups that support a child's natural enthusiasm and lust for life. A system that deemphasizes a child's childhood is not a system any human society should accept. These systems mold children into subjects and playthings, not competent adults or decent human beings. The school obliterates humanness, and it should thus be obliterated.

If people love their kids, they should seek to dismantle any organization that harms children. They should be tearing down the walls of all school institutions to save humanity from the incalculable wickedness perpetrated against its own young.

February 11, 2017

Female genital mutilation is a grotesque practice, but luckily, most people in the Western world condemn it as antiquated, evil, and misogynistic.

But what about rampant male genital mutilation in the West?

It is not only accepted but also praised as a mainstay of Western life. "Circumcision," as they call it, is defended as a valid "medical procedure," when in reality it is unneeded, antiquated, evil, and grotesque. People gladly, openly slice up the male sexual organs of their offspring.

To me, this is a tragic bit of hypocrisy. Cutting women is considered evil, but cutting men is considered normal and acceptable. I find this sentiment repulsive and loaded with misandry.

I know some folks will hit me with the "facts" about male genital mutilation being a preventive measure against disease, especially against HIV infection.

However, I find these "facts" to be underwhelming. Disease is prevented by taking proper care of the body, washing, and having safe sex.

In this vein of thought, the "disease prevention" argument just seems like a lazy excuse to mutilate infants. The argument is not compelling for me at all. It's not even compelling if someone makes the case that circumcision is necessary in Africa, where HIV transmission rates are notoriously high. I don't think there is any applicable medical excuse for genital mutilation of either males or females.

I prefer taking the compassionate approach: Don't cut the sexual organs of helpless infants. For God's sake, how long are people going to remain barbaric in the "civilized" age?

March 15, 2017

Hitting children is not an acceptable act, even if it is a final act of desperation. It's a form of abuse, even when it is euphemistically called "spanking."

In this sense, parents must not become desperate. They should remain patient, nurturing, and loving.

It's through this peaceful parenting that children learn hitting and violence are unacceptable for resolving disputes. When parents spank their children, they teach them volatility, anger, and the righteousness of hitting. There is also no such thing as "calm spanking," not to say that calm spanking would negate the effects of hitting.

Generally, when parents spank their children, they've already lost control of their emotions. Hitting by design is an aggressive, emotion-fueled act. When a parent hits a child, the parent's fight-or-flight response is in overdrive.

Instead of becoming desperate, which is an overloaded emotional state, the parent should take a minute to focus and gain clarity. Losing control of the self is the path to abuse and the continuation of violence.

To thrive, children require love, decency, and no personal harm from their primary caregiver.

As their parent, why would you want to give anything less?

Inhale. Exhale. Center yourself.

Don't hit.

April 15, 2017

The most destructive problem in society: not letting children express their emotions.

Anarchy and Emotion: Overcoming Childism and Healing Emotional Injuries

April 28, 2016

> The evolution of culture is ultimately determined by the amount of love, understanding and freedom experienced by its children... Every abandonment, every betrayal, every hateful act towards children returns tenfold a few decades later upon the historical stage, while every empathic act that helps a child become what he or she wants to become, every expression of love toward children heals society and moves it in unexpected, wondrous new directions.
>
> —Lloyd deMause

When we were children, some of our parents inadvertently betrayed us.

They smothered us and suffocated our emotional expressiveness. Our feelings were subdued and dimmed until nearly blotted out. We were ridiculed, shamed, or routinely hit. We were hardly allowed to feel, to truly experience life, or to explore our environments with security and freedom. We were not allowed to be kids. Our emotional sensitivity and curiosity were methodically amputated.

The culling of our emotional selves has led to the creation of an antiseptic and cold society where many of us now have difficulty navigating relationships and pursuing love.

This happened not because our parents were necessarily evil but because our culture embraces an anti-child mentality that has elevated emotional sterility above everything. This prejudice and nastiness toward children and their inner lives has rightly been called "childism" by Elisabeth Young-Bruehl.

Childism has been factually expressed in the cultural agreement that children can be condescended to, talked down to, hit, controlled, manipulated, coerced, and humiliated—on and on ad nauseam.

A *Toca Boca Magazine* piece articulated what childism *should* be: "Childism is the radical notion that kids need to be respected as human beings. It states that despite differences in size, experience and power, adults and children are inherently of equal worth, and that kids' perspectives and experiences should thus be considered on the same merits as those of adults."

But in our culture, children are not treated as equal to adults, as we have experienced first hand. They are often treated horribly. Psychotherapist Alice Miller expressed how this disrespect for children manifests from one generation to the next: "Children who are beaten will, in turn, give beatings, those who are intimidated will be intimidating, those who are humiliated will impose humiliation, and those whose souls are murdered will murder."

What Parents Have Done: Intergenerational Echoing

Parents who reenact this vicious cycle of childist torment often follow culturally standardized ways of treating children. They also employ emotionally injurious language when communicating.

When we were young, they told us to go to our rooms when we "misbehaved." But they said much worse things: "If you keep crying, I will give you something to cry about," or "I brought you into this world, and I can take you out." They issued threats like "Shut up. Do you want a spanking? You are annoying Mommy and Daddy."

We responded by expressing anger or hatred. We would wail, shake our heads, and stamp about in uproarious agitation. But instead of letting us vent, our parents did everything in their power to punish us and squash our desire to exist as small human beings. And when worse came to worst, they just beat the emotion out of us.

In doing so, they damaged our internal regulation processes and offset our ability to cry, laugh, become livid, or love in healthy ways. They inflicted deep wounds that have stayed with us into adulthood, which has caused us trouble in handling our intimate affairs.

These are a couple of reasons why many of us are emotionally repressed or aggressive, why we are afraid to share aspects of ourselves with the people we love, and why we sometimes have no clue what we are feeling and what it means. It is the reason men often focus on masculinity and emotional denial and why we see empathy and emotional sharing as weak. It is why women can become easily volatile or overly emotive.

A *Psychology Today* article explored how early childhood experiences might bring this about in relationships: "[Men] may experience an irresistible need to emotionally distance themselves from their wives whenever their partner exhibits the kind of behavior they can't help but identify with their own parents' disapproval and rejection."

It is this type of intergenerational echo that colors all future relationships and has also given the current world its violent and unstable character.

Ending Childism Starts with Us

To help mold society into something peaceful and emotionally salient, we must all be willing to let our children grow and feel. We cannot stop them from loving, venting, or raging, as this causes a host of psychological problems.

We have to acknowledge our prejudice toward our children, understand it, and examine its origins. We have to grasp why we behave in the manner we do. This means we must come to terms with our own childhoods.

If we do not, we will not be able to help our children, and we will fall into the cycle of enacting vengeance upon them.

Emotionally Focused Therapy Helps People Rediscover Their Bonds

How do we know that allowing children to feel and be emotionally free will help? There is a form of couples therapy called "Emotionally Focused Therapy," which was developed by clinical psychologist, professor, and researcher Sue Johnson. It is a therapy that teaches adults in relationships how to understand and communicate feelings.

A large body of research has given it scientific validity as a helpful form of therapy. In *Marriage and Family Therapy: A Practice-Oriented Approach*, Linda Metcalf notes that 70–75% of couples move from distress to recovery, while 90% show significant improvements.

These results suggest couples learn how to deal with their tumultuous emotional worlds and combat their old emotional injuries. The aforesaid information is of vital importance because as parents, we must understand and work with the emotional lives of our children instead of punishing them.

This not only means we must change and think differently about what it means to parent but that we must also aid in the manufacture of a new culture, one that focuses on allowing children to have the freedom to express their sentiments.

Currently, children do not have basic human rights. They have been abandoned and left to rot in the boneyard of emotional deprivation.

The Sensitive Society: Soft Anarchism, Soft Parenting

We are now trying to build a sensitive society.

This means focusing on care and love for children through the mechanisms of relationships. It takes the basic tenets of soft anarchism and applies them to parenting. That is, we maintain a softer, more caring attitude and do not attempt to lord over our children as authority figures. We do not repeat the sins of the past.

The idea is not that much different from peaceful parenting, except that the development of the relationship between parent and child is considered the central component. The moral implications are seen as subsidiary or peripheral because being sensitive toward children is predicated on not causing dysfunction or underdevelopment in the child.

Therefore, it not only requires parents to stop hitting but also to become kinder and gentler to their children—to treat them as equals and have an authentic bond with them. Love and connection are the focus. They are key because we now know that ignoring or squelching children's emotions causes wide-ranging harm.

To wit, parents must also understand the emotional injuries that childism causes and thus reject all variations of vengeance-based parenting. In Alice Miller's words, parents should reject the poisonous pedagogy and treat children as human beings who possess dignity and decency.

Psychohistorian Lloyd deMause was right: Our culture—especially all parents—will reap great rewards if they start responding to their children with empathy and compassion. If parents allow their children to experience the grandeur of life in any way they choose, we will begin building a more sensitive society.

"It is easier to build strong children than to repair broken men."

—Frederick Douglass, abolitionist and statesman

Inner Poetry of the Anarchist

May 6, 2010

Self-Analysis: The Ocean.

I let my defense mechanisms work without consent. Freud said defense mechanisms act to protect the ego from the harmful contents of the unconscious. I believe that through my closest relationships, I can overcome these defenses. I've struggled with this only recently. It feels like I'm barely dipping my toes into the surface of the water—and it's an ocean.

The problem is that I am in denial of my denial, and the only way to come to terms with this denial is to have it forcibly pumped out. I've gone through a lot of pain because of this, and I've always considered my defenses legitimized by my thoughts. This fails the truth test. It has come to me as a relief knowing that I deny and repress so much. However, by no means have I successfully negotiated the ocean. It's as if small fish, sometimes schools of fish, make it too close to the surface, then attempt to jump out. I relate this to unconscious forces trying to break through the hoot and jangle into the freedom of awareness. I want to let it all through, but there is too much fear below, and my mind is too wide and my reluctance too vast.

I think a lot. But I haven't been able to integrate my thinking into a retrievable whole. Honestly, I can't decide how I want to create myself. I can't decide who I am. Then again, there is this creepy need to exist in a kind of indeterminate zone as a doppelganger, naturally changing faces and designs when needed, when it suits me. But I imagine how tormenting, mind-wrenching, and frustrating it can be to those around me. They don't deserve my mental waffling. They deserve a real Sterlin. Then again, I can't break everything down into a small, tiny, naked truth. I'm at odds with the beauty of the world. I feel that everything deserves a part of me and me of it.

I'm not sure it's possible to self-psychoanalyze to complete understanding. I've tried, but denial keeps criticism out of my head. I ostracize myself. I say, "This is dumb. I'm too smart to fall victim to something shallow and dishonest." My intelligence overshadows my weaknesses. I regard this. But then my weaknesses come frothing to the surface, devouring my intelligence like a whale inhaling krill.

The ocean—so big. It swallows me whole.

Then I realize that I am the ocean. I'm also beyond it—in love with it.

January 28, 2011

I try hard to keep to myself. Solitude insulates me from human psychology. Though, by the same token, I'm immensely fascinated with psychology and social interaction. This seeming contradiction keeps me vigilant of my faults and follies.

March 25, 2011

The complexities of the human mind expose themselves tenfold in our ability to contradict ourselves and not realize it. The ability to take note of our own contradictions in thinking allows us to pave the way toward self-completion and a stronger awareness of all things.

August 16, 2011

There's something almost meditative and nostalgic about cleaning the apartment you just lived in for the last two and a half years. It makes me think I'm cleaning away the grime and waste of precious memories formed over that time. The longing it brings cannot be compared to anything.

September 28, 2011

Even though I am a bit cynical at times, I find great passion and joy in life and work. I see no shame in striving to better myself regardless of which endeavor or end I pursue. It's all part of the grand goal of feeling like I earned something and not feeling like I'm entitled to every nickel and dime that falls before me.

February 29, 2012

Don't just have an opinion about this or that. Instead, try having all the knowledge and facts at your disposal, and make your case from them. It's more honest.

April 26, 2012

If you're not challenging yourself in life and pushing yourself further and further down the toughest roads, you're simply not doing it right.

May 8, 2012

There's something seductive about skirting the edges of life and exploring the things society has deemed taboo. I've spent a lot of time enmeshed in these areas, and I have a richer life for it. I recommend that everyone explore things foreign to their comfort levels. Even if bad shit happens, you will be better for it in the end. You might even find a little truth in the unknown.

December 18, 2012

Some of the most beautiful things in life come from your inner world, but you must be patient and reflective enough to glimpse them.

August 28, 2013

Too often we see our past as shameful, or we regret the things that we have done. Instead of this, recognize that the past is what created us, and those things we see as shameful were really beautiful and allowed us to press onward.

September 29, 2013

Regret nothing.

Your decisions mold you and help create who you are. Without those decisions, you would have remained trapped in the mundane and trivial, and business as usual would have been all you'd ever known.

Beauty and wisdom grow with the struggle and the turmoil wrought by decisions, be they good or bad; live life to the fullest and allow yourself to mess up or go against the tide. It'll make you a better, stronger person.

March 12, 2014

I believe people suffer from anxiety, problems of everyday living, and a variety of issues associated with escaping reality or denying it. However, with current evidence, I cannot concede to the disease theory of mental functioning. This notion dehumanizes and demeans people. I believe it is a label that makes witches out of good people. I believe it creates a self-fulfilling prophecy where people think they are permanently sick. The power of the mind is strong, and if people accept the idea that they are not doomed, hope exists.

April 6, 2014

The thing about anarchism is that it is one of those truths you have to uncover through self-examination and then through viewing the world objectively, which requires some level of self-understanding.

I would never have ventured down this path had I not succumbed to introspection and deep thought. Without these necessary prerequisites, anarchism would have been just another brand of insanity, dubbed insane by the pantheon of social engineers.

Wake up and reconsider yourself and your surroundings. Things will make more sense, and anarchism won't just be a buzzword that elicits images of dead babies and Molotov cocktails.

April 11, 2014

Change scares people. They fear it. They enjoy predictability. I differ from this personality type. I have an adventurer's spirit. I embrace change and grow bored of business as usual. I find that part of the joy of living hinges on the variety of experiences. If I had to stagnate in one place for very long, I would become depressed and urgently desire something new. And right now, I feel change is coming. Isn't life based on its dynamism and evolving nature?

July 1, 2014

I've always thought of myself as an extrovert, but lately, I have moved more toward the introverted side of the scale. Sure, I have gone to public places, but even at these public places, if my darling is not with me, I go inward. I put headphones on and lose control. Then I write my stories. I write with whatever conviction I can muster because I just want to tell truths that have not been told. I want to tell stories about the age we live in and the battles we fight, which are much different from earlier times (but also similar in ways). Indeed, we are in an age of transformation on many levels, but I don't think some recognize this. It's obvious to me. I just want to point it out in every conceivable way with all the senses available to me.

July 25, 2014

Our worst fears often reside in the deepest parts of our psyche...because we put them there. We want to deny our fears, not confront them. But if we face them, we can learn control. We can learn what they mean and come to understand ourselves. Our fears tell us everything about our personal predicaments. They may even spare us pain in the future. Our fears are evolutionary descendants that motivate us into fight-or-flight, and if we disregard them, we may miss the opportunity for fight-or-flight and suffer the consequences of our denial.

September 5, 2014

Listen: Your brain chemicals do not control how you feel (insofar that you control them). Nor do subconscious desires propel you. Ultimately, *you* are in charge of how you feel. If you feel negative and emotionally distraught, reflect on your thinking. Harboring negative thought patterns and dwelling on fantasies can cause emotional distress. Learn to recognize these problems in your thinking, and you'll learn how to heal yourself. There's no magical formula for overcoming depression and anxiety. It requires a reworking of your thought processes. However, it also requires emotional intelligence. If you can also grasp your inner emotional world, it will allow you to heal completely. This is how thought and emotion converge to alter neurochemistry and create whole human beings.

September 20, 2014

Here's the rub. We're all narcissists. We're all self-absorbed. We all want to be heroes, to be recognized and remembered even if it's for only the small things.

Don't let people make you feel that your ego is running wild. Don't shut yourself down for fear that people will recognize you as arrogant or self-possessed.

Self-love is the only truth. Self-love is what keeps you functioning in this brutal and uncaring universe. Self-love is what you'll choose to either go to the grave with or without.

What others believe about you is ultimately irrelevant, so love the shit out of yourself, and make sure people know you do.

Perhaps, then, they will come to see the importance and significance of their own selves. Maybe one day, we'll all stop hiding from ourselves due to fear and cultural conventions.

For truth and beauty, let self-love reign. Free the ego and stand naked before your true self.

October 2, 2014

Every person is equipped with the ability to change, to see themselves and the world differently.

People are not chained to their personalities and behaviors. These things can be altered with enough introspection and through enough critical analysis of the self.

It does take courage to confront certain aspects of yourself and your behavior, but don't be scared to take the plunge. There await rewards for inspecting the naked marrow of the inner you, including a newfound conception of yourself or perception of the world.

This is essentially the crux of self-growth and transformation, and it is what will help heal the depression, anxiety, and other problems of everyday living.

Go for it. Take the leap and self-explore. You have nothing to lose and everything to gain.

I trust you. Just trust yourself.

February 4, 2015

Life has its ups and downs and difficulties but merely experiencing it is beautiful. Do everything to live with gusto and exuberance, even when life throws curve balls or tries to bury you under the weight of everything tough and terrible.

I have been through my own trials and tribulations, and they have only bettered me. I may be different than I was in the past. I may have changed, but there is not a day that goes by that I am not jubilant to be breathing and enjoying this existence.

Life is not a relentless tragedy. Comedy, redemption, and pleasure are embedded throughout.

Don't forget that. It is the hallmark of the wise.

March 23, 2015

One of the problems with our culture is that people don't easily express their feelings. People are not taught to display their emotions appropriately, and sometimes, they are unable to show any emotion at all. I also do this. I have had to work at learning proper emotional control and the ability to see and understand emotions in those close to me.

In other words, empathy does not come easy, and too many are taught to distrust people who try to empathize with them or get into their inner world. Therefore, when feelings come into play and people seek counsel, would-be counselors tend to band-aid problems by saying, "At least you're not as bad off as so-and-so" or suggest that the person just needs to "get over it, shit happens."

These responses do not validate emotions within the person, and they distort the way the person seeking help views themselves and those around them. In children, this problem seems to lead to ineffective emotional control, especially if they have suffered abuse.

Everyone should learn to empathize and express their inner worlds to each other. An empathetic society is a caring society. The next time someone expresses their feelings to you, try asking them what their feelings are like. Try to understand their inner world. Try to put yourself in their shoes. Also, if you happen to be a thinker, this will allow more room for intellectual growth because understanding other people emotionally leads to newer cognitive insights about them. Being cerebral does not mean you have to be cold. It can actually lead to a revelation in the way you work problems out.

Empathy is not the enemy.

November 27, 2015

Sometimes our thinking drifts into negative territory: "Life sucks, I am a horrible person, and everyone is bad," we think. Then we put these thoughts on repeat like a horror film. We chase them until we are overburdened with distress and anxiety. At this point, we have to stop ourselves and do some reality testing. We have to break down our faulty thinking.

Does life really suck so much? Am I that bad of a person? Is everyone else all bad, too?

We have to break the cycle of thought to control our emotions. In other words, we have to choose to not put ourselves down and paint everything in a negative light, especially if we want to quell anxiety. We must focus our thinking on positivity. This is the secret to what the Greeks called *eudaimonia*. It is the feeling of mental happiness and contentment with life, but it requires our effort. It does not magically or automatically happen.

In this sense, personal transformation is a kind of conscious alchemy. It is a process of changing negative or displeasing thoughts into positive or pleasant ones. However, we all must become psychologically minded to do this. That means we must be introspective and look inside ourselves for the demons—and then we must be our own exorcists. We must smite the negative thinking patterns, but we also must be objective and truthful. We cannot trap ourselves in a personal victim story and imagine everyone else and the world as our enemy. Instead, we must acknowledge what we are thinking and feeling and take responsibility for it. We must overcome that to activate our own beautiful inner machinery. This is one recipe for personal growth. It is how we make pleasant emotions. It is how we can know authentic happiness.

March 9, 2016

For all men out there:

We often strangulate our own emotional content. A variety of factors has taught us to be cold, detached, and alone in our ability to convey emotions. But for us to be truly intimate and vulnerable before our woman, we must let our guard down; we must not be as stoic as we pretend. We must be emotionally courageous and make that connection. A cold and calculated persona is not conducive to a developing and dynamic partnership, and it closes us off to the deepest and most beautiful aspects of her psyche. To make contact, we must truly disrobe and share the nakedness of our souls.

June 7, 2016

The beauty of counseling is it tackles what it means to be human. It is not merely talking about problems; it is not idle gossip or shallow banter. Counseling is delving into the recesses of the psyche where the drama of existence and all the contradictions of being human flow together. It is touching emotions that are generally unrecognizable and bringing them to bear, beholding and acknowledging them. It is a dynamic process of growth hinged on dialogues of pain, regret, love, passion, misled youth, murderous ideations, failed dreams, and harrowing fear. Counseling is the human profession of leading another soul into the black hole and finding out once and for all what lies beyond the event horizon—and then coming back from that abyss as a stronger person, a rejuvenated soul.

June 16, 2016

One of the largest contributing causes of social problems is that emotional expression is considered taboo. But it is emotional understanding and shared emotional states that allow people to fully grow and gain an understanding of themselves. They also provide them with a sense of empathy. When emotions are flattened, dulled, or considered bad, the result is repressed anger, arbitrary hatred, substance abuse, mass shootings, genocide, and statism. The problem is not one of policy, bad arguments, or entrenched interests. These are surface issues. The problem is that people are taught from a young age that emotions are weak, evil, or unhelpful. I submit to you that this idea runs contrary to the truth, and the most destruction done to people by people has come from a lack of emotional intelligence.

June 17, 2016

Laughing at pain is a coping mechanism. Sometimes things hurt so badly that the only relief is a strong dose of humor. At some point, though, we must stop laughing and come face to face with the pain. We must re-experience it in its full agony. It is through this process that we can integrate and understand where the pain resides, and it is in this moment of intimate and excruciating contact with ourselves that we can metamorphose into something stronger, more aware, and more beautiful. To laugh is good, but it is not always the appropriate response to trauma; much of the time it is a mask that helps us deal with the terror of handling threatening memories.

June 23, 2016

Stoicism is a disastrous philosophy for the growth of the self. The expression of emotion, emotional literacy, and the ability to process feelings are what help people grow. They create an integration in the brain, or the linkage of differentiated parts.

When people are either forced to suppress emotions or purposely try to deny that human aspect of themselves, they create more inner turmoil and suffering.

However, if people could somehow manage to understand and deal with their emotions while adopting stoicism, it might work. But overall, we now understand the importance of emotional expression and how it allows people to meet their needs and become whole.

Emotional awareness, communication, and ventilation are the secret gateways to the self-actualizing potential of humankind.

July 4, 2016

The cornerstone of being human is being in touch with emotions. We should revel in the glow of feeling, of acknowledging the emotions that make us up. Without understanding the vast depths of our bodies, we miss out on the gorgeousness of life. We take it for granted. There is something about feelings that provides our lives with a sense of meaning and depth. If we can't dance in the mystery of existence and become swept away by the intimacy we share with our significant others, we miss something profound and important. It eludes us. If we can't weep at the sight of a magnificent display of art or an overwhelming piece of music, we are lost to the depravities of nihilism and meaninglessness. We only get this life for a flash, for a single moment, and then it's finished. So, let's pour our souls into this exotic and strange revelation called life. Let us rejoice at the strength of our spirits, of the play of emotions that reminds us of our ephemeral nature. This is an ecstatic experience. Inhale it and quaver at its unrelenting beauty.

July 20, 2016

The degree to which children gain attachment bonds with their primary caregivers determines how they learn to regulate, employ, and appreciate emotions.

Paradoxically, emotional literacy also gives rise to more restrained and reasonable adults. It is not the cultivation of logic or reason themselves that allows for emotional control. Rather, it is the exploration of emotional content and the ability to put feelings into words. The acknowledgment of triggers and stressors is what produces more balanced people.

A person cannot just ignore, deny, or pretend he has mastered his emotions while simultaneously calling them "bad," "dangerous," or "for the weak." A person has to respect the primacy of emotions and the unique logic of emotional expression.

When humanity has gained emotional fluency and respect for emotions, we will grow toward freer societies with more emphasis on honest communication, empathy, and strong relationships.

October 13, 2016

Always be aware of your weaknesses and limitations. When you know these traits, you can use them to gain more insight into yourself and the world, and there is nothing more important than being able to grow because of self-knowledge.

Over the years, I have entered various phases of growth. In these stages, I have been able to propel myself forward and move into the future armed with more self-understanding.

Nonetheless, as I continue this journey through life, I always bear in mind any blind spots I may have. This constant self-scrutiny has helped me overcome many obstacles and take a breather from difficulties whenever they arise.

Without this kind of watchful eye, I might have fallen victim to myself or the myriad forces outside of my control and perhaps even entered a state of total ennui and melancholy.

The crux of survival and living the good life hinges on possessing a palpable sensitivity to everything, emotional understanding for others, open-minded intelligence, and most importantly, a comprehensive grasp of one's own failings and shortcomings. These are the traits I have tried to cultivate over the years.

But alas, I am only human. I am always learning. Always a student.

And the world is my classroom.

January 25, 2017

Compassion is something that can be learned and practiced. It is not something a person is born with. Some people may have a natural inclination to be more compassionate, but I view it as an interpersonal skill that anyone can adopt and develop.

It is also true that some people are disgusted and revolted by compassion. They seem to react against people who employ or practice it. But that's only because our society trumpets irrational egoism, narcissism, and other potentially unhealthy perspectives on human relations (not to be confused with healthy individualism).

More importantly, most people were traumatized and emotionally harmed as children, and trauma has a way of damaging the empathy circuitry in the brain. When this empathy wiring malfunctions, people's views on compassion can become warped. They may see it as inauthentic or tiresome.

However, their negative internal experience about compassion stems from the harm they have suffered in childhood, as well as cultural views on compassionate relations.

Nevertheless, if they start to understand why they react the way they do, they may be able to discover their compassionate side. They may be able to transform and evolve as human beings.

I am imperfect when it comes to compassion, but I realize through my psychological studies that many people deserve empathy. Their lives have been hard. They have been mistreated or abused; thus, their defense mechanisms and fight-or-flight responses are constantly on high alert.

With this perspective, I can accept another person's revulsion and disgust toward my compassion. I can accept their condemnation. They are merely hurting. They are struggling for connection. They just need time and love.

Perhaps this will allow them to realize and come to terms with their own compassionate nature.

April 7, 2017

A lot of people don't believe emotional insights will change their life.

That's likely false. Getting in touch with our emotions provides us with a newfound ability to introspect. It provides us with the ability to empathize and connect with other people.

These new behaviors are what allow people to heal from their childhood abuses and learn to resolve disputes with others without resorting to hate and violence.

Is there anything more important?

Passion, Exuberance, and Awe

October 2, 2011

When you go home and think about your work, contemplate what you did wrong while there, and work out in your head what you can do to fix it. Even if it is the most minuscule or mundane problem, it means you're both enjoying your job and passionate about what you do.

March 5, 2014

There are moments when I become so struck with the joy and beauty of living that it takes my breath away. And in this moment, I understand why freedom and truth echo in me as profoundly and immeasurably important. It has everything to do with these electric and awe-filled pieces of life, which remind me of everything wonderful and ecstatic.

March 24, 2014

A lot of different things have come to fruition in the last few weeks that have reminded me of the fragility and brevity of life. They have reminded me to live life to the fullest and to try to accomplish something worthwhile and lasting. These may be different things for different people based on personal preferences, but I now see my lasting intimate relationships, the creation of children, and writing as several of the most pressing and important things to me.

However, completion of these things in all their joy and glory will require more time and focus and energy on my part—but the payoff will be the best feeling I've ever had or known, more so than the fleeting and mundane pleasures and trivialities I have engaged in up to this point. I just have to keep myself floored with the notion that I am simply a piece of meat moving through the slaughterhouse of life, trying to do something—anything—before the impending and inevitable brush with the ax.

I know you may see this as almost cynical, but I see an ineffable beauty and lust in life that must be teased out to be appreciated...and this is where I stand as the world strays out of mortal sight, and I eventually pass on into dust, just calculating my next attempt at personal satisfaction and decency. And indeed, I say all of this with the hope that you might understand me and follow me in your own way, with your own path, of your own volition.

March 27, 2014

We all desire epiphanies if we regularly succumb to thought and contemplation. Some of us even go as far as to purposely invoke *satori*, the flash of insight. That is what I am doing now: sitting on my porch hoping for the eureka moment without any goal or idea or design in mind.

I don't know what knowledge I necessarily want to gain. I just know I seek it. So, I trust the chirping of birds, the grazing of a bullmastiff, the distant bellowing of a train, the aroma of spring, and the rustling of a chill wind to usher it into my arms. But then I realize that it is not an epiphany I am seeking in this second. I am merely letting the world overtake the senses and the joy of living run through me. It is a beautiful and monumental experience. You just must dig at the details and work the edges. You have to be willing to let go of all your hang-ups and fears to enjoy the magnitude of it all. Perhaps this was an epiphany. Perhaps the epiphany is a generalized joy of being.

April 15, 2014

People are often like insects. Their modus operandi is to stick with business as usual, the mundane drivel of everyday politics. Their work and political representatives are their masters. The world of ideas seems lost on them. The world seems lost on them. They are Alice without a rabbit hole. They are zombies without the inclination for flesh. This is what I feel and see from too many people, and it's a lonely vibration knowing so few want to experience the world wholly and completely.

This would make me feel more alone if it weren't for the few other stargazers and life- and love-mongers. I just wish more would care, wake from their apparent stupor, gaze into the abyss, and purposely allow it to gaze back at them. There's fear in this but also jest. There is a renewing and rekindling in tapping into the infinite complexity and oddity of this existence.

June 26, 2014

It's amazing how things in life change so drastically, and suddenly life ushers us toward new, more exciting destinations. Some people see this as scary or troublesome, but I welcome it in all of its unprecedented fury. I have a natural adventurer's spirit, and regardless of where the tide thrusts me, I'll do my best to make the best of it and perhaps learn a bit more about life and love in the process. After all, we only have the pleasure and joy of experiencing this rush called life a single time, so I choose to embrace it through all its turbulence and strangeness, through all of the fear and anxiety, through every bit of its majesty and glory.

Will you embrace it, too?

August 13, 2015

Life is a beautiful thing. Don't squander it. Time is too precious to waste. It passes quickly. Follow your loves and passions with gusto and let nothing stop you. With the right determination, much can be accomplished. Do not give haters and naysayers the time of day. Let them wallow in their mediocrity and envy. The future exists within the moment, at every draw of breath. Be unstoppable and without fear, for this mindset is the mark of excellence.

January 20, 2016

It is easy to see the negative and awful in everything. It is common to see the problems with people. It is simple to acknowledge faults, violence, and evil. As a human, seeing bad and ugly is almost second nature. It appears to be a part of the species. But if we constantly view the world in black, we are liable to miss the beatific and ecstatic. I also have to remind myself of this because I have a habit of constantly pointing out darkness, ghouls, and goblins. But I still keep a place of light in my heart: on the inside, I revel in love.

I enjoy trying to find the good in people and the world. I want to embrace the whole of existence with the rapture of being and sing an ode to happiness. If my soul became stuck in the harpy den of the world's maleficence, I would have trouble pressing forward and processing the pain and difficulty of life. My insides would swell with paranoia, fear, and insanity. Living would be unbearable, as if an assassin were lurking in my shadow. But I choose to radiate wonderment and excitement about all the amazing possibilities life has to offer. I don't get bogged down with the negative. I honestly admit to its existence, confront it with my chest puffed, and go about living so goddamned well that I feel an unstoppable glee grow inside me—and that glee manifests as an aura of compassion. I behold all the shimmering jewels in the world.

Thus, I beg all of you: If you get bogged down in the fear and excess of suffering in life, just imagine the glory and magnificence of the world. It is there. But you have to feel it as much as see it. You have to let go. Let it enfold you and burst outward and simply experience the sublime nature of being. Indeed, this is it.

June 26, 2016

It is amazing how things change so quickly and drastically. One moment I am just standing here, then all of the sudden life shifts, and wham, I am flung headlong toward more exciting, novel destinations.

Sadly, many people do not welcome change. They fear it. They do everything in their power to avoid alien territory.

I fear it, too...but I try to embrace change and cope with the impending terror.

Regardless of what shore the tide drops me on, I do my best to make the best of the situation. In the process, I attempt to learn more about life and love. I revel in the experience. I let it charge through me like stray lightning.

We only have the pleasure and joy of experiencing the ecstasy of this life a single time. And I choose to accept all of its turbulence and weirdness, all of the fear and anxiety, and every bit of its incomprehensible majesty.

Will you embrace it? Will you fight the terror and be swept up in the beauty and music of the unknown?

January 24, 2017

Now and again, I get the existential blues. But it is not depression or anything of the sort; I never get dramatically or suicidally emotional or nor do I wallow in ennui. I just get really excited about life, spending time and energy with my love Cecilia and the rest of my friends and family, reading and writing, and doing all the things we all enjoy together.

I call this the existential blues because I am reminded of how fragile and fleeting life is. I am reminded that every day is important, and I realize how dissociated I can get while inside my own head. The salience of it strikes home with tremendous force. Suddenly I am sorry for my aloofness and waywardness.

Then the blues subside, and I feel awe and joy at the sheer magnitude of living. I embrace the oddness of this adventure with both courage and strength, and I know I must not only live for myself, but I also must live to love. I must live for other people, but only the people closest to me—the people who matter and who likewise care for me—even if I tend to go space cadet from moment to moment and hide away from everything.

I at least know that people love me, trust me, and that I do have the ability to return the favor—existential blues be damned—because in the blues surfaces an extreme delight for this life in this temporary, sometimes pain-ridden world.

And it is in that precious moment that I doubly realize the importance of relationships and love.

March 19, 2017

One of the most epic insights you can have is the insight that you're doing everything you're supposed to be doing; the insight that you love your lover; that you love yourself; that you are making a positive impact on the world, and that you are living this life in the most meaningful and badass way possible. Now, seriously, that's a godly epic realization.

This is an ode to those who have done a great deal of introspection and who care deeply about this world and the precious lives we live.

Thank you so much. Love and respect.

March 22, 2017

Don't be afraid to live. We have one shot at this. Love and live as freely and widely as possible. Laugh. Dance. Sing and sex. There is a lot of beauty to be had. Lots of experiences. Lots of excitement. Give it 100 percent. Take it all in. It will be overwhelming, but the value it provides is unimaginable, dazzling, and wondrous. Life is the jazz at the center stage of the universe, so compelling and complex. Enjoy it. Embrace it. Be swept away by this ferocious journey we call existence.

February 21, 2019

I surround myself with beautiful people. I don't just mean physical beauty; physical beauty is ephemeral, like a springtime flurry of snow or the petrichor after a light rain.

I want to be surrounded by poets, artists, activists, iconoclasts, and mavericks. I want the people who dream of change and try to sing it into existence. I want the people who mold civilizations and move others to love. This is what I call beauty; these are beautiful beings, and I want them as confidants.

These awakened humans possess alchemical energy, and their souls cause the earth to quake through their mere presence. This is the beauty of enlightenment and of unfettered creativity. It is the beauty of the universe condensed down into living, breathing, talking matter.

I would have it no other way. Life is a precious gift, and if people don't radiate with the pulse of infinite creation, they will remain asleep among the flocks and the swineherds. They will remain unlit in their conscious expression.

Instead, I want the power and magnetism of the beautiful souls to stand near me so that I may soak up all their inspiration, light, and love—so that I may in turn light the world up with abundant beauty. This is what living and connecting are all about. This is the essence of friendship and the path to developing the power of soul.

Rhapsodic Creativity

January 11, 2011

I can't help thinking that my book collection is not only an outgrowth of my personality but also a story of who I am.

January 12, 2014

It feels good knowing you have the power to create something of value that other people may enjoy, as well.

January 17, 2014

Writing is my most beloved, cathartic outlet. It's an art that provides the freedom to make sense of this world, eliminate stress, and spread new and wholesome ideas.

February 10, 2014

I have noticed two key motivating factors in writing: fear and praise. I would say love and passion, but nothing ignites the creative drive like existential angst. Indeed, sometimes I think to myself, "What will I leave behind if I do not do this? What legacy? I could shuffle off this mortal coil at any moment, so what greater joy is there than producing something of value?" The other motivating factor, praise, is less deep and more surface-level, but it plays into the first factor. If someone compliments me, I feel like the praise validates the fact that I produced something of value; thus, it compels continuation of the work. Overall, it is the interplay and exchange of fear and praise that allows me to produce and maintain a spirit of raw creativity in writing. Without either, I might feel no self-compulsion to create anything or help anyone. At least, this is how I feel...and perhaps these are only my personal motivating factors.

April 27, 2014

I thought this was awesome. This is a journal entry from one of my journals four years ago. The entry is dated January 5, 2010.

> What is a writer? A writer is a person who challenges the future by mustering the courage to draw the next letter. A writer is a person who resolves to press on despite fear or ridicule or hatred for what he says. A writer is a person who revels in auspiciousness: Indeed, he cannot fear the future because the future is breathed into existence with each stroke of his pen. A writer is a person who explores emotion and expression. A writer is a

person who demonstrates spirit amid uncertainty and pain. I am a writer.

May 1, 2014

There's something sobering yet also disturbing about writing about my own childhood fears. It brings back the terror but also offers up a form of catharsis, as if I were settling and finally understanding those old night terrors, which used to make me cry and loathe going to bed as a youngster. Now, in writing, I look back and ponder why I feared this precise thing and why it specifically haunted me so often. I recommend everyone use the pen to introspect about their childhood monsters. Some things may come to light that you never considered.

July 12, 2014

Life is about pursuing love and passion. If you are neglecting your amorous needs and creative potential, you're just taking up space and whittling away precious time. This does not, however, mean you must be a Picasso or a Don Juan. It just means you need to activate your humanness. You need to recognize the deep needs and desires of your subconscious. Satiate these appetites and the despair and ennui will vanish.

August 18, 2014

I love to dive into a book, siphon the life out of it, and eat up all its grit and glory. But it's not just about the mental excitement of being in there, it's about the sensory exploration: the smell, texture, and look of the thing. Books are like magical artifacts in this sense, and to their beholders, they bestow a kind of overwhelming power and enchantment—one that's almost as ineffable as grasping at the precise rhythm and harmony of the cosmos. There's a kind of god, then, inside each book, and between the pages and paragraphs, it enters into the mind and commandeers the soul. It takes over, speaks, and moves me to rejoice at the ecstasy of living.

August 20, 2014

Writing is more than art. It is a logical exercise that follows the rules of flow and pattern recognition in the human brain. And if you don't meet these requirements, your art will likely suffer as incoherent at worst and amateur at best. For the beauty of your writing to shine as it is meant to, the work must be edited and re-edited. Indeed, writing is not just a natural gift, it is a learned skill based on the left-brained ability to understand organization and construction. These are the secrets of the craft. It is simply a process based on iteration after iteration that requires tremendous amounts of practice for quality.

January 14, 2015

Reading is such a pleasant, intoxicating joy. I cannot imagine living life without being able to know other minds, ideas, expressions, desires, and imaginations intimately and cathartically through the lens of their letters.

Devoid of this mental exploration, life would be a dreary, lackluster place where the mind would refuse to dance and frolic and thus forget about the overwhelming, enchanted beauty of this world.

January 24, 2015

For me, creativity is a byproduct of the existential question: how long do I have on this plane of existence?

But it is not as trivial as merely being about death. Even while living, shit changes—sometimes drastically—to the extent of incapacitating an individual.

The fear of uncertainty motivates me to produce material and use all of my intellectual faculties to their fullest. I might not achieve greatness, but at least I can let other people know that I lived—and lived for something—especially my children when I have them.

That is why I choose to write and get good at it.

I may not be Shakespeare, but I can articulate my points clearly and memorably.

February 23, 2015

I would have given anything to live in the 1960s. I see the modern anarchist movement as a more sober version of the hippy movement of the '60s. While it is arguably true that anarchists have more direction and purpose, the hippies had a more unique sense of freedom and more gusto about their art and creativity. I mean, they were almost always lit on something—probably LSD—so this explains the lack of structure, but it also explains their intense desire for producing art and waxing creative.

When I first read about the history of Haight-Ashbury in San Francisco, California, I fantasized about the possibility of being involved in that scene, of meeting some of the old Beat poets, like Allen Ginsberg, and other big names like Timothy Leary and Janis Joplin.

However, I know that the Haight inevitably devolved into a ratchet place of drugged burnouts and washed-out hippies. Still, it would have been amazing to even work around, converse, or experiment with those people. And you know, for as many folks who harp on the negativity and evil nature of so many drugs, a lot of brilliant pieces of music, writing, and art were produced because of the countercultural scene.

I don't know, sometimes I wonder if I was just born in the wrong era.

May 21, 2015

Reading is a meditative exercise; no wonder some people struggle with it. A person has to be able to quiet their mind to experience the minds of others, but the feeling of accomplishing this and gaining new knowledge and freedom of thought is unparalleled. Reading, indeed, is one of the greatest pleasures, but it is not necessarily easy, even if you know how.

August 22, 2015

Writing should be a dance. There should be moves, steps, and music. There should be elegance and grace and maybe some grit, lock, and pop. But there should be art, innovation, and innuendo. Writing should not be strained, re-strained, contrived, or held hostage. Like dancing, the writer should lay his soul naked upon the stage; this is where true beauty is found and marked. It is where the essence of a writer is distilled and refined. If one chooses to write, they must let the music of life guide them. Never look back. Never fear the future. Never self-censor. A myriad of new horizons and vistas lays before the pen as the sprawling and writhing canvas of the imagination. Writing, as in dance, is not idle communication. It is active adoration and selflessness. It is gangster life in perpetual motion and mission. Let the self go, and define the future with every step and mark.

November 19, 2015

I find such great pleasure and satisfaction in writing that I can hardly stop myself for breaks. It's like pulling a kid away from a video game. I looked up at my desktop the other day and saw that I have over a dozen drafts of half-completed material, including two or three book projects. I move in and out of these drafts as a spirit moves between worlds. I finally completed one I started half a year ago. That felt good. However, much of my time goes to writing essays for class, which I also enjoy so long as I retain the liberty to write what I want.

If you don't have a hobby or talent that occupies your place in this world and gives you meaning, you might try writing. It is a sublime art and a powerful method of catharsis. Writing keeps me sane, and I value the ability to communicate powerfully and clearly, so I will never stop. It is in my blood.

April 14, 2016

One of the things I enjoy is motivating and inspiring people to be the best they can be. I love helping build communities with direct participation while helping as many members as possible unlock their creative potential. Unlike some theorists, I believe creative motivation and expression of talent comes from without as much as from within.

In this regard, community-building is a lot like counseling. A counselor does not necessarily advise or direct a client. Instead, the counselor helps unveil a client's own inner strengths and resources. A counselor develops a working rapport with the client, and it is this emotional mechanism that gives another the courage to live and love.

I find great joy in the idea that I can be of service to others in so many contexts.

May 3, 2016

Friends, I just watched one of the most badass dystopian films I have ever seen. I know it sounds strange to be excited about a dystopian piece, but this film justified and defended the anarchist sentiment in the most poignant and compelling way. It is called *Children of Men*. I am surprised this was the first time I watched it because it came out back in 2006.

The film captures humanity at its worst as a result of governmental coercion and is a powerful criticism of the anti-immigration mindset. It also contains perfectly placed historical and intellectual references, including a display of Picasso's painting of Guernica, a Spanish town the Germans razed during the Spanish Civil War. Lastly, toward the end, the film has one of the most emotionally salient scenes I have ever witnessed in film. It put tears in my eyes.

I highly recommend this for anyone, but especially the world-savvy anarchists.

September 16, 2016

Is there a connection between the Quakers and the Hobbits in the *Lord of the Rings*? I had not even considered this idea until I started reading the book *Mad in America* by Robert Whitaker.

The Quakers were simple people, but they were also highly distrustful of authority and preferred a life of peace and hard work. Even a common Quaker had the last name of Took. To me, the relationship between this religious group and the Hobbits is uncanny.

It is also cool to note that the Quakers were almost solely responsible for the invention of the non-medical, moral treatment of the "insane."

April 15, 2017

Words committed to paper should be backed by artistic integrity. Prose should be poetic; prose as poetry—poetry prose. Writing is an extension of a person's soul.

Written communication represents someone's essential energy—their evolving creativity and humanness. Underlying all written words should be an emotional valence that charges the words with the personality of the writer. If this distinct character is missing, we might as well assume the author is dead.

They died of blandness. Of infirmity. They committed intellectual and imaginative suicide. They will be remembered as mediocrities, scrawling lifeless and listless words from a sense of fear and falsity instead of reveling in the joyousness of their life.

This type of creativity takes guts. Someone should be willing to express everything that resides inside. They should write as if they are on the verge of death, as if the only thing that matters is spilling their intestines on the desk before them—giving their heart and soul to the world. They should imagine they can murder all the evil in the world with their pen and then elevate their most romantic and private desires without shame or guilt.

This is what writing is about. This is what communication is about. It's giving zero fucks and pressing forward despite all the insecurities that push back against the writer like a demonic force. It's moving forward even if the territory defies the map. Keep writing. Keep communicating. The mixture of truth and emotion will set the world free...and set you free.

Writing is raving.

Persuasive Anarchy: Using Change-Talk to Create Freedom Lovers

01/18/2016

Many people complain that anarchists are idealists who imagine a utopia that will never exist. They call anarchists stupid and naive and delusional. They say anarchists do nothing but fantasize about dreams with no way to realize them. They do not give anarchism a second thought. These anarchophobes go about their lackadaisical lives and never weigh or consider the plight of the freeman. They absentmindedly reject freedom, thus missing the beauty of the vision and ignoring the *raison d'être* for living anarchically.

People harbor anti-anarchist thoughts because they fear change. They feel safe and secure in their lives, work, and livelihoods; they fail to grasp the necessity of change. But if they took Alan Watts's advice, their life might be vastly improved. As Watts said, "The only way to make sense out of change is to plunge into it, move with it, and join the dance."

If people plunged into change for the sake of freedom, the idea of anarchy would evoke less dread and hesitation. It is true the anarchist perspective is replete with images of a disorderly and mad world; but in truth, this new world is not stricken with doom and chaos. Instead, it promises freedom from institutional violence, less war, zero taxation, and greater personal autonomy. Whereas science was the revolution of the old world, anarchism is the rebellion of the new one; it is the sun breaking the horizon and flash-burning all the vampires of culture and convention. Anarchism is not a fear-invoking idea. It is the dawn of a golden new epoch.

But for most people, anarchy is death and destruction regardless of how it is presented. It is fetters and chains even though anarchists desire freedom; it is desolation even though no one argues for widespread destruction or nuclear warfare.

People believe this nonsense because the freedom of anarchy implies a departure from social and cultural norms. It means people's lives might be utterly different, abnormal, or extraterrestrial. The human animal yearns for simplicity, structure, order, and security. Any vaguely alien idea about reordering and reorganizing society will send people spiraling into a maniacal state of terror.

But there are psychological methods to help people, to persuade them of the brilliance of anarchism and ease them into the philosophy with newfound appreciation and curiosity. Change-talk through motivational interviewing is a potentially great tool for the anarchist.

Motivational Interviewing and Change-Talk

In psychotherapy, clinicians often look for moments of clarity and change in their client's language. There is a technique that substance abuse therapists use to promote intrinsic growth and behavioral change in their clients. It is called motivational interviewing.

Case Western Reserve University's Center for Evidence-Based Practices expanded on the definition: "Motivational Interviewing is an evidence-based treatment that addresses ambivalence to change. It is a conversational approach designed to help people identify their readiness, willingness, and ability to change and to make use of their own change-talk."

Anarchists can also use change-talk, just not in the same professional capacity because an anarchist is not a counseling therapist—but he is a cultural therapist of sorts. He is trying to help people work through the trauma of everyday living. He is trying to help people understand why they agonize over existential issues, why the world is so violent, and why they see anarchy as strife. He is playing the role of social healer and visionary and giving people the ability to change by articulating truths and providing a clear image of the future.

Of course, this visionary anarchist will only notice change-talk in people he or she converses with daily, so the anarchist must speak with people about the ideas regularly and attend to all of their reactions and thought processes. Change-talk is difficult if not impossible to identify in people who anarchists rarely confront. A trusting relationship is a necessary prerequisite for recognizing this kind of speech.

The signals for change-talk are readily available. The individual will start to become less emotional, but they will still be visibly aroused in the sense that they fidget or appear nervous. They may start to pose serious questions for the anarchist out of raw curiosity, though a hint of combativeness may still permeate their rhetoric. Nonetheless, this is a signal that the person might be ready for change.

The individual will suggest their desire, need, reason, commitment, and ability to make the change over to anarchism, but the anarchist might have to help spur this kind of talk and thought process by making himself or herself available.

It is also up to the anarchist to exercise patience and employ nonviolent communication to ease the process. When someone is in a state of "change-talk," they can be quite vulnerable. The anarchist should remain calm and not become volatile. As a general rule of thumb, the more poised and level-headed the anarchist, the more likely people are to listen. The anarchist can use similar questions that motivational interviewers use during substance abuse counseling to determine the desire, ability, reason, commitment, and need to change. These are the five:

1. Desire: Why would you want to make this change?
2. Ability: How would you do it if you decided?
3. Reason: What are the three best reasons?
4. Need: How important is it? Why?
5. Commitment: What do you think you'll do?

If these questions are asked in an empathetic and caring tone, it can help create new anarchists by allowing them to consider and accept the possibility of a changing world. It will help them consider why they want to start living differently and why they might want to help others change. It may aid them in seeing the world in a better light and realizing that anarchism is not a visage of a broken, hostile world. They may start to realize how anarchism can heal everyone as a kind of social panacea.

That said, sometimes using change-talk and motivational interviewing is not enough to spur outright change. For more difficult or stubborn personalities, confrontation might be a necessary strategy to inspire change for freedom.

Using Confrontation: Expertly Raising Arousal Levels

Things get trickier when it comes to using confrontation, though. Most people tend to believe confrontation means getting aggressive and hostile. In a therapeutic setting, confrontation just means pointing out discrepancies between a person's thoughts and actions, or just their thoughts. It does not mean berating the individual or purposely making them feel stupid.

An anarchist goes about this by trying to expertly point out the errors in thinking, as well as providing examples of the cognitive dissonance the person is experiencing. Cognitive dissonance refers to entertaining two contradictory thoughts simultaneously. For example, a lot of people think murder is bad but will justify it if it is called war. The anarchist can politely "confront" the individual and point out their discrepancy. However, regardless of how caring and empathetic the anarchist tries to be, it is likely that the person will get flustered or angry.

This is normal, but the anarchist should not further antagonize the person and incite anger. They should adjust the levels of confrontation they are using in the discussion to spur more change-talk and a possible epiphany in the other person. Here is why some confrontation is important: it raises cortisol levels, as well as other neurohormones.

Cortisol is the neurohormone that modulates the fight-or-flight response in humans. It is released whenever a person feels threatened or endangered in any way. Generally speaking, too much cortisol can actually damage protein synthesis in the brain. However, studies have shown that medium levels of arousal, or a small amount of cortisol release, can increase a person's attention, learning, and susceptibility to change.

Psychologist Louis Cozolino discussed this concept in his book *The Neuroscience of Psychotherapy*. "Mild to moderate stress (MMS) activates neural growth hormones supportive of new learning. Thus, MMS may be utilized to enlist naturally occurring neurobiological processes in the service of new learning," he explained.

This is vital knowledge for the visionary anarchist because it will give them an understanding of how the change and learning process functions biologically.

For instance, when the anarchist notices the person starting to get aroused, he will know to keep them at the current level of arousal. If he overuses confrontation, it may break the "therapeutic window" and send the person into full-blown fight-or-flight mode. This, of course, would be counterproductive to the anarchist's goal of helping persuade people to accept anarchy and change for freedom. And sadly, too many anarchists turn people off by becoming aggressive.

Hostile Anarchists: The Art of Persuasion

Helping inspire people to change without turning them off requires patience and a touch of élan. The anarchist should also be somewhat advanced in his communication ability and understand the tenets of nonviolent communication.

Nonviolent communication was a communication style created by Marshall Rosenberg in the 1960s. The primary goal of nonviolent communication is to access people's needs during a dispute rather than issuing counterattacks. Rosenberg said all humans have basic needs, and if we can inquire about those needs and try to meet them, we can resolve any problem without resorting to hostility or violence.

Indeed, a lot of anarchists in the community seem to be hostile and aggressive by virtue of their mindset. They tend to troll feeds or lob attacks at people simply for their viewpoints, but anarchists would do well to remember where people come from.

Most folks were introduced into cultural statism in the same manner a cow is introduced into the feedlot. They were born into it, and their thought processes have matured to believe that grazing and chewing the cud is business as usual. To break this trance, the anarchist must be an artist of persuasion. He must be able to articulate his ideas skillfully and authentically while maintaining empathy. This is a necessity if he is to give the other person room to think and eventually grow beyond the confines of the pen.

Discontinuing groupthink and shedding the herd mentality is not an easy feat to accomplish, but if the anarchist employs therapeutic techniques like change-talk and confrontation, he has a decent framework to help people, and he will no longer have to rely on arbitrarily arguing with them. As mentioned, this is crucially important for those individuals who are close to the anarchist, who he communicates with daily. If he can transform friends and family into anarchists by allowing them to embrace change, he may eventually help the whole world embrace it and prepare for a paradigm shift into anarchism.

After all, the *raison d'être* for living anarchically is the ability to dance in change; it is the deep yearning to be free of toxic convention. What good can anarchists do if they cannot help heal the world by persuading people of the dignity and decency of the anarchist future? People have to be baby-stepped into believing that anarchy is not a delusion and that it matters on a global scale. They need help with the deconditioning process in order to grow and accept the inevitable change toward anarchism proper.

The Anarchist Communication Lexicon

July 22, 2015

When I make posts over Facebook about anarchism, my mission is not to condescend to people who believe in government and support statist or socialist agendas. I know some of my material can come across as if that is the intention.

My goal is to grab your attention and shake you out of business as usual. My goal is to inject the red pill and spur critical thought about old dogmas. If you had an emotional reaction when you saw my post, that is because I hooked you. I caused you to stop thinking about day-to-day activities revolving around the silent and obedient acceptance of government.

This is a good thing. It means I have given us the opportunity for civil discussion about these issues. If this has happened to you, please do not hesitate to post your thoughts on my wall or message me directly for a more direct conversation. I believe it is staggeringly important to discuss these things and get everyone on the same page. The acceptance of these ideas may affect the future of our species and thus the future of your children.

February 23, 2016

What I really love about the advancement of anarchism is that there are so many different people discussing and promulgating it in unique ways. We are growing at such an unprecedented rate that new talent is coming on board every moment. It is spectacular because everyone, with their own style and creativity, can uniquely convey the ideas. This allows them to get at some people in ways others would not. For instance, I am coming from the empathic and behavioral perspective, which has a certain group of people it appeals to, including psychological researchers, therapists, professionals, academicians, and sensitive types. But besides me, there are singers, artists, communication experts, economists, philosophers, shamans, healers, novelists, cryptologists, journalists, and so many more. And they are all attacking the legitimacy of government and spreading the idea of freedom in their specialized niches and cultural environs. Never doubt that we are on a crash course toward the total dissolution of the establishment. Anarchism is no longer a trend or fad but an explosive shift in the paradigm.

March 1, 2016

Empathetic use of the Socratic or elenctic method is one of the most valuable techniques in the anarchist's tool belt. It allows the anarchist to gather information and debate others in a mutually appreciative way so long as the anarchist remains tactful. The use of this method is how all anarchists will effectively weave together nonviolent communication and thought-provoking rhetoric to create a dynamic and evolving anarchistic community. It is the one skill that may help push other people in the direction of absolute freedom. It is the technique that can telegraph love if wielded by the right people. The ability to communicate anarchism without arousing defenses and the suspicions of others is quintessential to overcoming the many biases about anarchism.

As an aside, it is also important for the anarchist to employ confrontation when necessary. In this context, confrontation means challenging discrepancies in a person's thinking and telling the truth. It does not mean becoming vulgar or ugly.

So far, I feel like I have reaped dividends by employing these tactics in my mission to bring people over to peaceful anarchism. Nothing can be gained if both people are merely triggered, emotionally volatile, and too stressed for conversation.

> "People are just as wonderful as sunsets if you let them be. When I look at a sunset, I don't find myself saying, 'Soften the orange a bit on the right-hand corner.' I don't try to control a sunset. I watch with awe as it unfolds."

—Carl R. Rogers

March 2, 2016

If you are not an anarchist but see my posts and the ideas upset and fluster you, I have accomplished part of my mission. I want you annoyed, frustrated, and on edge. I want to snap you out of your trance and shake you from your cultural coma. I need you hot and bothered with a bit of cortisol leaking into your blood and brain. I need you to talk about my views behind my back, to hiss and spit and sometimes curse me. I want you sleepwalking to anarchism, day-walking and speaking in tongues to it. I need my philosophy to infiltrate your soul so you share it with everyone—so that it pulsates so profoundly in your mind that you cannot rightly ignore it. Yes. I need it to stir you, to inflame you, and to put you on guard. You must be provoked to action. I want your spirit rioting and raging, yearning for truth. Then, I want you reaching out, crying to be released from the torturous and dangerous aura of statism. And it is in that moment that you may fully awaken, burst from the cocoon of servitude to become what you did not know you could ever become: sovereign—fully free from all fetters.

June 10, 2016

Nothing saddens me more than anarchist or libertarian figures who use their platform to spread male hatred, victim mentalities, sexism, and divisive philosophies.

I understand they have their own struggles and have suffered in their own way, but to spend energy condemning males is a gross misapplication of vital intellectual ability. It is good for arousing feminists and causing bitterness between anarchist camps, but it doesn't seem viable for helping transform society.

Why not preach compassion, love, unity, and freedom from tyrants, instead? Why not help inspire people with courage and a desire for change rather than making certain individuals feel low, disgusting, or hated?

I am by no means condoning actual sexual violence or misogyny, but the fervor of feminist libertarianism is tragically wrongheaded and shortsighted and seems to act as a form of male hatred rather than a legitimate philosophy for the expression of accurate grievances.

I hope the leadership in these feminist camps can overcome their inner turmoil and start uniting all sexes, races, creeds, and classes to focus on the problems of authority, violence, and lack of relational enthusiasm in society.

What do you guys think? I know this is a contentious topic, but relational anarchist communities should address it.

September 6, 2016

A guy said this to me today:

"I heard you were an anarchist. Can you explain that to me?"

Sometimes I am skeptical when people ask this. I often feel like they might just want to start an intellectual battle of wits with me. However, some people harbor a genuine curiosity, so I try to cater to that and use "we first" communication no matter how I feel.

But it is sometimes hard for me to tell who is authentic and who is just looking to poke fun at the philosophy because most people tend to ask the same questions about how anarchy "will work," and I usually sense defensiveness or scorn in their tone.

Nonetheless, I try to treat them all with dignity, as if they are interested in learning about anarchism. That is how I treated this gentleman, although I did not have time to provide him with all the nuances of freedom.

I did leverage my best pitch, though. And when I do this, I try to invoke the poeticism of Voltairine De Cleyre. I feel like the passion of her explanations and fire of her words are representative of the more evocative word-smithery in the anarchist literary lexicon.

If I can just channel this type of magic and intensity, I feel positive I can leave a lasting impression of our philosophy—the kind of impression that leaves someone wanting more, like sampling a taste of that sweet ambrosia.

I think I was successful today. But fuck, I think I am successful every day I can actively and compassionately express and live my hard-earned values.

September 10, 2016

One of the struggles of the anarchist is feeling free enough to speak openly and candidly. Political correctness is a plague that stifles thought and communication. Political correctness exists to prevent change and disallow long-standing beliefs from being scrutinized.

If anarchists are to progress, we must not be afraid to speak our minds. There are influences and interests out there that would have us squelched and censored because our ideals and goals undermine silly traditions and violent rituals. Some people will even take what an anarchist says personally and attack or hamstring that anarchist as a form of petty vengeance.

In this sense, anarchists are some of the most courageous people because we risk ostracism and social alienation for the sake of helping catalyze progress in this shithole, debauched world.

Therefore, it is a sign of success if we experience pushback from people who react antagonistically to what we say. That means our words are having an impact. They are stirring a person to question their consensus delusion. And it is through our rhetorical impact that a seed of change is planted in that person. With any luck, our sacrifices will cause that seed to sprout.

After it takes root, that person may come to realize that the anarchists were right and that condemning them for speaking truth was not such a good idea because it has contributed to the nastiness and decadence of this world.

So, anarchists, don't be afraid to slice through political correctness. In the long term, our efforts will be rewarded handsomely. If people are trying to shut us up, that means what we are saying has merit. Sometimes people just don't want to acknowledge the truth.

October 24, 2016

Someone on my feed kept asking me to provide evidence for how anarchism "will work" if it is established.

I have been an anarchist for many years now, and I have probably heard this question over a thousand times from people trying to understand the philosophy.

Sometimes I legitimately do provide evidence, but other times I demonstrate that trying to understand how it will work and function in society is irrelevant.

This is how I expressed this sentiment (as compassionately as possible) to the individual on my feed just now.

> I don't think evidence is even needed to move toward anarchy. There is a deeper, more fundamental reason for pursuing anarchism. Anarchism is the more morally palatable philosophy and the only sane option.
>
> Allow me to provide an example to help clarify this position.
>
> For instance, take antebellum slavery. Most people involved in that enterprise thought an America without slaves was unthinkable. And some of them even argued that the world would collapse into chaos without people to involuntarily pick that cotton. They took a position similar to the anti-anarchist one. They thought that without cotton-picking chattel, the economy would collapse.
>
> But for the abolitionists, this was an irrelevant argument. The primary reason to end slavery was that it was morally reprehensible and wrong. They wanted to end slavery for those reasons instead of worrying about how the world would look after the fact. In this sense, concerning oneself with practical implications of a new social or cultural paradigm is superficial and a non-issue.
>
> Many anarchists take a stance like the anti-slavery abolitionists. We want to end government because it is wrong, because it is corrupt, because it murders and enslaves people.
>
> Therefore, instead of busying ourselves with theoretical questions about how anarchy would work, we take initiative to abolish the State and figure it out after the fact.

This is a common anarchist argument, but I think it is powerful, which is why people often repeat it.

If we know some cultural trend is evil or equates to a net negative for society, the arguments from fear about how to proceed after its demise ring hollow.

November 8, 2016

I have a feeling more people would share my posts if they didn't fear such opinions could have them ostracized or tormented by friends, family, and co-workers. It makes me tremendously sad that people are afraid to express themselves and share controversial commentary because the world is populated by people who are easily triggered by new ideas and will harangue their friends and family members for being too "radical."

But I submit to you that there is nothing bad or unwholesome about sharing truth. There is nothing to be ashamed of by loving the world and yourself so fucking much that you convey your values and tribulations to everyone around you. The only way for us to proceed is by not sparing people of their insecurities regarding ideas and change. We may sacrifice some of our opportunities by expressing ideas, but without professors of these notions, the world will continue to march on in its shamed state of oppression, incivility, and despair.

Indeed, the Western world was initially built on the philosophical idea of questioning established authorities and working to create new visions of society for humanity. If we fall prey to our states of fear and reluctance, we deprive the world of our youthful vigor. We trade practicality and the illusion of safety for standing up to principle and the virtues of absolute freedom from despots. We choose our fear over self-preservation and the preservation of our children.

Try not to be afraid to talk, to persuade people, and to preach truth with uncanny poetic candor. Dissenting speech is the cornerstone of creating paradigm shifts, and without a doubt, we do not want to be left alone in the dark.

November 14, 2016

A lot of people believe humans can't change—that we are violent, greedy, and evil by nature. This is the nature of humanity, they say.

As a person interested in humanistic and choice theory psychology, I ardently reject this position.

Even if people have the capacity to commit evil and do bad, they also possess the capacity to commit good and do right. I believe not only in the evolution of the individual but also the evolution of the species.

It is true. I do not expect a utopia to emerge from our collective behavior. But I do think cultural considerations can be shifted to align more rightfully with humanity's fluid and less airtight nature. I believe people can change their worldview and adopt principles that create personalities that are more geared to shun greed, evil, violence, and ultimately government.

Just because there is a vast history of men doing bad does not mean there isn't likewise a vast history of men doing good. Just because the benevolent deeds are less written about and worshiped does not mean they cease to exist. Currently, history is just a written genuflection to bad men with power. The good deeds often go unobserved and are less revered.

Let's change that for the sake of reason and dignity.

Humanity is a chemical admixture of various traits and characteristics, and the predominant cultures and paradigms will determine which ones bubble to the surface. The interesting thing about individual psychology is that it is largely determined by the social forces that shape it. Let's wield this knowledge and alter society to fit the image we most longingly desire: one of peace and freedom.

November 14, 2016

The number of people who ignore anarchists as they continue to beg for more political control, bombing campaigns, enforced servitude, and their favorite presidential personality astonishes me.

How much destruction and chaos do you want to see play out before you finally pause and say, "FUCK, this is not working out!" When will compassion, tenderness, and love for other humans finally be a consideration? How many centuries of stupidity, sociopathy, abject violence, and carelessness do we all have to be subjected to before the world wakes up?

It's not difficult nor does it take a powerhouse intellect to acknowledge the current state of affairs—to see that government has caused great harm globally. It just takes one moment of personal vulnerability. It takes a minute to let the truth of the world and our predicament sink in.

Most people are not evil. They are just born into a situation and their worldview is colored by it. Then the shepherds of culture tend to the charade of running society politely while in reality using violence readily.

If you are one of these people who are good but happen to buy into the system, I urge you to STOP. Think. Start looking at alternatives. Quit believing social bromides. Realize the political pond scum is manufacturing your consent. See the bombs. Feel where the annihilation originates. Know that you do not have to be culpable, that you can choose nonviolent and peaceful philosophies. Grasp that you are a creature of virtue and decency. Ascend to something better.

Together, we can stop this bulkhead of madness. Will you live with me for change? Will you join the anarchists in their march to save humanity from itself and to finally be able to live freely and prosper?

Come.

You are needed.

November 19, 2016

I want to let everyone know that I have an open platform. Anyone can post their ideas, and I encourage everyone to maintain civility and enact any degree of compassion they can muster. I endearingly accept most everyone so long as they have ideas to share to help condemn government and create productive dialogue.

I notice that many anarchist feeds and blogs are replete with angry mobs of "anarchists" calling each other cucks, libtards, and other choice names. But I am glad to provide a feed that acts as an exception to that, where people can disagree with grace and class.

However, my feed is still not a safe space.

Many of these ideas will hurt feelings, and even though I advocate compassion, that does not mean I promote political correctness. I expect people to challenge each other and talk about difficult things. However, I don't expect people to go into unproductive rants filled with name-calling and backbiting. These types of tantrums are exhausting and do not contribute to more knowledge and understanding. They contribute to hatred and are ultimately pointless other than to satisfy fragile egos.

As a psychologically motivated and introspective group, I expect us all to behave in ways that reflect that. Paths are cropping up in "anarchist communities" that are geared toward being as volatile, unsophisticated, and reactive as possible because doing so does not violate any principles or standards.

This may be true, but I am a strong proponent of compassion, community, human connection, and dignity. I think if anarchists cultivate these traits, they will thrust humanity forward. Being ugly to each other for the sake of being ugly will only tear us apart, burn bridges, and ultimately contribute to nothing more than the continued stigma toward anarchists and voluntaryists.

Much love.

November 26, 2016

It saddens me that so many anarchists are at each other's throats. The lack of communication and mutual understanding boggles my mind. It appears their philosophical differences are mostly superficial or of little consequence. And if they aren't attacking each other on a philosophical plane, they are attacking each other on a personal level for no meaningful reason. But let me ask: What productive ends do these attacks serve other than to caress bruised egos and inflate the sense of self? Is it about being right or wrong? Or is it something more?

Know that I am not attempting to take a position of moral superiority or claim I am better. I am just pointing this out because it speaks to my desire for anarchists to improve their communication skills, and I mean not just communicating ideas but also communicating emotions and needs. If we are unable to understand each other on a fundamental level, it is unlikely we will be able to help anyone understand our philosophy. I am ashamed that there are camps that have taken infighting to levels of outright hate, condemnation, and gang rivalry.

For as long as I am empowered to push forward, I will continue to evangelize the truth of love and compassion. I will continue to promote peace between everyone, especially since it starts with our communication and connection. And if anarchists can't properly relate to each other, understand each other, and share in a common relationship, how can everyone else come to commiserate with anarchists and grasp their vision?

I disagree with some of the ideas being shared as part of the anarchist lexicon, but this chemical admixture of them is what ultimately produces the uniqueness and vitality of anarchist culture. And for that, I do not shun any idea or person...I welcome all with the hope that our mutual compassion will allow us to finally work together without a need for tyrants to rule and control us.

I truly believe that connection to each other will triumph over philosophical differences.

November 30, 2016

I sometimes wonder how many people have blocked my feed in response to me posting "political" stuff. I know there are casualties I could not have prevented, but I feel like there are some people I pushed away because I was too hostile several years ago. Now I have lost the opportunity to express the compassionate side of anarchism—the compassionate side of myself.

Then again, there are probably those people who would cover their ears to anything I say even if it is only vaguely outside the status quo. Nonetheless, I would be remiss to not mention that I could have hooked them better with this vector of anarchism.

To those of you who didn't brush me aside for how volatile I was, I appreciate the unconditional positive regard you showed me. That speaks a lot to your character even if you still disagree with my apolitical belief in no rulers. Perhaps we can now have another discussion about anarchism—about how love and belonging fit into this philosophy.

Doesn't that sound more appealing? If you have stuck around this long, it's likely that you get the basis of the ideas and that you have already made some connection with me.

December 6, 2016

It is common for anarchists to say they can't change others or help alter people's perspectives.

However, when anarchists use this as an excuse to resign themselves from providing ideas and using social interventions, they miss a key opportunity to help shift the dominant paradigm away from statism.

And this is also why anarchists still talk about the ideas even if they believe a person has to discover the philosophy on their own. The anarchist wants both to fit in and feel loved, as well as bring others over into their mold.

People are group animals, and their virtues, principles, and ideas shift along with the herd. Since people desire connection and attachment, they will often adopt a group identity to fit in and feel loved. Love and belonging are two of the most predominant, genetic human needs—and they often trump the desire for individuality.

Thus, compassionate anarchists see themselves as cultural therapists. They use social interventions to help people heal from the wounds of statism and move away from the old ways of thinking and feeling. They realize that people's behavior and attitudes reflect the dominant paradigm, which has arisen because of abuse, maltreatment, and childhood violence.

In this sense, the words that compassionate anarchists utter can act as a "corrective emotional experience" in the sense that they help people awaken to their desire for freedom, connection, and love. They help mend wounds, heal, and effectively alter the functioning of society. They bring everyone together.

Soft anarchists suggest that group activity and social interaction provide fertile ground for the seeds of anarchy to sprout.

This is why we should never underestimate the power of words and connection in human relations. Our words and direct interactions with other people are what can help alter their perspectives. It is why they harbor such powerful transformative magic.

Let's keep speaking.

December 23, 2016

A lot of anarchists get so focused on logical debate and discussion that they believe they can divorce emotional content from the argument or philosophy.

I want to remind anarchists that this is biologically impossible.

Humans are creatures of high emotional expressivity. Only a very small percentage of the population has little access to emotional content. These are labeled "sociopaths" or who have flattened emotions because of extensive trauma.

Indeed, whenever we have any type of philosophy or coveted idea, our emotions become intimately intertwined with those notions. The emotional connections in the brain are intricately wired with the prefrontal cortex, where executive functioning and higher thinking occur.

It is true that we can use the frontal cortex to help mitigate emotional reactions, but every time we express our ideas or philosophies the emotional centers will become active.

This is especially visible when people debate, become "triggered," and set off the fight-or-flight response. These defense mechanisms for ideas are simply the fallout of our evolutionary birthright. In this sense, we are all susceptible to becoming invested and thus triggered by specific ideas. And all we can do is become aware of these triggers and emotions so we can temper and take control of how we respond to others.

This is extremely important to remember because it will allow us to employ compassion and empathy in the heat of an intense debate or discussion about ideas.

In my opinion, this understanding is part of the process of developing wisdom.

I am still learning, as well.

December 29, 2016

Anarchism does not have to be volatile, unsophisticated, and tasteless.

It can be polite, classy, and refined.

January 6, 2017

Communication is difficult because sometimes people aren't interested in listening, sharing, or empathizing.

However, I think patience and perseverance will help put everyone on an even keel. An individual's passion for connection creates mutuality among individuals, and this sentiment is contagious.

The desire to connect and the ongoing struggle of making a connection are much better than being at perpetual war with each other.

Non-communication is the path to bloodshed in its final incarnation. Let's not go down that path if possible. Let's fight to talk. Let's fight to love.

January 30, 2017

When all else fails, simply call your "opponent" a leftist, mock them, and then virtue signal about the importance of statist erotica and extol the virtues of a favorite politician.

I wish we could all have compassionate discussions without resorting to uncivil mockery and internet pseudo-machismo. I think some of these factions of anarchism have become so cancerous that decent chit-chat has been replaced by bloated egoism and maniacal character attacks. This strategy or path to anarchism is inherently doomed to failure.

Did I mention it's ironic when these folks virtue signal while claiming that nonpolitical anarchists are the ones virtue signaling?

February 3, 2017

I feared that jokes about helicopter rides would be escalated into calls for outright genocide, which is starting to happen.

Some "anarchists" or "alt-right" adherents have begun the dehumanization process of a group of people by generalizing them all as "degenerates."

For those familiar with history, this is the same thing Hitler started doing to the Jews, except he based his dehumanization tactics on an ethnic/religious group rather than a political group.

This mentality shakes me to the core because I have maintained the idea that anarchists can keep their perspective and dignity and that their beliefs are the opposite of murder and mayhem. But it seems like their dignity and decency have been perverted by recent culture wars.

With that said, this is not to justify people on the economic left who choose to vandalize or destroy property. It is not to condone this childish, aggressive behavior. Indeed, I rail against this aggression and weakness of philosophy, as well. However, I honestly had higher expectations for people who promote modern libertarian anarchism. I thought they knew the dangers of dehumanizing others and trumpeting violence against economic groups as the answer. I thought they could move beyond this urgency to shed blood.

It turns out they were weak-minded and desirous of warfare. Turns out they were not true freedom lovers but hate mongers hellbent on tasting the blood of their enemies.

So, I will ask any "anarchist" who has these Freudian murder fantasies a few questions: What can you do for peace instead? How can you deescalate an increasingly volatile situation without stoking the fire? How can you reign in your growing desire to hurt others? How can you better relate to others even if they are unhinged and ready for violence? How can this be resolved?

I hope these people talking loosely and non-jokingly about extermination can come to terms with their impulses and that we can find better ways to solve the current cultural crises.

I don't want to see this escalate any further.

February 20, 2017

Some people talk about "leftism" infiltrating the anarchist philosophy and claim many anarchists are turning into zealous, rabid leftists.

That's certainly a concern. I can see and acknowledge why that may be happening.

However, this so-called "culture war" of the modern era has created a diametrical reaction from anarchists and other individualists. In this sense, I see that anarchism is also being infiltrated by the "right."

There are as many anarchists joining the ranks of right-aligned politics as there are the left, and it's a tragic state of affairs to watch unfold. This devolution into rightism acts as a counterbalance to rampant identity politics and leftism, but it's still not a positive development. It just seems like a reactionary regression back into the cave of old statist dogmas.

Nonetheless, I will continue to sit back and preach the gospel of decent and dignified communication for ending the State and finding common ground with other anarchists.

Initiating an economic battle between two seemingly opposed factions has harmed communication. It has just inflamed either side into adopting greater and greater levels of statism as they attempt to tear down the economic and moral arguments of the other. And now we are witnessing the breakdown of understanding as each party talks past one another and no one focuses on solutions other than their own.

Therefore, I hope we can all move beyond this culture war phase and begin to find the anarchism we keep tucked away inside of ourselves. Everyone needs to step back from the "election" and take a deep look at their beliefs and ideas. Then they should remember where they come from and how they got where they are now. This kind of calm and considered introspection may help anarchists figure out how they can come to terms with each other.

If not, there could be more trouble looming on the horizon.

The State thrives on this ongoing battle of leftism versus rightism. It gorges itself on the sumptuous feast of political and patriotic correctness, of divisiveness and hatred—and it will cash in its chips with the lifeblood of anarchists. It will grow and evolve as it tries to bring anarchists into the fold of its political machinations.

Let us disallow that.

Let us come together as freedom lovers without having to obsess over economic erotica. There are other ways to build a society than to constantly mock each other's logical, economic, and moral aspirations. There are humanitarian ways to figure things out in society without moralizing.

This is what I am interested in trying.

What about you?

March 1, 2017

Drawing hard economic lines in the sand is not always useful for creating a more anarchic society. Mostly, economic divisions only inspire people to hate. They drive them to violence.

Instead, I recommend communicating with people and discovering common ground. It is through this channel of mutual interaction that a relationship forms, and it is through the struggle, purity, stress, love, and joy of having a relationship that people learn to cooperate for the sake of spreading anarchism.

Indeed, individuals cannot form a deep and powerful bond with every person, but the glimmer of the relational interaction can help bring more people together than any economic ideology ever will.

Relationships are the crucible of the anarchist world.

March 5, 2017

I reject any splintering off into left or right political factions from anarchism. I think it's toxic and unhealthy. However, I will not purposely let this splintering off strain my relationships with these people. The problem is that thanks to their misadventures into politics, they exacerbate their relationship problems with everyone. It's tough finding common ground with people who want to toss you out of a helicopter or slit your throat because you enjoy entrepreneurship and the beauty business brings. Their ideas are dangerous because they are inherently anti-human and anti-cooperation.

April 1, 2017

Arguing with people to the point of emotional exhaustion is a waste of time. Literally.

April 8, 2017

I can't wait to see the descriptive analysis report on Trump's awesomeness surface from the alt-right Molyneux camp.

Don't get me wrong. I hold nothing personal against these folks. I believe many of them will return to the sanity of anarchism rather than continuing to worship nationalism and their Führer.

However, there will probably be more "I told you so" incidents like this Syria airstrike cluster fuck.

The question remains: How many more lies will it take to bring people back to not wanting a master?

Hopefully not many.

April 25, 2017

Sometimes it is good for anarchists to be vulnerable and tell stories. Narratives can be powerful methods for spreading truth. Usually, we get in the habit of arguing, of trying to pigeonhole people into anarchism with raw logic.

How about this, instead? Talk about what the State did to us. Tell people about how they threw us into cages, beat us, and held us for ransom. Talk about how they threatened us with violence for holding a plant or pill. Reiterate stories about the IRS, CPS, and other coercive agencies. Let people identify with the hurt and anguish.

Share tears. Convey burning anger. Many will react emotionally to this sentiment and thus comprehend the power of our words and the adversity we suffered. Do not be afraid to disclose all the brutishness of our experiences.

In this way, the more emotional pockets of society will respond and consider our plight. We will then bring other types of individuals into the fray. Anarchism will rise out of a heartfelt and loving need to end oppressive violence.

Per aspera ad astra.

The Relational Anarchist Primer

12/14/2016

> "When you show deep empathy toward others, their defensive energy goes down, and positive energy replaces it. That's when you can get more creative in solving problems."
>
> —Stephen Covey

Relational anarchism is a standalone vector or field of thought under the umbrella of anarchism. In this perspective, relationships determine levels of human freedom. The process of human interaction is more important than content.

The way people relate to each other is considered the process. It necessitates freedom from governments and rulers through communication efforts rather than relying on freedom to crop up as a result of providing better arguments or information (the content). Ways of relating—using communication processes—include narrative conversation, nonviolent communication, compassion, empathy, gentle confrontation, appraisal of body language, and other aspects of communication between people.

How Relational Anarchists Think

According to relational anarchists, the better humans connect with each other, the more peace and understanding will exist between them. The greater the strength of the relationships, the less likely people are to believe rulers are necessary to control society.

Anarchism means "without rulers," and besides being a political assertion, this is a psychological and relational preference. It is apolitical and based on preferred relationship standards. Instead of dispensing violence, these anarchists dispense compassion.

To be "without rulers" is a state of human interaction. It is how most people prefer to make contact with others and how human connection unfolds when certain skill sets and forms of communication are employed. Most people do not want to be ruled. Yet they often end up in a ruler-serf dynamic as a result of cultural modes of interaction and attachment, which are generally anti-empathetic and detached.

The Content of Anarcho-Politics

Forms of political anarchism, namely anarcho-communism and anarcho-capitalism, tend to focus on the content of change rather than processes and interactions (in the very least, on the surface, processes are not emphasized compared to economic or moral considerations).

These modes of thought suggest society should be arranged according to economic precedent or standard. Their defenders say pure logic, argumentation, historical analysis, class analysis, moral positions, or other rhetorical tools will bring people over to anarchism. They also point to practical strategies like counter-economics, cryptography, protest, peaceful resistance, violent resistance, riots, and other means to bring about a stateless society.

The Relational Solution

Relational anarchists take a more novel approach. They say anarchism will emerge within the context of human connections and the presence of empathy within relationships. It is through the conduit of connection that differences of economic opinion can be dismantled. The mutual struggle for property ownership versus non-property ownership can be worked out through connection, bonding, and the process of communication.

The hope is that all competing parties can figure out how to maintain their economic preferences and lifestyles without seeking to force their views on others. This is because the truth is that no party is going to be able to change the minds of all their detractors.

In place of an infinite struggle of deciding on the best economic model for society, the relational anarchist asks everyone to come to the table and figure out how to cooperatively coexist in a state of anarchy. Indeed, the partial reason governments have maintained their power is the ongoing battle between "left" and "right."

As an aside, relational anarchists do not necessarily oppose or support defensive violence. The use of defensive violence will differ from person to person and depend largely on their preferences and principles. I believe that if a person initiates violence, they have sacrificed any opportunity for compassionate connection, and the most loving thing a person can do is defend themselves from that act of violent hatred.

Relational Anarchism in Practice

Relational anarchism does contain a lot of theory and speculation. The evidence that this could work stems from counseling psychology and attachment theory.

In counseling psychology, evidenced-based practice suggests people are more likely to heal not as a result of some strategy or rhetorical intervention the counselor uses but because of the bond that develops between counselor and client.

Laurie Meyers, writing for *Counseling Today*, confirmed the importance of the therapeutic alliance or "counseling relationship," noting that, "in 2001, a comprehensive research summary published in the journal *Psychotherapy* found that a strong therapeutic alliance was more closely correlated with positive client outcomes than any specific treatment interventions." In this regard, I believe anarchists can improve their outcomes for persuasion and getting people involved in anarchism if they focus on social therapy, connection processes, and their relationship with society-at-large.

As a last bit of working evidence, attachment theory has taught us that humans thrive when their bonds with other humans are strong. They not only thrive but also learn how to connect with others and work through problems. In relationship settings with adults, securely attached adults seem to have more satisfactory and less hostile relationships. In terms of society, if this theory is applied on a grand scale, it could determine how quickly society moves toward relational anarchism.

However, there needs to be research conducted in all of these areas. Perhaps it will start a new research trend with a goal of understanding how "social healing" can take place via different communities and movements.

A Plurality of Strategies: Psychologically Minded

As a final thought, relational anarchists understand the need for a plurality of strategies and thought processes to bring about freedom and social healing, but they also believe that without proper communication, differences in economic or political theory cannot be resolved in practice. Communication— or the processes of interaction—must be completely open and unblocked for positive change to occur.

It is difficult to work things out for peace, social cohesion, and spontaneous order when humans have not opened to the idea of being psychologically minded or focusing on processes. Without this prerequisite for building anarchism, the political gainsaying, economic overtures, practical advice, and pleas for freedom will be lost on the deaf ears of a non-empathetic and uncaring audience.

In this culture, people are taught to focus on content rather than process. Observing emotions and relationship transactions in public settings is considered awkward and taboo. I believe the superficial focus on content has damaged people's self-awareness. Paradoxically, it has been the cause of hyper-emotionality, volatility, and an inability to control emotional content. When people have been taught to ignore or repress their feelings, they lose awareness of their inner worlds. On the other side of the token, when people have been given the freedom and the opportunity to feel, they gain a sense of emotional intelligence. They start to understand their own emotions, and they can finally relate and empathize with other humans.

—From my journal, early 2016

Beauty and Truth: The Anarchist as Psychological Muse

December 27, 2013

Anarchists do not want to watch the world burn; they only want to expose its beauty.

March 29, 2014

This is my truth: I crave anarchism because I acknowledge and embrace mortality. I see the brevity of life. I see the drying and withering of leaves. I see violence and corruption, and I realize that freedom from cages and rulers sets my fleeting time here above barbarism and wanton indulgences. In this, anarchism equates to the supreme and most affectionate desire to live and be without interruption. I am here for a mere milli-frame in this theater of the vast cosmos, and I intend to relish and enjoy every second despite those clamoring stupidly to control and thwart my love of this life. Everything experienced happens too quickly and ends too unpleasantly to allow tyrants to ruin this most pleasurable moment. This position, while existential and scary, sums up my attitude of anarchism and why it should matter so much to everyone.

March 14, 2015

Being an anarchist is not just a catchy and trendy temporary way of life, nor is it a passing fancy or a cool philosophy to use for the sake of winning arguments.

Anarchism is deeply, intimately personal.

I chose anarchism because I do not believe I should have to obey someone for the sake of obeying. I chose it because I know "governmental authority" is a useless and dangerous concept that only gets innocent people caged, harmed, or killed. I chose anarchism because I enjoy independence, because I loathe the idea of being ruled, and because I acknowledge that freedom from institutional and social violence leads to happiness and love. I chose it because I believe people are innately free and that they have the power and decency to live their own lives and solve their own problems without a perpetual father figure looming over and judging their decisions.

Anarchism, under this light, is more than a philosophy. It is the soul and fire of the authentic person. Anarchism denotes a spirit and strength of character that other philosophies fail to discern, that other people fail to grasp or care about. Anarchism screams for acceptance of humanity, and it declares all individuals totally sovereign, only governable by the will and moral compass of their passions. To not accept anarchism, then, is to throw oneself down at the altar of slavery and insert oneself into a kind of hell on earth.

June 1, 2015

Would you enjoy a non-consensual or coerced intimate relationship? In other words, if you were forced to love a person, would that relationship benefit you in any way? Or would that relationship be detrimental to your well-being and dampen your experience of eudaemonia? Correct, the relationship would not be good. It would be abusive.

Here is the thing: you also have relationships with people involved with the institutions that make up society-at-large.

Now, if you do not enjoy coercive and deleterious personal and intimate relationships and would not voluntarily enter one, why would you enter socially coercive relationships?

For instance, it is not therapeutic to have *any* relationships you are compelled to enter, so why do people, overall, choose not to apply their personal relationship ideals to society-at-large? Why do they see their relationships with government or other social entities as beneficial if they are compelled to love and worship them under the threat of harm?

Therefore, anarchism is ultimately therapeutic. It teaches us the value of good, healthy relationships and that we cannot harbor double standards in terms of how we relate and interact with other people, even if those relationships are short-lived.

Life is always better when our relationships allow us to grow and change as people. Conversely, being forced into relationships causes us to stagnate as individuals. It hampers self-actualization.

It is time to take our social relationships as seriously as we take our personal ones.

June 5, 2015

Anarchism is not just a political idea or a personal philosophy. It is a psychological expression. Anarchists and libertarians are saying they want the freedom to choose their relationships voluntarily. They want all their interactions with humans to allow for the most growth and change because this is how relationships function. Coercion condemns a relationship to psychological turmoil and stifles development.

Anarchism will move forward, then, not because it will alter the economic or philosophical direction of society but because it will transform humanity's view of social relationships and business partnerships.

This is the therapeutic renaissance that will arise because of absolute liberty.

August 22, 2015

Anarchism is not just a political philosophy. It is a medium of exchange. It is a medium of emotional transfer. If a person self-discloses that they accept anarchism, they are saying they want to have a harmonious, authentic relationship. In other words, they have shunned force and fraud from their intimate and personal attachments. They have given up on the social more that drives people to control and coerce friends and family. Anarchism is the ultimate medium of emotional exchange because it surpasses political philosophies. It moves into a realm of pure love. If a person identifies as an anarchist, they are denoting an anti-political stance, which means they are ready to live as a true human being devoid of the inclination to harm, manipulate, and control. It is the next step in human moral and logical development. If a person encounters an anarchist, they should hug them—surrender themselves to the purity of their soul. Anarchists are miles ahead of their time and culture. They will teach people what it means to truly care about humanity. They are the non-charlatan shamans, the neo-lovers, the modern-day Jesus without dogma and damnation.

October 16, 2015

I appear wrapped up in negative thoughts to many of my friends. A lot of anarchists share this temperament because the goal of our philosophy is to show people the truth, to expose them to realities that may be too uncomfortable or painful to bear. We hope that by unveiling these ugly things, we can wake people from the cultural coma, from all the fictions and fantasies they have created to cope with reality.

We focus on the negative because we have realized how precious and beautiful life is, how ecstatic and amazing it is to be alive, and we wish only to share and promote these feelings of awe to heal the world.

This life represents the one opportunity we must connect with ourselves, others, and nature. We merely want to encourage others to experience this solidarity, but anarchists can only share their emotional sensitivity if everyone acknowledges the bad, negative, and evil and works toward ending or lessening it. Achieving this requires a true appreciation for existence, a kind of love that is unparalleled and pervasive. This is where anarchists acquire their courage to do what they do and live how they live.

So the question remains: will more people choose this path of beauty and worldly love?

March 24, 2016

I am trying to bring something superbly high-brow and sophisticated to the anarchist community. I want to inject more poetics and dialogue into the fray. I want to see beauty and understanding spread among everyone—among government apologists and beggars on the street corners.

I want to be the change I espouse, to breathe it in and exhale it. I want to drag everyone along for the ride. I have dreams, ambitions, and visions, and they include a respect for subtlety and nuance. They involve the synthesis of disparate elements, like economics and depth psychology; like neurology and anarcho-capitalism, like love and hate—neuro-radical and neuro-basic.

I see a sensitive and diverse generation of anarchists cropping up, a group that respects everything compelling about human creativity and passion. I desire an anarchic society made up of more than disquieting echo chambers, repetitive idolatry, and manufactured truths.

I want a joyous philosophy; one that resonates with the soul and light of every person, not just the adopters and lip-syncers. I want anarchism to spill over into the rough and tumble day-to-day life of the world. I want to help communicate it with a fashionable and unique cadence, one that touches the innermost humanness of everyone. I want anarchism to be the new dialogue, held in high esteem by every individual far and wide.

April 1, 2016

Anarchists are natural poets. They wish to sing a new society into existence with the beauty and rhythm of their verse. They are thus visionaries. With every utterance and action, they mold society into something more palatable, worthwhile, and ecstatic. They want to unmake the damage wrought by the leech class and their scheming, kleptomania, and psychopathy. This is why anarchists manifest their artistry through the grace of movement and principle, highlighting their convictions with a passion they exemplify and live by.

Anarchists are tired of the drear and tedium of the workaday drudgery, of the silent violence that seeps into every nook and corner of culture. Anarchists thus manufacture truth from the pit of their being, serving as a wellspring of love shot into the decaying heart of humankind. In this regard, anarchists are the revivalists and the truth junkies. They feel the agony of society deeply. It slithers through their consciousness and reverberates wildly. It is this explosive sensation that sparks the magnificent change they constantly paint onto the world. This is how their poetry dances, how the magic functions, and where the evolution erupts.

April 3, 2016

The rave scene and the interpersonal love that arise in that diverse and joyous atmosphere characterize the underlying reality of relationalism.

Inside the rave, bursts of intense care are telegraphed between partygoers, and different people with different backgrounds and styles come together without distrust, fear, or rancor. It is a relationship culture where empathy and dialogue come easier insofar that people listen and respond.

The dancing and rhythmic aspect of the experience only adds to the sensuality and communicative nature of the total experience.

Obviously, we cannot rave throughout our lives and within everyday reality, but we can use that atmosphere as a metaphor for relating to one another. We can understand that being naturally empathetic and together is possible without being in that environment or necessarily an altered state of mind.

In this sense, relational anarchism is a kind of altered-state experience, a culture of emotional awareness.

As an aside, the rave scene is not perfect; it is composed of imperfect humans. Nonetheless, it is one of the few crowd gatherings that manifests a kind of spiritual belonging rather than stupefied barbarism.

April 4, 2016

I want to join with you to have a peaceful relationship, even if we are different and do not know each other deeply. We are naturally social animals, and harmonious interactions dictate the relative peace of our coexistence. If you encumber our relationship with violence or destruction, you are not only doing us a disservice, but you are also undermining your close relations and putting everyone at risk of barbaric, uncivilized acts.

Humans grow with love and connection, not anger, hatred, or coercion. Let us work this out and respect each other's humanness and shared appreciation. I have faith in our ability to connect and revel in the beauty of being together, even if it is only for a moment. This is how I believe we can build a culture of empathy and compassion.

April 6, 2016

Healthy relationships are non-coercive, violence-free, and peaceful by nature. If we strive for healthy relationships with everyone, even a brief acquaintanceship or business partnership, those relationships will naturally yield anarchistic results. The relationship vector of social interaction negates the need to invoke logic or economics to abolish government. Government naturally declines as healthy relationships grow since government itself is a relationship pattern based on the consequences of cultural trends in how people interact with one another.

Therefore, I believe one new goal of any anarchist should be to maintain healthy relationships and teach others about the importance of building a culture centered around empathy, communication, and emotional intelligence even with people they may not know. These traits foster anarchism from the ground up.

It is the path toward building a sensual society, or anarchism by way of love.

April 9, 2016

My goal as an anarchist is not just to convey a political truth or position. It is to create a new community and culture based on relationships and genuine dialogue. It is to prevent the trauma of alienation and develop emotional health in whole groups of people. It is to distill psychological truths into socially workable solutions.

Thus, anarchism is not just political realignment in practice but also a form of therapy initiated on society at-large, and anarchists are the new class of wounded healers. If anarchists are not thinking and feeling along these lines, they are liable to miss the new big-picture method for spreading love and appreciation for anarchism.

April 21, 2016

Why should you be an anarchist?

Because anarchism is not rampant destruction or a bomb-flinging bonanza. Instead, it is a joyous dance between sentient beings who wish to live in harmony with one another and resolve conflicts with dignity and decency.

I believe in the power of this relationship and our ability to work out differences. I think we can live in proximity or relative distance without feeling like we should employ control or coercion to get our way.

I think you, like most people, operate with a desire for love and attachment, and this type of connection is opposed to violence or destruction. I know we can solve any disputes that arise and live as freely and independently as possible with shared respect and without any kind of government interference in our business.

This is the kind of anarchism I see existing between the space you and I occupy. Isn't it grand?

June 8, 2016

Anarchists are not merely philosophers or political activists. Anarchists are social healers. They are the modern shamans, the medicine folk of this age.

When anarchists vie for State abolition, social reconstruction, and deconstruction of the throne, they are saying "I know how to help repair this broken culture. I know how to sing life into every person's soul."

Anarchists are offering a cure for the pandemic of authoritarian violence, and in doing so, they will help alleviate other systemic problems.

Psychiatric "illnesses," mass school shootings, rampant suicide, alienation, disconnectedness, emotional repression, poor relationships, and unbridled hatred are symptoms of authoritarian social structures.

Caged animals behave in ways that mirror their station in life; it is no wonder most humans exhibit erratic behavior, self-destruction, mental injury, and moral corruption.

It is this servitude society that causes it, and contrary to popular belief, most human behavior is not a non-negotiable part of human nature. It is the consequence of the control freak and totalitarian structures society has erected.

The evidence exists regarding how the brain develops and integrates—or, in this case, fails to integrate—under the barbaric supremacy of statism at home and abroad.

Time to unmake the system, allow anarchists to work their magic, and build freer cultures without kings and impossible expectations. The product may not be perfect, but it will allow for greater neural integration in society's individuals, and this will likely translate as love.

November 8, 2016

Where can we find real power? Not in the men of always; not in politicians and men of violence. Real power is found in the courage of love. It is discovered in the depths of individual human beings who are willing to take risks and share themselves with their intimate partners and closest allies. Real power is practiced through making lasting friendships, finding companionship, and striving to relate to others. Real power is the power of the soul. It is the shrine of character that is emblazoned with the spirit of compassion and concern for the well-being of those around you. Real power is the ability to face difficulties and confrontations with tact and dignity. Real power is not discovered in the halls of great buildings with giant colonnades. Real power is inside. It is right here, before us, for everyone to wield. Do you see it? Can you feel it? It is here.

December 27, 2016

When I was younger, my intellectual curiosity developed rapidly, and it quickly became boundless.

I explored and considered every subject I came across.

Philosophy. Science. Religion. Literature. Gardening. Economics. Technology. Everything.

Nothing was safe from my voracious hunger for knowledge. I became especially intrigued with what neuroscientists and philosophers of mind came to refer to as the "hard problem of consciousness."

The "hard problem" relates to human consciousness and how it arises—how our "subjective experiences" come into existence. Scientists have little understanding of this area. They don't even know what consciousness or subjectivity is. How exactly does a physical substrate, the brain, produce imagery in the human mind? Is this just a manifestation of brain processes? Is the mind something separate or part of the body? Can science explain the mechanisms of how consciousness arises and what it is?

These are fascinating questions, indeed, and I probably would have focused 100 percent of my intellectual energies trying to solve these kinds of problems. However, I stopped thinking as hard about these issues. I changed direction and placed my focus elsewhere.

After I had a run-in with the State and started learning about anarchism, I realized there are more pressing matters than laboring over obscure and arcane questions regarding the nature of human subjective experience and consciousness.

With that said, I would sometimes rather focus on these intriguing philosophical and scientific conundrums. Even though they seem vaguely relevant, a discovery in these areas could bring about a paradigm shift or change the course of human history. It could perhaps even lead to a new technological invention that would reshape medicine, neurology, or engineering.

You never know. Anything could happen. I am probably not smart enough to make a huge impact, but because of our current social problems, I have decided my talents and abilities are best spent trying to convince people of better ways to live together. I honestly think I can save more people doing that than by working strictly in advanced fields on specialized subject matter.

But there is an even deeper insight hidden inside this thought.

The presence of governments and the existence of politicians have dashed many hopes. Think about how their violence, arbitrary rules, and red tape have dissuaded people from going after their passions in life.

If this parasitical demon of statism did not exist, I would probably be using my time and talents to do other things. So would many other people. But governments have created a situation where the brightest people have been driven to battle for their lives and livelihoods rather than spend their time pursuing other things and ignoring the looming threat of annihilation.

Sadly, we are in a situation where the most good will likely come from abolishing government rather than building new technologies or gaining more insight into the human brain.

It goes to show how dire humanity's situation really is.

Those who focus on other intellectual issues will indeed help humankind in some way, anyway. But what happens to all that good when people destroy each other because of their bad ideas?

Those discoveries will be for naught.

Nevertheless, I have hope that anarchists will help end this crisis by wet nursing humanity out of the womb of violence and into an adulthood of peace and love.

February 27, 2017

I just returned safely home from the Anarchapulco conference. I had an amazing time and met many amazing people doing amazing things. My head is still swimming with thoughts about the experience.

I was so proud to be able to speak to a large public forum about my ideas for the first time. This was a crowning moment in my career as an anarchist speaker. It meant a lot to me to be invited and shown so much love and respect from my fellow anarchists. I hope to do plenty more public talks in the future.

I was also blown away by how amazing Acapulco was. It was basically anarchic. You could move around in the town without fear of being gunned down by the cops. You could do what you pleased without worrying about the eye of the law always watching.

There's a bunch of nasty propaganda about Mexico being pushed around, but I can attest that it's mostly nonsense. The place was magical. There are things wrong, of course, but at least it's not a fascist slave state that constantly monitors all the people. In comparison to the USSA, it's an anarchist's wet dream.

Finally, props to all the friendly anarchists who mingled with me and put up with my eccentric antics. You guys rock. You're all doing God's work. Keep pushing forward, and we will build the society we seek.

I can see it before us, right there on the horizon, and it's brimming with love and compassion.

I Was Spanked and I Turned Out OK—or Did I?

05/16/2016

Most everyone has heard or used the phrase, "I was spanked, and I turned out ok." This expression represents the acceptance of hitting kids. It sits at the heart of American spanking culture and conjures similar phrases, like "My parents spanked me, and that is why I spank my kids," and "If more children were spanked there would be fewer brats running around."

Clichés like these not only promote spanking but also encourage and praise this type of punishment, which research evidence overwhelmingly suggests can damage children.

Parents use corporal punishment to allegedly correct unacceptable behavior or stop a child from disobeying or hurting themselves, but they usually "do not intend" to injure the child. They only want to command the child's attention and correct bad or dangerous behavior.

Definition and Statistics of Spanking

Spanking generally includes soft swats on the buttocks with the use of implements like a board, rod, or flyswatter. It could also be a slap across the face or other parts of the body. Some may even beat their child with a belt and call it spanking.

One issue here is that parents and professionals disagree on a clear definition of spanking, especially since most parents refer to any physical discipline as spanking in order to justify the act. In reality, spanking is just a euphemism for hitting.

The American Academy of Pediatrics defines spanking precisely as "striking a child with an open hand on the buttocks or extremities with the intention of modifying behavior without causing physical injury."

Taking this definition into account, and as previously mentioned, the prevalence of spanking is high. Studies suggest a decline in spanking in the last few years, but the majority of parents still administer it.

According to a Harris Poll conducted in 2013, four in five, or 81% of parents, said it is sometimes appropriate to spank children. Two-thirds, or 67%, say they were spanked as a child, which is down from 80% in 1995 (most polls and studies today vary between 65% and 90%).

A Columbia University study and a similar Harris poll said most parents spanked their children consistently at ages three to five. The poll also validated the cycle of spanking. Roughly 73% of parents who spank were spanked as children, whereas 25% were not.

This frequency of spanking implies that many people see it as a valid form of punishment. But why?

Hitting in a Calm Manner

Proponents of spanking argue spanking is acceptable if parents perform it calmly. They argue that if parents explain to their children why they are being spanked, it is a reasonable form of punishment. Problems only arise, say pro-spankers, when people hit out of anger or impatience.

In a 2014 *TIME* article, Dr. Jared Pingleton defended this view. "If he or she deliberately disobeys, the child should be informed of the upcoming spanking and escorted to a private area. The spanking should be lovingly administered in a clear and consistent manner," he wrote.

Although hitting in a loving manner is an odd and perplexing take, there is some evidence to support Pingleton's argument.

Dr. Robert Larzelere and his colleagues at Oklahoma State University conducted a positive study on spanking. It concluded that "two open hand swats to the buttocks after a child has defied an authority figure led to greater reduction of child defiance or anti-social behavior than 10 of 13 alternative discipline techniques."

Another argument against the non-hitting position suggests that anti-spanking studies cannot prove whether the practice directly causes misbehavior, mental illness, hostility, or other problems.

A *New York Times* article also defended this idea, asserting that "[s]tudies cited by opponents of corporal punishment...often do not adequately distinguish the effects of spanking, as practiced by non-abusive parents, from the impact of severe physical punishment and abuse."

Spanking Causes Long-Term Harm

Opponents of spanking have a different perspective, though, and at least one major institution discourages the practice of spanking altogether.

In a 2012 pressroom comment, the American Pediatric Association said: "The use of physical punishment to discipline children has been linked to a range of mental health problems and is strongly opposed by the American Academy of Pediatrics."

Not only have a few articles hinted that spanking causes mental health problems, but dozens of scientific journals have also stated that spanking causes a variety of long-term effects, including hostility and the use of violence through multiple generations.

A 2012 article from the American Psychological Association cited one such piece:

"A study published last year in Child Abuse and Neglect revealed an intergenerational cycle of violence in homes where physical punishment was used. Researchers interviewed parents and children age 3 to 7 from more than 100 families. Children who were physically punished were more likely to endorse hitting as a means of resolving their conflicts with peers and siblings."

There are more damning studies than ones that suggest an increased likelihood of hostility or mental health problems due to hitting. Newer research claims physical punishment damages children's brains. These studies confirmed that children who were spanked (received harsh corporal punishment) were likely to lose some grey matter tissue.

According to a 2014 *CNN* article, "Researchers found children who were regularly spanked had less gray matter in certain areas of the prefrontal cortex that have been linked to depression, addiction and other mental health disorders…"

Where the Debate Stands

This is where the current debate stands: it shuffles between experts and parents marshaling these arguments or similar ones based on the evidence.

Overall, advocates of spanking contend that spanking can be acceptable and effective if done gently and with love and care, but very little data support this view. They also argue that most evidence against spanking is only softly linked and not an exact cause.

Still, most pro-spanking researchers do not advocate harsh corporal punishment with implements, as this tends to "escalate to abuse." Finally, pro-spankers complain that anti-spanking studies often neglect to define the differences between spanking and harsher forms of physical punishment.

Anti-spankers Are Winning

By contrast, anti-spankers argue there is an immediate risk that spanking could cause permanent brain damage, so they ask: "Is hitting your child worth the risk of permanently damaging their brain?" Anti-spankers say that even if their data is sometimes unclear, there are dozens of studies that refute spanking and only a few that defend it.

Leading researcher Elizabeth Gershoff of the University of Texas echoed this. "I can just about count on one hand the studies that have found anything positive about physical punishment and hundreds that have been negative," she said.

This means parents should weigh and consider the evidence before rushing to the conclusion they should "spank because their parents spanked them" or because they "were spanked and turned out okay."

These phrases hold little water in the face of most of the evidence, and even though there is a minority of evidence that suggests "soft" spanking may help, most of the research literature rejects the practice as dangerous. If a person is saying they were hit and turned out okay as a justification for hitting their children, they likely did not turn out okay.

It is time to stop hitting children. The evidence is in.

Break the cycle.

Sovereign Minds Versus Mental Straitjackets

January 11, 2011

Drapetomania was a "mental illness" in 1851 proposed by Samuel Cartwright. It supposedly caused slaves to flee from captivity. How does this make us feel about the mental disorders proposed today?

August 28, 2013

It's sad when someone self-labels as suffering from mental illness because when they do this, they're ultimately condemning themselves to the behaviors that illness entails. It's like a self-fulfilling prophecy, and the social engineers love it.

December 3, 2013

What does "chemical imbalance" mean? Even if you could establish variations in neurotransmitters in people, what would the measuring stick for "normal" be? Would you judge a person by their behaviors? Use your magic Harry Potter wand to tell you? What?

Don't be duped into believing you are "mentally diseased" because you are different, because some "professional" says so, or because you have bad days. The evidence for chemical imbalances is scanty, and when you label yourself, you create a self-fulfilling prophecy the social controllers and engineers love because you lose your ability to think. You become numb and docile and obedient. This self-fulfilling prophecy makes you think you are damaged and useless, which makes you easier to manipulate and control.

February 26, 2014

If mental illness is a disease, why do ivory tower psychiatrists vote on which of these so-called diseases get put in or taken out of a book every few years? Do diseases sometimes not matter or fall out of fashion? What about the radical idea that you are not diseased and are actually a healthy and awesome and unique person? What if your behaviors just do not coincide with what modern brainless sheeple should look like?

Modern psychiatry is worse than charlatanism. It is outright fraudulent chicanery that is hurting people. Don't fall into their trap by believing the labels they give you. You are beautiful. So is your brain—without their chemical lobotomies.

February 28, 2014

I do not dismiss a person's internal suffering because I dismiss mental illness as a useful or valid concept. Instead, I recognize and understand people's suffering by providing them with the truth that they are not stricken with a permanent illness, that they are not a diseased outcast. The ones who do not care about them and think of them as degenerates are those who want to label them as witches and see to it that they are chemically lobotomized.

June 3, 2014

For the so-called mentally sick:

Mental illness is not a disease; you are not stricken with a sickness from which you will never recover —or recover from only if you are lucky. Mental illness as described by psychiatry is just an observation of behavior; it is not caused by insufficient chemicals in the brain or any other brain anomaly or genetic pattern. When you start to believe you are diseased, you start behaving in a way consistent with your label, making yourself feel worse and worse.

So, I bring you good news today: You simply have to work with your environment and your thinking, behavior, and habits. If you can break the mold of old destructive routines, you can start to overcome the problems that cause psychiatrists to label you as sick. I say this now because I believe you are well and healthy. I believe you are beautiful and that you have a gift. I do not think you are a social outcast or misfit or an ugly person. You just have to hone what has been given to you as a personality trait and make the best of it—or change it completely. Just don't allow yourself to fall into a pity pit where you feel entitled because of your "disease." Don't use the nonsense as a crutch and likewise make yourself feel like shit.

I love you enough to pass this message onto you and help you in any way I can. It's all about motivation. It's about teaching yourself to change. It's about finding the right support group. It's about doing your own research and fact-finding. You must realize that your brain is fine; it may even be better than fine—stronger than the rest of ours. But you must not be duped into believing you are toxic or a witch. Stay positive. Move forward. Succeed in anything.

July 5, 2014

The problem with claiming that depression is an illness or a disease is that it takes away from the personhood of the individual. The contents of the individual's mind are no longer important. According to this perspective, it's not a negative thought or feeling that is causing their discontent; it's their brain that is malfunctioning. It's their chemicals that are out of whack, but this can be corrected with drugs—no talking, no therapy necessary.

However, studies have shown that placebo studies have been at least as successful as antidepressants and drugs. It's also true that there's no litmus test for chemical imbalances, so why not just work with the individual? Why not help them see, grow, change, and come to understand themselves through talk therapy?

Sometimes people just need other people. Sometimes people just need to feel they're not alone in their suffering. When psychiatry denies and robotizes a person, they take away individual meaning and the possibility of understanding the deep reasons why people suffer. It's understandable that in medical science only the bodily lesion or injury is important, but when psychiatry takes this mode of thinking, the discipline ignores the most important factor of the person: their mind, thoughts, beliefs, desires, goals, fears, and traumas. If psychiatry wants to prevail and truly help people, it has to take a step back and reconsider its mission.

August 15, 2014

People have been so conditioned into accepting the idea that mental illness is a disease that they cannot decouple disease from sadness. They cannot understand how a person can be sad without being diseased. This goes to show that the everyday societal mindset is that if you have negative feelings or prolonged sadness, your brain is malfunctioning.

This does not bode well because it gives people the impression that they're damaged and irreparable. The reality is that there is little evidence suggesting sadness means the brain is damaged. It's natural for all of us to be sad and anxious at times.

These are evolutionarily derived emotions that help us survive. They're also utterly human emotions that expose the nature of what we are: beings who think and feel and sometimes come to fear our surroundings and our thoughts. These fears, however, are not unnatural. They are not based on brain damage. They are just a part of our humanness, part of what it means to live.

So, don't go on behaving as if you're permanently stunted or ill. Just try to live the best you can and overcome your feelings of sadness and seek help and guidance if you need it. You're beautiful and awesome and healthy. You don't have to live as if you're damaged goods, as if you need sedatives and "mood stabilizers" to live.

August 15, 2014

Thoughts about the sad and depressed among us:

A common theme in society is that people who suffer from "mental diseases" have chemical imbalances that manipulate their moods and make them feel sad, among other negative emotions. Doctors then claim these unbalanced chemicals can be corrected with drugs, thereby healing the sufferer.

However, there is no measuring stick—no test—to accurately gauge what levels of brain chemicals exist in people's brains at any given time, much less what levels constitute "normal." The only studies that currently exist from the chemical imbalance perspective are based on levels of neurotransmitter metabolites found in spinal fluid.

For example, serotonin has been shown as the primary brain chemical involved in mood, and several studies have been done on its metabolite, which is called 5-HIAA. However, none of the studies found a "statistically significant" difference in the metabolite between depressed persons and normal persons. This study was conducted in 1969 and was improved upon and repeated throughout the years with similar results (see Robert Whitaker's book *Anatomy of an Epidemic*).

Sadly, studies like these that contradict prevailing views on depression and bipolar disorder have been swept under the rug by governments and special interest groups. This lie-mongering keeps the myth alive that people are sick and need drugs to heal them, which ultimately allows governments to amass more control and power and pharmaceutical companies more growth and money.

This is a terrible, sickening tragedy because it keeps people locked into the belief that drugs are helping them and that they are truly diseased when the reality is that most of the drugs used to combat chemical imbalances have caused some of the behaviors they were created to defeat. This has simply worsened the feelings in people whose souls are already crippled and aching.

I believe people do suffer from terrible anguish and sadness and that sometimes it's necessary for people to seek help and guidance for it. But we all need to come together and be honest about what we are dealing with and start treating people like humans rather than machines with damaged brains that can be fixed with concoctions of poisons. This only destroys their spirit and will to live and paves the path toward self-annihilation.

People are beautiful in all of their many personalities and quirks, even those who feel like they should give up on life. But we should do what we can to love them completely and try to salvage them. We should care for them to the best of our ability without defrauding them or trying to control them with drugs or lying to them. We should be honest with them in all regards and let them know there is hope for change, and they are not permanently diseased or stricken with any tangible illness.

We should let all the truth be known to them.

September 22, 2014

More philosophical shenanigans during class because I can't keep my mouth shut. But that's probably due to the inherent doublethink embedded in the university and academic mentality.

We covered the Adlerian method of psychotherapy today, and one of the ideas behind this school of thought is that they shun diagnostic and pathological labels.

This prompted the question I asked the professor: "But based on our last class discussion, a diagnostic assessment of a mental health issue has to be made, correct?"

"Yes," he responded.

"But then how do Adlerians practice what they believe if they are forced to commit to a diagnostic and pathological label for their clients?" I retorted.

I was met from the class with dumbfounded hand-waving and grunt-like gesticulations.

Apparently, a pathological label is accepted for diagnoses, but it is simply not discussed during therapy, meaning the label is not applied to that person while they receive psychotherapy.

I argued that this was silly because the person is still labeled. You can't dance around this issue and pretend that the tenets of your own therapy are being adhered to because the person *does*, indeed, have a nice fancy mental health diagnosis behind them.

I was happy for a moment until I realized that the Adlerian school does not adhere to its own ideas due to clinical rules. In therapeutic practices, the practitioner is usually required to label the client with a diagnosis, especially for insurance purposes. In this sense, it is extremely difficult for a therapist to abide by their values. It means they have to practice without accepting most types of insurance, which also means they will only be catering to the wealthy.

Sucks.

October 10, 2014

Further thoughts on mental illness:

When the psychiatrist diagnoses mental illness, he does not use tests. He does not hook you up to a machine that reads your neurotransmitter balance or uncovers a problem with the brain. Mental illness is wholly diagnosed based on patient behavior. If that behavior fits the guidelines of psychiatry's holy bible, the *DSM*, then you'll likely be diagnosed with that illness.

This simply means you're not acting right according to the professionals in ivory tower psychiatric circles. It does not mean you have a physical disease. It means dick-all for your overall physical and psychological functioning.

The only evidence for mental illness is a cluster of behaviors and symptoms based on genetic and environmental factors. They do not stick out as an absolute problem that can be viewed under a microscope or pinpointed to one location in the brain or body. The diagnosis is simply made up and voted on by the less-than-scientific process of looking at vague aspects of body, mind, and behavior. If you suffered from a mental illness before death, an autopsy would not show any signs that you had a mental disease in life. If you asked a psychiatrist to prove to you that you were diseased, he would simply point out your disease classification in his holy manual (which would be based on behavior and a vague or ill-defined set of symptoms). He could not rigorously and objectively identify it.

Just remember that mental illness is defined around what people *do* and *feel* rather than what people *have*. People have cancer. People have AIDS. People do not have depression. They become depressed; they feel sad. But suggesting that they *have* something gives a medical air of disease permanence, and that is just not the case.

But does that imply people are lying about their sickness?

It could be, but probably not. Malingering, or faking illness, is tragically common, but everyone still suffers from the problems of everyday living. Indeed, people become depressed and have ups and downs and highs and lows. But this does not mean that one is irrevocably sick from something permanent in the body or brain. It just means that one might need therapy or guidance on what to do next in life. It means one is struggling, but there is nothing in the brain that can be cured in a medical sense. Sometimes people just need assistance and another person to listen to them and be there for them. Life is harrowing. It's a given that problems of the spirit will manifest as behavioral and mental disturbances.

So this is my ultimate goal: to carve out a space in psychotherapy and psychiatric circles for practitioners who want to work from a non-disease model of counseling and psychiatry that places the patient or client as number one, much like Carl Rogers did with his person-centered therapy—except I'd also like to disregard modern psychiatry since it is a haven for quacks and charlatans. It's time for the social control emphasis of psychiatry to finally come to an end so the needs and personhood of the client can be placed above finding "problems" and "diseases." What this really means is that laws hovering around the assessments and diagnoses need to be completely abolished. The whole notion of the "therapeutic State," which rests on collusion between psychiatry and the State, must be dismantled so counseling can be practiced with complete autonomy.

February 16, 2015

So, the idea that mental health struggles amount to disease is scientific? Schizophrenia—the holy grail of psychiatry—is a "real" disease/disorder, right?

Okay. I offer a challenge.

What are the falsification criteria for schizophrenia? In other words, what evidence or proof could falsify its existence?

This simple inquiry destroys the whole foundation for mental illness as a brain disease because if someone falsified the brain evidence (for which very little exists, anyway), they would simply point to genetics, invoke a nonexistent virus, or fabricate some other cause, maybe witchcraft.

Indeed, there is no way to falsify mental illness because "mental illness" is nothing but an observation of personality and behaviors that society deems unacceptable or wrong. The majority of psychiatry is built upon the foundation of cultural bias. This problem of psychiatry is also why the *DSM* has been revised and altered and why some diseases have been "removed" while others have been "added."

Recently, the *DSM-5* added hoarding as a brain "disorder," and a few years back it added "Oppositional Defiant Disorder." Notice that homosexuality and sexual addiction were variations of disorders that have been removed from the psychiatric bible.

This adds another question: If you can remove a "disease" or "disorder," was the "problem" ever a disease or disorder to begin with? Was the "problem" just a behavioral trait that changed with the times, shifting from socially unacceptable to socially acceptable?

Psychiatry is a joke if it contends that any behaviors are diseases or disorders. Looking at people under the light of the psychiatric medical model, which is not medical at all, only hurts clients and makes people distrustful of the field.

I do not deny that people suffer and have problems with everyday living. However, using pseudoscience to make cattle out of people and legitimize chemical lobotomies and other forms of "treatment" is a stain on human decency and dignity that will never easily be wiped away.

April 10, 2015

People often simplify the "nature versus nurture" argument to mean it is *either* nature or nurture that determines personality, attachment styles, suicide risk, etc. Rather, nature and nurture interact and blend in complex ways to determine the structure of personality.

Say an individual attempts suicide. What was it that drove him to do it? Was it his nature or the way he was nurtured? The answer is both. For instance, if the individual was spanked as a child, it is likely the spanking caused physical alterations in his brain and reduced gray matter. Physical punishment would have likewise caused the child to resent his parents and be more prone to avoiding and distrusting them, leading to an avoidant attachment style (nurture), thus affecting his interactions in and perceptions of future relationships. This would also trigger changes in his neural networks, and his brain would rewire itself based on his environments and experiences.

Thus, the association between the individual's environment, emotions, and brain all led to the feelings of self-disgust and learned helplessness that culminated in the suicide attempt. Now, bear in mind that I am not trying to label the individual as pathological but to paint a picture of how nature and nurture interact to cause problems of everyday living and persistent trauma states. I feel like neurology and psychology have done a poor job connecting all the dots, but then again, neuropsychology is in its infancy. This is an exciting new realm that may help explain certain behavior in novel ways.

November 28, 2015

This is the trend I am seeing on my page: "I don't trust government, but I trust psychiatry."

Everyone has to remember that statism plays a huge role in educating psychiatrists, propping up Big Pharma, approving so-called psychiatric cures, making people sick and docile with these "cures," and allowing psychiatrists to lock people up in institutions without due process.

This is a monstrous beast that relies directly on State approval to hurt people across the board. It is an issue that deserves honesty and attention from anarchists because psychiatry is helping to numb and incapacitate the population.

How are people going to contribute to a movement for liberty if they have become so medicated, entitled, and psychotic that they can't function coherently enough to care?

February 18, 2016

If one thing needs to change in psychiatry and some branches of psychology, it is the use of medical metaphors to describe problems of living, psychache, and existential woes. But tragically, some areas of the helping professions have adopted the mechanistic and reductionist model of the world, which suggests that all human problems must be biological in origin and are thus diseases or illnesses.

Humans are natural organisms, but by virtue of its observations, this model eliminates the relational, the humanistic, the deeply emotional, and the poetic. The psychiatric model takes the life out of living. It views people not as humans with problems to solve and pent-up anger to unleash but as robots with broken circuitry and faulty wiring to repair.

This position is summed up like this: "Behind every twisted thought there lies a twisted molecule." And this idea has been devastating. It has caused massive undue harm with the belief that drug cocktails can cure people of their depression and anxiety and that people's relationships and lifestyles do not factor into their psychological wholeness and happiness.

Neurology and genetics do play into the wiring of the human brain, but modern psychiatry has nearly abandoned the idea that nurture and nature dance together to fully develop our humanness. These pseudo-doctors forget that nurture, thinking, and environment also inform genetic expression, neural wiring, and the transmission of biochemicals—and ultimately, they create consciousness, emotionality, and personhood.

March 21, 2016

Psychiatry is another apparatus of the State, except psychiatric clerics do not respect due process. They feed toxic pills to their wards, and they employ electroconvulsive therapy as they see fit. Psychiatry is the modern church. It conducts witch hunts on those who are neurodivergent, rebellious, or think and feel outside the scope of cultural norms. The institution of psychiatry pretends to dictate what constitutes normal levels of stress and abnormal forms of functioning. Psychiatry is an infection that whittles society down one pill at a time, creating an unthinking army of catatonic people who shrug off State drudgery and servitude as business as usual. Psychiatry must be abolished.

March 28, 2016

It is no surprise that antidepressants and antipsychotics don't work over the long term. Besides the fact that the brain compensates for the effects of these drugs and creates more problems with neurotransmission, these drugs do not solve the underlying psychological problems that alter brain function and structure. It is not a "brain disorder" that causes psychological disturbances, it is psychological disturbances that cause "brain disorder." Currently, modern psychiatry has not been able to admit how much behavior and thinking contribute to what they refer to as "mental illness." They believe the brain is broken from the start or that genetics ultimately led to the problem. But this theory represents a gross misunderstanding of the mind-body relationship.

June 6, 2016

What is a "normal" functioning person in terms of mental health? What measures baseline normalcy?

Here is the rub.

There can be no such thing as normal since any behavior can be characterized as normal or abnormal depending on the circumstance, biases of observers, and meaning of "normal."

Normalcy is a myth dreamt up by psychiatric engineers to claim some people are mentally unwell or diseased.

In truth, most of the ways people react to distress and shitty cultural circumstances can be considered perfectly "normal." There is nothing "abnormal" about human evolutionary reactions to problematic life circumstances, rampant statism, or servitude.

July 17, 2016

In our society, where children are treated despicably daily, where government escalates violence, where relationships suffer, and where social alienation peaks, it is no wonder psychiatry's influence has grown.

When "civilization" erodes, institutions that feed off its carcass arise. Psychiatry is the fallout of statism. It makes sense that it has profited from the vast hordes of walking dead—and that the antidepressant and antipsychotic markets are a multibillion-dollar industry. People rely on their regular chemical lobotomies to cope with the agony of being alive.

I just hope they can finally acknowledge the core of their suffering, realize the truth of this violent environment, and discover a modicum of peace.

Though some may be skeptical of this, love and solace arise from gaining knowledge and discovering truth and compassion.

September 16, 2016

Schizophrenia is a pseudo-medical invention used for scapegoating the downtrodden, different, and impoverished people in society. The creation of these "mental illnesses" has provided outlets for sadists and other individuals who likely qualify as more "mentally ill" than the people they allege to help.

As an aside, I am not saying people do not suffer from problems of living or the traumatic exigencies of life. Nor am I discounting people's experiences of hearing voices or seeing things. I realize that people suffer in a variety of ways, but I think they have been harmed more by psychiatry than they have been helped.

This is why I think we need a complete revolution in how we think about the people who experience different states of mind or who perceive the world differently. Just because their experiences fall outside the norm does not mean they are sick or that their brain is broken.

They are simply unique. They may experience distress from their lives and mental states, but how we help them should not involve half-baked medical treatments and pharmacological agents that make their experiences worse or affect their brain functioning.

It is time to start seeing different people as people and not as subhuman beings who constantly need to be chemically lobotomized, discriminated against, fed poisons, locked in institutions, or otherwise harmed by the medical and State establishments.

Psychiatry is an embarrassing pockmark on the face of humankind.

September 19, 2016

Psychiatric, biological-based "therapies" have always been erroneously touted as cures and important "medical advances."

Here are a few:

Insulin coma therapies, electroshock therapy, frontal lobotomies, hydrotherapy (includes drowning a person), and nowadays, chemical therapies that deaden and zombify people.

We can see that psychiatry has barely progressed over the years. It has moved from deeply inhumane therapies to other, slightly less atrocious inhumane therapies.

In this light, psychiatry has always amounted to thinly veiled social control. It has not been meant to help anyone deal with their psychological problems. It has been used to quieten, subdue, and harm those who are different or strange within society.

Ever consider psychiatric "remedies" in a cultural context?

It's eye-opening.

December 28, 2016

Psychiatry is worse than pseudoscience. It is pseudo-medicine. It is not even snake oil. Most of its "remedies" are either toxic, non-efficacious, or tranquilizing.

The people it allegedly helps aren't being truly "helped." They are being emotionally subdued and chemically sedated. At best, these psychiatric compounds are palliative. At worst, they are dangerous.

I trust the shaman to provide me with better "medicine for the soul" than I trust Western psychiatry. The shamans seem to have a better understanding of mind and behavior problems than the PhD psychiatrist.

Then again, the shaman will not claim he is the doctor or the healer per se.

He will simply point to a couple of plants and explain how to take them.

He may sing some songs and guide the experience, but in the end, the magic of the plant and the client do all the work.

February 11, 2017

Psychiatry is an adverse side effect of statism. When people become institutionalized and coerced under a government, psychological suffering occurs. This is akin to the caged animal metaphor. Caged animals act out rabidly, especially if they are higher-functioning animals, such as great apes. The problem, however, is that psychiatry manifests not as a cure or remedy but as another layer of control meant to subdue and control people. Psychiatry is a side effect or fallout because a proper cure cannot be created or managed by the same systems that cause the initial harm. It's a tragic situation.

April 5, 2017

Psychiatry is the medicalization of morality. It is upheld by cultural statism.

April 5, 2017

Thomas Szasz was the great psychiatrist who wrote the classic *The Myth of Mental Illness*. Many of Szasz's opponents believe modern medicine has invalidated his arguments. They claim technology has laid bare the biological foundations of mental illness.

But the people who make these claims are ignorant of Szasz's arguments. Szasz claimed his position would be vindicated if mental illnesses were discovered via biological instruments.

He said this because "mental illness" would then be put under the domain of medical science and not psychiatry. If mental illnesses were a "brain disease"— i.e., they actually existed—they would not be considered "mental illnesses." Szasz was praying that some mental illnesses would be found to be brain diseases so that psychiatry would be rendered obsolete (save for consensual counseling).

The problem with psychiatry is not only that it attempts to persuade people that its diseases are real, but also that it is loaded with linguistic charlatanism. It uses language to disguise its nature. Psychiatrists talk as if abstractions like "mental illness" have a basis in biological functioning when really, they are just syntactic descriptors of human behavior and thinking processes some people dislike.

What makes matters worse and further vindicates Szasz is that modern technology has *not* uncovered the precise mechanism of "mental disorder" or "mental illness." Almost every known mental illness is labeled as having an "unknown cause." Therefore, psychiatry continues onward with unconfirmed claims of mental health as being embedded in the brain as disease processes.

Mental disorder as brain malfunction should never be considered a foregone conclusion. The consequences of doing this already weigh heavily on society, and we will continue counting bodies and mopping up blood so long as this nonsense continues. Too many people are called diseased and left for dead when they are beautiful souls in need of love and human connection.

Cognitive Liberty and the Question of Drugs

August 26, 2013

Meth is illegal and horrible, and it causes undesirable behavior.

However, we must feed it to unruly and disobedient children. We can just call it ADD (Attention Deficit Disorder) medication and have a psychiatrist prescribe it, and everything is fine.

August 18, 2014

Have you ever been so caffeinated that your eyes start to bug out of your head and you begin experiencing synesthesia? That's me right now. It's at this point that I remember that coffee used to be banned in many parts of the world and that during the reign of the Ottoman empire, one could be beheaded for drinking coffee in public. Once upon a time, coffee houses were associated with political dissent and outright rebellion. So what's the moral of this story? Coffee fucks you up and makes you want to revolt. It's bad kids, very bad. Use it at your own risk.

November 16, 2014

People with "drug abuse" problems aren't hopeless and depraved. They're just people who have made choices to help them cope with reality. They only need guidance and a plan to cope better in ways that are not detrimental to their health and well-being. However, since people who "abuse drugs" aren't hurting anyone but themselves, criminalizing their bad habits isn't helping—and it isn't justice. It's giving up. It's labeling drug users as witches. It's violating their right to choose. It's saying that something is fundamentally, morally wrong with them.

The truth is they're just people like everyone else—except they've chosen habits that are considered taboo and dangerous. But sadly, most people who level these condemning criticisms at "drug abusers" know jack shit about drug culture and drug use. If they had any experience with how this world functions and what types of individuals populate it, there would be a change of tune. Right now, most people are just deluded about drug life, so they examine it from a tainted and culturally indoctrinated perspective with no personal experience or logic to rely on. They simply scream "Hang 'em all" as their misguided anthem of hate.

November 17, 2014

I just read a journal article that claimed ADD is a "neurological disorder." But what they mean in plain English is that the children aren't obeying authority. There's nothing wrong "neurologically." And what is a "disorder," anyway? All this fancy language is used to conceal the reality that there's nothing medically or physically wrong. These children are just refusing to follow the boring and brain-shrinking curriculums that "public education" provides.

What's worse is the popular solution for this misbehavior is a strong dose of speed.

But I thought speed was a horrible and evil drug in society? It must be bad for adults but good for misbehaving boys.

March 19, 2015

The war on drugs is a huge success.

The government and special interest groups reap great profits from continuing to wage their war against drugs and drug users. Limiting the supply of psychedelics and other mind-expanding drugs has allowed pharmaceutical companies to profit by soliciting their tranquilizers and mind-numbing agents. The government reaps its dividends by participating in the solicitation of "illegal" drugs on the black market and extorting money from those unfortunate enough to be caught with banned substances. Thus, in the eyes of the elite, the war on drugs has been super successful and vitally important.

In truth, from the people's perspective, the drug war has utterly failed. It is a war on innocent people. It has cost taxpayers billions of dollars, but that is not the real cost. Many people have been caught in the crossfire between mobs and police forces, including women and children, and their body count rises every day. Between botched police raids, adulterated drugs, and thousands of innocent people locked in cages, the number of families ruined and destroyed has multiplied beyond sanity.

Yet every day, drug warriors continue to spew their nonsensical propaganda at the expense of innocents everywhere. Is this what you intended for the result of the drug war? Is the death and destruction of good people what you wanted? Are you still buying into the poisonous lies and vicious talking points?

It is time to reassess this situation and get government out of people's lives. As usual, their interference is causing more harm than good.

April 12, 2015

I do not advocate current pharmaceutical drugs to help people overcome substance abuse (and most counselors and psychologists won't, either) because they compound psychological problems. Most drugs are shit when it comes to helping people deal with their issues, drug abuse or not.

Psychiatric drugs are laden with iatrogenic effects (unintentional harmful side effects caused by medical intervention), and they are dangerous. But more importantly, they do not help people cope with internal problems. They do not allow anyone to process thoughts and feelings.

A lot of these drugs—especially in the benzodiazepine class—are meant to tranquilize people, not promote health. Here is the paradox: Certain psychedelic drugs are potentially beneficial to drug and alcohol abusers. According to research, these plant-based compounds bring about states of mind that allow for introspection regarding a person's *reasons* for their need to self-medicate with booze or other chemicals. These plant-based medicines attack the center of the psychological problem rather than just numbing the brain or slowly causing neurological changes.

Tragically, most American universities do not discuss psychedelics because of the rampant paranoia and stigma against drugs that do not already enjoy medical recognition from the State. However, in both New Zealand and Mexico, there are studies underway regarding the effect of ibogaine (an African ritualistic psychedelic plant), which may reduce a person's craving for alcohol and opioids. New Zealand has, indeed, legalized ibogaine for medicinal purposes.

The political insanity and drug schizophrenia in America have caused counseling psychology to lag. They have created an environment where troubled people cannot receive the best possible help for their problems. The medicinal and palliative effects of cannabis for cancer are longstanding examples of this issue and show how infantile and fearful people get when it comes to drugs that are not already sanctioned by daddy government.

I believe we'd all be better off if the State just went away. Practitioners and researchers could work on solutions without interference from bureaucrats who do not know better and who allow the continued suffering of millions because of their unequaled desire for power.

I encourage everyone to check out current ibogaine studies on alcohol abuse. This information needs to be spread and discussed regularly by all the sane people among us.

May 15, 2015

There is a ghastly idea floating around that addiction is a disease.

Having a bad habit is not a disease. A certain pattern of behaviors does not fit the medical model for disease classification. People can only refer to addiction as a "disease" metaphorically, meaning it is a "disease" when society shuns that behavior, or it is not benefiting the person.

However, a complicated aspect of brain activity accompanies addiction and might lead one to think it is a disease.

When people become hooked on substances, many changes occur in the brain, including overactivity of the reward and pleasure centers and a rewiring of neurocircuitry. But this does not mean the brain is broken. It only means the brain has adapted to certain behaviors and the environment. In other words, brain alterations are a natural response to a person's choices and proclivities.

Yes, the person chose to become "addicted," and their brain followed suit. But the person can rewire themselves by making different choices and changing their environment. This is, of course, easier to say than do, but it explains why people can escape addiction and change their lives for the better.

Free will and choice are the emergent properties of higher cortical activities in humans, and they explain the vast array of behaviors that humans display. They also explain why genetics is not destiny. Thus, even a person with a predisposition toward drinking or drugs can think and "behave" themselves out of their biological cages. This is the feedback loop that demonstrates how thinking and behaving can work to one's benefit or detriment.

People must choose wisely. They are in more control of their brains than they think. Tragically, society has taught everyone that they are victims of their neurology. This stance is inaccurate, dangerous, and causes more harm than good. People must start to believe in themselves...and in their brains.

May 16, 2015

Drug use is a paradoxical problem in society; most "normal" people love their drugs, but only if they are socially acceptable and given in the form of a prescription or purchased legally from the counter of a pharmacy or liquor store.

In contrast, there is a whole movement of counterculture hipsters, cancer patients, and neo-shamans who experiment regularly with psychedelics and designer drugs to reach higher states of consciousness, alleviate their medical symptoms, or just escape the mundane.

Many "socially acceptable" drugs are used for some of the same reasons—primarily to heal symptoms of pain and escape—but some are "abused" for the sole purpose of feeling good, which is the next best thing to experiencing states of "quantum consciousness," or reaching God.

Society has got to get to the point where this drug hypocrisy and insanity is annihilated, and it is understood that even "normal," law-abiding citizens like to feel good, experience altered states of mind, and self-medicate. This rampant drug schizophrenia has got to end. It is hurting good people and scaring scientists away from studying potentially beneficial compounds and plants.

Drug use is a personal choice, and just because a doctor or politician says it is okay to use a certain chemical does not automatically mean the rest are bad or useless. It is an ugly bit of hypocrisy to claim some drugs are safer and better, while other drugs are wicked and harmful. Ironically, many "legal" drugs are much worse.

If an individual enjoys their sanctioned drugs, why can't other people enjoy their drugs equally?

The ability to experiment with drugs is one of the main principles of freedom and dignity, and to dispose of this freedom is to create a violent and hostile society.

Everyone must dispel their delusions and hysteria about drug culture because drug culture is a rich part of every domain of human life and society, and it always will be regardless of how many people are caged, beaten, and murdered over social dissonance and dogma.

Think about the children.

Undoubtedly, they will want drugs of some kind when they come of age. Should they be shot or put in a cage for making a personal choice? Or should they be educated about the benefits or harmfulness of a given chemical without a looming threat of violence against them?

May 30, 2015

I am livid about what happened to Ross Ulbricht. That guy deserved a Nobel prize, not life in a cage. To add insult to injury, all the bootlickers and government worshipers are blabbering about how he deserved it, that he was an accused murderer.

For starters, the court never indicted Ulbricht for murder nor was proof presented showing that his alleged hits were carried out. What he did was innovate. He created the safest way for people to avoid dealing with a criminal government via an anonymous server with quasi-anonymous methods of purchasing goods.

He showed the world that free trade is possible. He showed the world that people can trade in drugs safely without having to incite gang turf wars. In other words, Ulbricht was a genius entrepreneur. He effectively paved the way forward for humanity. If I were to provide historical examples, I would say that what happened to Giordano Bruno and Socrates loosely matches what happened to Ulbricht.

History will not look back kindly on governments, and Ulbricht will be a martyr for progress like so many others. When will humans stop being so culturally brainwashed and susceptible to dogmas that cause the suffering and deaths of so many? This world is truly batshit crazy. Sometimes it shames me to be part of it.

June 14, 2015

Psychedelics are more useful than argumentation for convincing people of anarchism. When people have their boundaries dissolved and realize they have very little control, they are more likely to understand that trying to control others is fruitless and dangerous. It is just a matter of teaching people that these psychospiritual agents are not evil or depraved. Matter of fact, they may have contributed to the developing compass of our humanity. They may have even had something to do with helping internalize the feeling we call "love."

September 15, 2015

A recent story was floating around claiming a girl in the UK took MDMA at a party and ended up bound to a wheelchair, stricken with brain damage, and drooling on herself. Of course, most websites covering the story are spinning it as a cautionary tale against the ravages and evils of drugs like ecstasy.

Let me tell you: I have seen people on MDMA, and I know the pharmacology of the compound. One pill, or roughly a 125-milligram dose of ecstasy, is not going to give anyone brain damage. That is called propaganda.

Now, it is true that the pill could have been something else entirely, like a poison, but if that is the case, the last thing anyone needs are drug laws that create situations like this. How can anyone expect their drug to be good and pure if they are relying on black market manufacturers and sources?

This is the problem of government enforcement through the vicious war on drugs. It is what puts teenagers into wheelchairs with brain damage—not drugs. Don't fall for the government's idiotic and senseless policies. Ecstasy has the potential to wake you up and make you smarter, not turn you into a braindead, drooling zombie. However, we should still be smart about what we put in our bodies. Research and care are of the utmost importance.

September 18, 2015

Life is a drug-induced experience. Our consciousness is held together by electrochemical signals in the brain, which also transport the drugs of subjectivity. These endogenous chemicals help regulate our experience of life because they control the speed of impulses in the brain. They also regulate other drug-like compounds in the body, which control everything from sexual arousal to the circadian rhythm. For instance, serotonin, a ubiquitous neurotransmitter in the brain, has implications in mood, hunger, and sleep-wake modulation.

Governments ban drugs, but they are really banning elements of our own neural makeup. When the government says psilocybin (magic mushroom's psychoactive chemical) is wrong and bad, what they are claiming is serotonin is also wrong and bad because psilocybin is nearly identical to naturally existing serotonin. In their mind, both internally and externally induced control of consciousness is illegal.

The war on drugs, then, is essentially a war on our consciousness, a war on the sovereignty of neurochemistry. The government is attempting to claim kingship over nature, over the molecular makeup of humans. This is insane and impossible. If we took the government's anti-drug mentality to its logical conclusion, consciousness and subjectivity of the individual would be banned because serotonin helps activate one of the most amazing and precious experiences: life.

Governments have banned DMT, too.

This is the direst grievance against life—and reflects a deep irony. DMT is another compound closely related to serotonin—mere atoms worth of difference—but DMT is also naturally occurring in most plant and animal life. It has been speculated that it occurs in humans, as well. If this is the case, governments have banned chemicals that currently exist in the body, making life illegal at all times. These laws go against nature in every way and make little sense. How insane does a species have to be when it claims its own nature and consciousness are immoral and illegal? It is essentially setting the precedent for self-hate, self-flagellation, and suicidality. It is suggesting that humans should hate themselves since they are naturally evil based on the dictums of chemistry and evolution.

September 29, 2015

Beware: rant of the evening...

I opened my substance abuse book to the chapter on psychedelics. Right out of the door, the second sentence exposed the ignorance of the authors. They implied that hallucinogens are like all addictive compounds by referring to them as "drugs of abuse." Wrong. Wrong. And wrong.

I would like to see somebody "abuse" psilocybin mushrooms or DMT. I don't even believe LSD can be abused. If anything, these compounds can negate patterns of addiction in people who have habituated themselves to actual horrible drugs.

The psychedelics, ironically, wake people up from believing in the nonsense spouted about drugs. The plant chemicals are antithetical to everything bad and abusive. They are pro-empathy, pro-life, and pro-consciousness. It is obvious that cultural biases regarding illegal drugs are shining through, and the authors have not the faintest clue what these chemicals can do.

One of my biggest problems with Western culture is that subjective experience is brushed aside for sterile (yet icky) rationalizations regarding certain classes of compounds. Even many professional researchers refuse to address the healing potential and anti-addictive properties of psychedelics. They also smugly dismiss these emotional experiences as unimportant in comparison to the physiological aspects.

Their demeanor illustrates finely why people feel so alienated and out of touch in society. The only thing that matters to some of these "researchers" is the number of heart beats per minute and the amount of sweat that accumulates on the skin. Are you kidding me? The fact that a person's whole mind is turned inside out and that they shake hands with oblivion is irrelevant to them. These researchers and their preoccupation with the inane and trivial blows my mind. "Drugs of abuse." Don't make me laugh. You have no clue what you are dealing with or talking about. I am at least glad that more intelligent and sensitive people are picking up studying these compounds to better understand their beneficial and mind-expanding properties.

January 12, 2016

Psychedelics are a useful way to augment perception and creativity. If a person takes psilocybin mushrooms or LSD at higher doses and with focused intent, they can hone their creative talents. These compounds allow people to tap into purely artistic areas of consciousness and drown out editorial and critical voices. The plant hallucinogens inspire people to tap into new abilities, but they also allow people to gain insights into their personalities.

These compounds are not "dangerous drugs." They are tools. They are medicines. They are aids in healing the world's weary souls and eradicating the mundane and trivial. It is through these enlightened perceptual channels that individuals can develop any aptitude or endeavor imaginable. Don't buy into bullshit and fearmongering about psychedelics. These compounds are nature's equivalent of a godsend. They are the flesh of the gods. Spiritual honey. Ambrosia.

However, one must have ample courage and mental fortitude to brave the bizarre worlds they unveil. Never underestimate their utter strangeness and capacity to dissolve cultural mechanisms and rend business as usual. That is all part of the game these chemicals play. But it is worth it for the sake of becoming a better, more well-rounded, and innovative person.

January 14, 2016

I have one major pet peeve. I usually just gripe to myself about this issue because I cannot control it. But I have to articulate it now: it drives me up the wall when people get online and attempt to discuss a subject they know nothing about, especially regarding drugs.

For instance, I cringe when the uneducated and uninitiated attempt to discuss psychedelic mushrooms. Sadly, the first couple of sentences they type contain anecdotal stories about how these are dangerous drugs, and they have "friends" who were permanently damaged from using them. Then, after I correct them, these plebeians continue to spin urban myths about the aforesaid compounds without really knowing the pharmacology or pharmacodynamics involved. What motivates people to recite nonsense and propaganda? Why not just admit ignorance?

I suppose it is a mixture of fear and the erroneous belief that "psychedelics" are what caused their friend or whoever to go crazy even if their friend was crazy to begin with.

It is true that these compounds can precipitate latent psychological problems, but it is certainly not characteristic of the compound to cause them. It is rare. The research suggests the opposite. Psilocybin mushrooms may spur neuroplasticity and positive cross-hemispheric communication in the brain. This means mushrooms may intensify creativity, heighten elements of intelligence, and augment personality. Psychedelic mushrooms have a track record of hundreds of thousands of years. Humans have used them since time immemorial, and they are not associated with psychosis or brain damage. They never have been. They are incredibly safe.

Further, even if these naysayers want to accuse LSD of being a "dangerous drug," the evidence that it causes brain damage or permanent psychosis is also glaringly absent from the literature. The only place people will find these stories is within propaganda articles and exaggerated government-funded "studies."

Here is a quote from a *Wondergressive* article covering LSD:

> "Psychedelics of all types have been studied and found almost across the board to be incredibly safe and highly effective tools in psychotherapy. Despite this clearly illustrated fact, psychedelics continue to be irrationally feared and demonized in the same ignorant fashion as cannabis. Interested in LSD? Let's go for a trip."

Indeed. Go for a trip and stop making up nonsense about hallucinogens without the proper knowledge and understanding.

February 11, 2016

Being numb to life is not the same as being emotionally healthy, and psychiatry would rather numb people than heal them. A lot of the pills psychiatrists prescribe for anxiety, bipolar disorder, and schizophrenia merely work to stunt emotional responses and disorient thinking. People only feel better because their thinking and feeling have been chemically subdued. Psychiatry is the profession of locking people inside themselves without physically putting them in a cage; it is the institution that works to make the sane go insane through tranquilizers or poisons posing as remedies.

For people to genuinely feel better and live in good psychological health, they have to learn to cope with their struggles without taking psychiatric snake oil. There is not an SSRI or benzo that can solve relationship problems, make life easier, or provide existential hope.

There are hallucinatory plant teachers that may aid this process, but nothing psychiatry offers will enliven and heal the individual. The consequences of psychiatric work are now obvious: It has turned people into the walking dead. Don't fall for its chicanery. Look elsewhere to deal with mental and emotional difficulties. Personal exploration, spirituality, and individual counseling are all options to help people cope with the exigencies of life.

February 25, 2016

Psychiatrists can legally give people chemical lobotomies with tranquilizers and psychosis-inducing drugs.

However, it is largely illegal for them to prescribe drugs like MDMA and psilocybin, which can allow people to deeply introspect and understand their emotional selves. (Not that they would want people to be "healed" after one or two uses, anyway.)

To me, this cultural drug schizophrenia shows where people's priorities lie: in being comatose, numb, and stupefied to the sheer grandeur and phantasmagorical nature of life.

It is a tragedy.

March 13, 2016

The beautiful thing about psychedelic drugs is that they put you into a state of consciousness that is intrinsically at odds with consensus culture. Therefore, they are inherently anti-authoritarian and anti-subservience. Once you augment your consciousness away from the asinine world of day-walking delirium and business as usual, you can never return. The monotony and monotone feeling of the servile life is forever exposed as unbearable and unacceptable. It is in this frame of mind that you may finally realize the full value of your humanity.

April 8, 2016

You know why "hard" drugs like LSD, mushrooms, and MDMA are banned, right?

What if I told you it is not because they are bad for you? They are banned because they cause inner awakening. They instill a sense of freedom and incite you to rebel against the State apparatus, and the politicians cannot have that. They hate freethinkers and free-feelers. They hate people who are liberated from the cycle of statist dogma and abuse.

This is the key.

It is the reason why LSD was banned in the 1960s. The drug was a threat to business as usual. It aroused the control freak nature of the bureaucrats. Thus, they started suppressing the population. Too many people were waking up, protesting, and condemning government. People suddenly knew the truth. They realized they were slaves. LSD allowed them to awaken from the matrix of illusion.

Hallucinogens cause people to think and exist outside the box. Psychedelic experiences show them how controlled and coerced their lives are and make them want to live more creatively and without restraint. Politicians are opposed to this and thus continue spewing rampant anti-drug propaganda. This keeps people asleep and numb, but don't fall for the disinformation.

Realize the facts. Research the drugs yourself. Look into the history. Talk to the plant.

May 22, 2016

Psychedelics are plant or chemical teachers that restore balance to our psyches. They provide us with the ability to see things from different angles, uncover hidden truths, understand our emotions, and connect with other beings.

These chemicals foster psychological growth and put a strain on violent and coercive influences that live inside of us. That is why they have been called entheogens and why they harbor the ability to summon the divine within. It is why they can help heal our wounded and tormented souls.

In modern government-controlled industrial societies, then, it is no surprise that these compounds are feared, dismissed, hated, and banned. Anything that softens the ego and dissolves boundaries has the capacity to turn people on to various truths about their living conditions and oppression.

July 18, 2016

This is the poppycock that chemical dependency graduate-level college courses are peddling:

Remember the alcoholic or addict is sick. He/she has the disease of chemical dependency. When they lie to us, it is their disease talking. Do not take it personally. As we will discuss later in this book, an individual with chemical dependency is not himself/herself. They often have a changed personality and an altered value system. The only way for the user to get better is to abstain from all alcohol and drugs.

I won't go into details on my views because I am writing an article on this topic. However, I will provide a few thoughts.

The way this is worded conveys to me a sentiment of pretentious moralizing, which biases people's views toward those who use drugs and their ability to stop using. It lowers them to "patient" or "sinner" while elevating the caretaker to "doctor" or "priest." The wording within the disease model context removes the human relations aspect of care and healing and makes the matter one of authority and paternalistic browbeating.

This disease model idea of substance abuse also only works to create self-fulfilling prophecies for people who choose to use drugs, which perpetuates the cycle of use and makes it seem like the problem is drugs or alcohol alone.

It pretends there were not precipitating events that led to the use and neglects the idea that they may just enjoy getting hammered. It denies self-responsibility and independent choice, which likewise denies humanity. It also stifles the development of a real relationship between client and therapist because the game is rigged by a moralistic power imbalance.

I won't even get into debunking the spurious claims about how alcoholism or drug use constitute "disease." The term is not even used appropriately.

September 7, 2016

Want to stop your suicidal thoughts and depression?

Here, take this antidepressant!

Suicidal thoughts and depression intensify.

This is true. Research has suggested that long-term antidepressant use can cause suicidal tendencies and more depression. This is referred to as tardive dysphoria.

These compounds could help some people in the short term, but is the risk of addiction by psychiatric proxy worth the consequences? Are worse depression and more suicidal thoughts good things?

There are much better ways to deal with depression than ingesting psychiatric toxins.

September 21, 2016

Think about this:

Lithium is prescribed to treat bipolar disorder. Its therapeutic window, or dosage required to gain a "therapeutic effect," is very narrow. In other words, the regular dosage is close to the lethal or toxic dosage. Yet for people who are diagnosed with "bipolar disorder," it has been doled out like candy.

The shit is so toxic that the patients who are on the medication have to have their blood levels screened regularly to prevent them from accidentally overdosing.

While understanding this, realize that nontoxic and harmless drugs like cannabis or psychedelic mushrooms have been demonized and made illegal for a long time.

But it is perfectly legal for psychiatrists and physicians to prescribe literal poisons for people daily.

The hypocrisy and insanity of this world never cease to shock and amaze me.

October 3, 2016

The drug war is a pseudo-moral crusade without any end in sight that creates a multitude of casualties.

The policemen and politicians involved in the drug war rarely consider the consequences of their actions, but they continue to wage their war with blind audacity.

Sadly, their self-righteousness and vigor for eliminating drugs and drug users have caused a mound of corpses to pile high.

If they only stopped for a few minutes of introspection, they would realize the drug war cannot be won and that they are directly responsible for creating these battlefields and perpetuating unfathomable harm and destruction.

It's an irony of staggering awe.

Indeed, whenever one attempts to use authoritarian clout to thwart people from using drugs or altering their conscious awareness, there will be a natural backlash against those who issue the anti-drug dictates.

It was the creation and maintenance of various prohibitions that created monsters like Arnold Rothstein, Al Capone, Pablo Escobar, Lucky Luciano, Chapo Guzman, and all the other killers and psychopaths who have made millions or billions from the drug trade while intimidating or murdering anyone who gets in their way.

In this sense, many cops and politicians have just been the alternate side of this evil coin. In setting out to stop these "villains," they have become the very thing they have sworn to destroy (assuming they did not already harbor the desire to extort, murder, and harm vast swaths of people to begin with).

In either case, so long as people continue to profit handsomely from bloodshed on the streets and the overcrowding of prison cells—regardless of whether that profit is money or power—there will continue to be collateral damage of unimaginable proportions.

To mitigate this insanity, we need more people speaking up and telling the truth. It is about time we started screaming "STOP THIS INSANITY" as loudly as possible from the ramparts.

Enough is enough.

October 13, 2016

It looks like many people are railing against the DEA's attempts to ban the kratom plant. As a result of pressure from various groups and efforts from decentralized grassroots organizations, the DEA has withdrawn its immediate ban of kratom.

This represents another assault against the war on drugs. But as my buddy Derrick Broze has pointed out, we still need to get everyone on board with the idea that the war on drugs has failed and that no drug should be banned. The war on drugs has caused mass suffering, imprisonment, and the deaths of thousands of people.

I think many are starting to realize that prohibition has only exacerbated social problems. It has not stopped people from using drugs, and it certainly has not stopped the flow of them. It has only gotten people killed, broken up families, and torn society asunder.

If you still support the drug war, it is time for some deep introspection and consideration of why you feel the need to control others and use violence against them.

The drug war is a war against the innocent and a monopoly for the powerful.

October 15, 2016

Addiction is not a disease.

It is not a moral failing, either.

Addiction is an adaptation.

People fall into addictive patterns of behavior because they want to escape terrible environments, emotional injuries, and the ravages of abusive relationships.

There are studies with rats that demonstrate how this works on a basic level.

Most people are only familiar with the study that showed the singly caged rat (inside a "Skinner box") who constantly chose cocaine over water until it died. However, when rats live with their families in safe and playful environments, they will rarely choose heroin over their familial connections.

There was an experimental study called "Rat Park" that demonstrated this. The rats within Rat Park played often and mingled with other rats. When opioids were introduced, the rats seldom touched the substance, much less became "addicted" to it. They preferred to play instead of taking dope.

Compare this to humans. Whenever we suffer various forms of abuse and live in difficult environments—whenever we feel alone—we may turn to drugs, booze, and other "addictive" habits. In this sense, addiction is only a choice made for survival and psychological equilibrium.

However, we have been duped into believing the drugs themselves cause addiction. This is one of the biggest lies ever peddled, and it is used to prop up the drug war and condemn drug users as worthless junkies.

But armed with new knowledge and understanding, we see that the root cause of addiction is safety. People want to feel safe, and that is why they escape with drug abuse. That is why they choose these chemicals over anything else.

Next time you see a relative doing hard drugs, instead of judging them, perhaps try to empathize with their plight and understand what traumas and abuses may have led to their need to rescue themselves with drugs.

December 15, 2016

"My kid died from smoking weed"—said no parent ever.

December 19, 2016

Psychedelics are popular in anarchist circles for a couple of reasons, but there is one predominant factor.

Anarchists seek enlightenment about the world and themselves. They want to heal their wounds and find ways to prevent these emotional injuries from occurring in the future.

This is precisely what the psychedelic experience offers. It substantiates the anarchist's worldview and explains how to make it happen.

Psychedelics are a portal to discovering a 360-degree perspective on freedom.

Contrary to popular belief, psychedelics do not make you crazy.

They make you uncrazy. They show anarchists how to unfuck themselves and the world.

December 22, 2016

As early as the 1930s, people talked about the dangers of cannabis. They said it killed brain cells. They said it made you crazy. The plant was associated with racist perceptions of the time. People thought it was vile and heinous.

Nearly a century later, the propaganda and hysteria are finally starting to wear off. More people are talking about cannabis as acceptable, and some rulers are allowing the serfs to smoke at their leisure.

But this situation provides me with a thought: what other propagandized drugs will start to be seen as safe and useful, as they should be?

LSD, MDMA, psilocybin?

Will these drugs be next?

I hope it doesn't take another century for people to escape their ignorance. Lots of people have lost their livelihoods or lives as a result of the shortsighted and fanatical war on drugs.

Let's help people wake up faster.

March 6, 2017

The most elegant feature of the MDMA experience is that it amps up our ability to connect with other humans. Our emotional sensitivity to others becomes heightened, and we can then empathize deeply with them. While on MDMA, other people's needs are put into focus, and we can address their needs and demonstrate true love for them in a non-judgmental fashion.

This is important for anarchists to know because how well we relate to others will determine how well we build anarchist societies. MDMA can allow us to bridge any divides to create freer communities.

In my mind, freedom cells and friendship circles are first created from re-lational understanding rather than ideological considerations. If people have deep attunement with each other, any economic or philosophical difference can be resolved after the fact.

This is why MDMA is a powerful diplomatic and negotiation tool. It is a human-centric drug rather than an idea-centric drug. One can certainly discuss ideas, but the conversation will always be mediated by extreme compassion between all individuals within that group. That means any differences can be resolved with honesty and integrity.

March 22, 2017

Awakening for the first time in the world can be traumatizing. I remember mine. It was years ago. I disobeyed social rules and took MDMA.

Suddenly, the drug made me realize that established social rules are bullshit and that my life is meaningful. Before this experience, I didn't perceive the grandeur and majesty of life. I just shambled through life like a sleepwalking, hungry-for-brains zombie.

This experience was traumatizing because I didn't expect to realize how many lies I had been fed since my youth. It was traumatizing because it brought back old memories and put them in a new perspective. It was traumatizing because all at once I realized how much others had been trying to control and subdue me.

Then the trauma turned to beauty, and I came to the realization that I am beautiful, powerful, and without regret. Immediately I started questioning the alleged truths I had been told. I started questioning authority, and long-held myths about society started to vaporize in my mind.

I knew drug laws were based on lies told to prevent people from experiencing and expanding their consciousness. I knew that the education system was more akin to a prison. I knew something terrible and painful was wrong with society.

At the time, I couldn't put my finger on the exact reason, but my awakening so many years ago put me on the correct path to anarchism. And since I have been navigating this road, I have felt no urge to turn back or cower before the authorities and capitulate.

Instead, I have grown and evolved as a human. I have continuously said "fuck you" to the self-righteous people who would try to rule me and force me to kiss the ring. I have matured into an awesome human being because I have not allowed any force in this world to halt my progression toward absolute self-love and total freedom.

Indeed, something tells me this life is all about the experience of transcendence. It's almost spiritual in a way, and there is much pain that comes with this kind of hero's journey.

Are you prepared for your own?

To See the World in a Grain of Sand:
A Short Guide to Everything MDMA

11/28/2016

The designer drug MDMA has caught a lot of flak from mainstream media over the years. Journalists, politicians, and other antediluvian types have failed to understand it and neglected to research it beyond biased governmental sources. This intellectual dishonesty, of course, has led to the mass spread of myths and disinformation. But contrary to the rampant lie-mongering, the drug has been a godsend for people suffering from a variety of problems, especially latent traumas.

MDMA behaves like a periscope turned inward toward the soul. It allows individuals to become deeply introspective and examine their lives. For this reason, when the drug was first introduced to psychotherapy during the 1960s and 1970s, it was the therapeutic tool *par excellence* in couples counseling.

Psychotherapist Claudio Naranjo even wrote an insightful, albeit obscure book about his clinical experiences with the compound. The book is called *The Healing Journey*. It is recommended for anyone interested in how MDMA was used in therapy. Naranjo implies that the drug was a communication and empathy enhancer. It inspired quarreling couples to solve their interpersonal problems without fear and with ample love in their hearts.

MDMA Psychotherapy Goes Underground—but Returns

Not long after Nixon initiated the war on drugs, MDMA psychotherapy went underground or vanished entirely. The government had effectively removed one of psychology's greatest boons from clinical use. Just over the last decade, the drug has finally started to regain popularity in psychological and medical circles.

Today, researchers use it again to help "PTSD" populations overcome flashbacks and night terrors. The results have been positive thus far. Clinicians have found that it helps trauma survivors face and accept what they have been through and learn to cope with issues. MAPS, or the Multidisciplinary Association of Psychedelic Studies, is one of the few organizations that has conducted this kind of legal research. They have plans to make MDMA a prescription medication by 2023.

As an aside, the compound should be completely legal, anyway. People should be able to use it of their own volition. It is too therapeutic and useful to pretend that governments know what's best for everyone and to let the State determine who needs this medicine most. Individuals should have free reign to augment their psychology without coercion or interference.

Still, it wouldn't hurt anyone to know what they're putting in their bodies.

To See the World in a Grain of Sand

MDMA is fascinating because it invokes a powerful psychoactive experience characterized by intense feelings of bliss, euphoria, wonderment, awe of nature, and love.

In the brain, the chemical triggers a massive serotonin "dump," which is said to cause the altered state of consciousness it brings forth. However, some researchers believe the serotonin dump may also cause a cascade of other effects, including the release of oxytocin and other neurochemicals.

Some researchers have referred to MDMA as an "entactogen" and "empathogen." The former means it enhances sensual and tactile pleasures, and the latter means it induces intense empathy, as Naranjo suggested. It is the combined effect of these pharmacological features that makes it such a powerful agent. The experience it creates is so profound that it has been compared to a poem William Blake wrote called "The Auguries of Innocence." The poem starts like this:

> To see a World in a Grain of Sand
>
> And a Heaven in a Wild Flower
>
> Hold Infinity in the palm of your hand
>
> And Eternity in an hour.

An MDMA.net article summed up what the poem was getting at.

> As well as acting as a "gateway to the soul," MDMA "opens up the heart." Taking MDMA induces an amazing feeling of closeness and connectedness to one's fellow human beings. MDMA triggers intense emotional release beyond the bounds of everyday experience. The drug also enhances the felt intensity of the senses—most exquisitely perhaps the sense of touch. The body-image looks and feels wonderful. Other people look and feel wonderful too. Minutes after dropping a pill, a lifetime of Judaeo-Christian guilt, shame or disgust at the flesh melt away to oblivion.

Anyone who has experienced the drug or witnessed people on it will instantly understand the aforementioned experiential description. What is truly fascinating is how people interact and behave on the compound.

MDMA Behavior and Quantum Personality Changes

People on MDMA can be seen holding each other tightly, kissing, touching, caressing, petting, talking deeply and incessantly about their shared love, and calling each other beautiful. Their eyes may be "rolling," and they might be grinding their teeth, which is a side effect of the amphetamine aspect of the drug.

To outsiders, people on MDMA might appear "drunk" and also improperly happy. They might think the people on it are crazy or strange. It might cause those unfamiliar with the compound's effects to be fearful and nervous about those who are on it.

This is ironic, though, because someone who has taken ecstasy may have a stronger sense of their emotional content and more internal awareness. This fact goes to show how emotionally detached and out of touch modern people are, especially since they are not normally in an "ecstatic" and emotionally vulnerable state of mind. The drug is so intense that some people claim it has augmented their personality forever.

Psychologists refer to this experience as a "quantum personality change." This is a kind of personality shift that happens because of insight or a spiritual epiphany. It is intense and immediate. Zen Buddhists call it *satori*, or the flash of insight. Close relatives of that person even recognize that his personality has changed drastically—most often for the better.

If any drug could alter the psychological makeup of an individual, it would be MDMA, although classical psychedelics like mushrooms and LSD can accomplish a similar personality alteration.

This is all great information, but an individual should also be aware of the possible dangers of consuming MDMA.

Possible Dangers of MDMA

As powerful as the drug is, it may not be completely safe. At high dosage levels, it can cause neurotoxicity, or damage to the brain or nervous system as a result of chemical ingestion.

An Erowid article elaborates on the neurotoxicity of MDMA.

> The acute toxic effects of MDMA are well documented by hundreds of case reports of adverse events in illicit users. Considering how many people use MDMA, serious acute adverse events seem rare. MDMA appears generally similar to psychostimulants such as methamphetamine with respect to the risks of acute toxicity. With trained personnel, properly screened volunteers, and established protocols for monitoring and treating adverse

events, these acute risks appear modest and do not present a strong argument against carefully conducted clinical research with MDMA.

There is also a chance that a person who uses it could overheat and become dangerously dehydrated. Historically, MDMA has been associated with the club and rave scenes because, as stated, the compound is often tied together by amphetamine compounds, which gives people the stamina to dance all night long.

All the dancing and edginess caused by the speedy effects can intensify a person's desire to drink water. But because of the psychoactive effects, sometimes they forget to drink, and their bodies overheat. In worst-case scenarios, death can occur from heatstroke.

Everyone should do adequate research on any drug before deciding to partake. There are other possible consequences of using this compound, especially since it is synthetic, but so far there do not seem to be any negative long-term effects so long as it is used in moderation. If taken with caution, a person could free themselves from the stranglehold of modern culture and experience a quantum personality change.

Curing Drug Schizophrenia: Toward an MDMA Culture

Before people are freed from culture and able to acknowledge MDMA's power, its taboo nature must be eradicated from people's minds. This cannot happen through legislation or the abolition of government alone. It must occur from people living spontaneously and embracing the MDMA experience. It must happen through people displaying their emotionally sensitive sides, which are germane to problems of our time.

So long as people continue to feel uneasy about altered states of consciousness and being sensitive and emotive, MDMA will not be a culturally accepted compound even if it gains a socially "legal" status and is widely adopted in psychotherapy settings. This will likewise prevent people from wanting to broaden their horizons or change their personality. To bust all the myths and hysteria surrounding designer drugs, people must be cured of their drug schizophrenia.

Currently, people only believe in the efficacy of tranquilizers, downers, sedatives, opiates, crawlers, and a whole host of psychiatric snake oils to "cure" them. But they do not seem to want to live, to be, to feel, and to absorb all the vicissitudes of life. This is tragic because MDMA invokes the opposite of the modern social plague. It promotes fully being, youthful exuberance, awareness, felt presence of existence, and unbridled humanness. It is the drug for the enlightened and awakened, for the crowd that has escaped the coma culture in the hopes of building something new and powerful—an MDMA culture.

"The artist's task is to save the soul of humankind; and anything less is a dithering while Rome burns. If artists cannot find the way, then the way cannot be found."

—Terence McKenna

PART 3: CRYPTO-ANARCHY AND INNOVATIVE FREEDOM

The Power of Cryptocurrency: Undermining the Fed

08/03/2015

The Federal Reserve central banking system of the United States is a destructive organization. Freethinkers and anarchists seek to abolish it. In their minds, the Fed has maintained a death grip on society for far too long. It has led to myriad economic calamities. Luckily, technology now exists to push humanity into the next epoch by upending the current state of monetary despotism. The tools to propel an economic reformation have arisen from underground capitalism, online shadow markets, and the fringes of society.

This new tool, or technology, is referred to as cryptocurrency. It was established without the guiding hand of authority overseeing its manufacture. It was created by cypherpunks to escape clumsy and heavy-handed bureaucracy. It was built to be decentralized and to evade institutional control. It was meant to be the people's money, to liberate the populace from the oppression and corruption of State banking. It was forged to shatter financial totalitarianism and level the playing field. Cryptocurrency is the ultimate form of technological nonviolent disruption and disobedience.

The White Paper

Many different cryptocurrencies exist. The most popular is bitcoin. It first emerged in 2008 when an enigmatic figure named Satoshi Nakamoto submitted a paper to the cypherpunk mailing list referred to as the bitcoin white paper. In the abstract of the paper, Nakamoto elaborated on his intention.

"A purely peer-to-peer version of electronic cash would allow online payments to be sent directly from one party to another without going through a financial institution," he said.

A year later, this culminated in the creation of the bitcoin software and the blockchain it is founded on. The blockchain is a public ledger that documents every transaction ever made through the protocol and publishes it transparently. The blockchain is essentially the vertebrae of bitcoin. It gives it all its fundamental characteristics.

It is not readily apparent how bitcoin is going to revolutionize finance much less bring down the banking conglomerate and Federal Reserve system. However, several major characteristics give bitcoin and its protocol the capacity to disrupt and disempower those who wield too much control over the economic infrastructure.

The Disruptive Power of Bitcoin

The underlying disruptive power of bitcoin is simple yet elegant. It is disruptive because it is decentralized. It does not rely on central planners. It is also automated. It is programmed to spit out a limited number of bitcoins over the course of years. The implications of this are huge. There will never be a crypto-authority or a few guys sitting in a room deciding what is best for people, the economy, or the country. The technology puts a check on human corruptibility and invalidates the Federal Reserve.

Bitcoin is peer-to-peer. Transactions only occur between the people directly involved. There is no middleman and no institutional stranglehold. People no longer must rely on a third party. They can send their money to each other without going through an organization. People can essentially debank or become unbanked. Viewed another way, they become their own bank. They are the masters of their own money. They do not have to worry about having their accounts frozen, either. No one besides the users has access to their funds. This feature removes the possibility of institutions stopping transfers or confiscating money. Bitcoin is uncensorable.

Bitcoin represents the height of computer wizardry insofar that it is tamper resistant. If a group of tyrants or banksters wanted to access the money supply and control it for themselves, they could accomplish that easily. The bitcoin protocol is distributed over a large network and operates via many computers, which increases its strength and security, deterring hackers and tyrants alike. In its current state, it is almost impossible to acquire the computational power to successfully hack the protocol. Several security experts and professionals have already tried. They openly admitted failure. Bitcoin is extremely antifragile and can withstand a variety of attacks.

As an aside, some bitcoin exchanges, such as Mt. Gox, have been hacked, but it was not the bitcoin protocol itself that failed—only Mt. Gox's servers. The protocol is currently resistant to outside threats because of its size. Bitcoin's distributed nature is what makes it astoundingly tough to crack.

You Can't Target the CEO

The aforesaid reasons are why the Fed cannot deal with cryptocurrency on a practical level. Usually, when someone tries to compete with the Federal Reserve and government, they are simply arrested for counterfeiting or another bogus charge.

Bernard von Nothaus is a monetary architect who created the Liberty Dollar. His money was backed by gold, and it looked "authentic." As a result, it gained immediate popularity. But the Feds caught on. They arrested Nothaus for alleged domestic terrorism and then confiscated his money. He ended up getting a light sentence and not going to prison, but he lost all his revenue.

Bitcoin does not suffer from the same weakness. Since the system is decentralized and no one person controls it, the State cannot issue a warrant and arrest a CEO for "domestic terrorism" or counterfeiting.

Indeed, there is no central commander at "bitcoin headquarters." The Feds would have to round up all the miners and programmers involved in the network. In other words, they can't act against bitcoin in an efficacious manner. The system does not care about authority and bureaucracy. It will function regardless.

Even if government agents did arrest everyone, new miners would emerge and create new nodes on the network, just as new dealers crop up to sell more pills in the drug market. There is a potential threat to individuals who choose to use bitcoin, but there are few real threats that target the protocol itself.

The Age of Economic Freedom

The most important reason the Fed will perish is bitcoin's utility. It is safe, secure, and efficient. It works—and works well. There is incentive to use it. Anyone can send bitcoin anywhere around the world. The fear of being defrauded is reduced because users don't have to share private data. They can also keep multiple wallets with bitcoin and spend their money from anywhere so long as they have an internet connection, which is becoming easier to access even in third-world countries.

Bitcoin will not dismantle the governmental banking empire by assaulting it with guerrilla warfare; it will abolish the system with guerrilla economics. The central bankers must compete with it. Since they can't arrest anyone, they will be forced to outpace it. Their attempts will fail, though.

Decentralized currencies, not improvements on existing money and payment infrastructures, are the next step in innovation. This truth implies the Fed has been subjected to a zugzwang: all their potential moves worsen their situation, while all cryptocurrencies have to do is continue growing.

And grow they will. It is not a matter of if bitcoin and cryptocurrency will go mainstream—only when. The age of economic freedom has arrived, it's sounding the Fed's death knell. Nonetheless, there will be battles over bitcoin neutrality that must be fought and won. The Fed and bankers will not go down without a fight.

The Cryptocurrency Evolution

January 22, 2014

I love bitcoin not just for its efficiency as a currency but also for its sheer beauty and elegance. There's a deep iconoclastic core to bitcoin that shuns all master-slave relationships through its decentralized and cryptographic nature. Bitcoin has risen out of humanity's desire for total freedom and pseudo-anonymity in trade, and nothing can stop it.

April 1, 2014

You know what I am reminded of when people doom-speak and naysay bitcoin? The Age of Enlightenment. Back then, scientists would ask people to look through a telescope to objectively view the heavens, and those people would simply lash out in disbelief and scorn. Today, if you ask people to investigate bitcoin as the legitimate currency that it is, they turn into Dark Age priests, calling you a witch and demanding your head. The amount of superstition people have is insane, and they will go to great lengths to ignore obvious truths.

July 6, 2015

When bitcoin and other cryptocurrencies fully burst into the mainstream, people aren't going to know what has hit them. These digital currencies not only offer secure and private personal "banking" but also a hyper-efficient means of trading and connecting with others economically. The possibilities are endless, and they will expand and diversify even more as governments lose their grip on individual finance. Overall, blockchain technology represents a new frontier in internet interactions. We are on the verge of experiencing and living in the new crypto-digitalia.

July 11, 2015

Some people complain that bitcoin is too complicated for the average person. That is a ridiculous argument. Contemplate fiat currency for a moment. What do you think goes on when central bureaucrats print money arbitrarily and control interest rates? Think about the complexity that exists within the economic environment. Just imagine the hidden information about fiat currency you aren't privy to. It is insane. Bitcoin dodges all that nonsense. It is transparent, open source, and allows a person to be his own bank. No central controllers oversee it. It is completely decentralized and accessible. This is the future, and you are either in or you are out. Fiat currency is totally incomprehensible. Bitcoin is easy to understand in comparison...and it is literally in your wallet all the time.

July 18, 2015

A lot of people are not grasping the impact cryptocurrencies are going to have on every aspect of society.

July 23, 2015

One of the big fears of digitization is that we will sacrifice our identity as unique humans. The beautiful thing about blockchain technology is that we can preserve our individuality while maintaining a sense of community. What we are witnessing is an unprecedented development in internet-based applications. The blockchain protocol is all about individuality because it preserves the secrecies and privacy of the individual while simultaneously blending him into the collective. This paradox is just arriving on the scene, and few people have grasped the enormity of influence this will have on the social and economic development of humankind.

Most people do not realize that blockchain technology is not merely a part of the Internet. It is on another plane, another playing field within the ether. This is fascinating stuff.

Humans are learning to whisper into the void.

July 24, 2015

A lot of people believe "money" has to be in a paper "fiat" format and that they have to be told by governments or banks that it is legitimate. However, money can have value simply because people assign value to it, not because it is enforced. Currently, new decentralized forms of digital money are gaining popularity and value. For instance, bitcoin is now accepted by major online retailers and private individuals even though it is just a series of zeros and ones and does not exist in a physical sense. People are coveting it even though no government controls the underlying protocol that it rests on. Do you guys believe that money must be controlled by a government, or should people be free to choose what money they use and value?

August 29, 2015

Bitcoin has already proven immensely useful in my life. Instead of relying on expensive money transfers and remittance services, I only have to rely on myself as my bank. I have been able to send decently sized sums of money to friends at super low costs—instantaneously. Bitcoin has been advantageous in every imaginable way. Even in first-world geographies, bitcoin has demonstrated its utility and versatility. Why some people call it a hard sell in an industrialized world beats me. Everything about bitcoin is better than the centralized money transmitters and the cartelized bank tyrants. Now, if only people would stop spewing their nonsensical, ignorant smear campaigns. Just try it. It is beautiful technology.

August 6, 2016

For the first time ever, people are learning that transferable value can exist in different "monies" or competing, abstract tokens.

We don't have to rely on our day jobs or government fiat scams to generate valuable assets. Culture, as it stands, is drastically moving toward more fairness, transparency, wealth, and inclusion. The powers are finally being balanced.

There is now technology that allows you to gain value in cryptocurrency doing whatever kind of work you can imagine (depending on what kind of blockchain activity or decentralized organization you are involved in). And it won't have to be strictly fiat currency.

Value isn't something that some government or other coercive agency decides. It is whatever *you* decide based on your interests, skills, and talent. That is the kind of world we are building right now.

Are you tired of playing the old games? You may not have to anymore.

October 4, 2016

I have never felt more in control of my financial life since cryptocurrencies came onto the scene. There is so much we can do with these currencies without having to rely on banks and other agencies. There is a real feeling of power and financial independence when it comes to using these tools. There is also incentive to save, hoard, and trade because many of these currencies have the potential to be extremely valuable in the future.

I never felt the same way when I was constantly using USD. Cryptocurrencies have provided new ways to generate income without necessarily having to do it the old way and constantly worrying about governments or banks devaluing or stealing those funds.

The age of collaborative consumption and decentralized economies is upon us.

January 4, 2017

Hate that your government coerces you into using its money? Hate having to trust the central banks that print it? Hate not knowing if your funds will be frozen or stolen at any moment?

Don't worry. Cypherpunks and anarchists have created cryptocurrencies for all of your monetary and revolutionary needs—and they are skyrocketing in price because fiat currencies have failed.

As people increasingly lose faith in government currencies, freedom lovers will continue to let algorithms mint theirs since mathematics is fairer and more trustworthy than the sociopaths who run the central banks.

April 24, 2017

Blockchain technology combined with changing visions of society is enough to bootstrap humanity to a new beginning.

Bitcoin Was Built to Incite Peaceful Anarchy

01/09/2016

B itcoin is the catalyst for peaceful anarchy and freedom. It was built as a reaction against corrupt governments and financial institutions. It was not solely created for the sake of improving financial technology, though some people adulterate this truth. Bitcoin was meant to function as a monetary weapon, as a cryptocurrency poised to undermine authority.

Now it is whitewashed. It is often presented as a polite and unassuming technology to appease politicians, banksters, and soccer moms. Its purpose is sometimes concealed to make the tech palatable to the unwashed masses and power elite. However, no one should forget or deny why the protocol was written.

The enigmatic creator, Satoshi Nakamoto, expressed the truth in his white paper. He mentioned that bitcoin was supposed to eliminate redundant middlemen and banks. The intent was to thwart corrupting influences and put money back into the hands of the people.

If anyone looks at history, they can see that the cypherpunks started building bitcoin right after the financial crisis of 2007. The timing was not coincidental. It was initiated as a counter-offensive against political machinations, mass extortion, fiat inflation, and extensive banking fraud.

In October 2008, Satoshi Nakamoto unveiled the white paper, saying, "I've been working on a new electronic cash system that's fully peer-to-peer, with no trusted third party." Although there is no direct reference to challenging government authority, the idea of being trustless contains anarchist sentiment.

Satoshi elaborated on this view in the white paper.

> While the system works well enough for most transactions, it still suffers from the inherent weaknesses of the trust-based model. Completely non-reversible transactions are not really possible, since financial institutions cannot avoid mediating disputes. The cost of mediation increases transaction costs, limiting the minimum practical transaction size and cutting off the possibility for small casual transactions, and there is a broader cost in the loss of ability to make non-reversible payments for nonreversible services.

Thus, bitcoin was not created strictly as a better financial technology (although no one is denying that it is a superior form of currency with value and efficiency). Bitcoin was built as trustless and borderless money. It was created to destroy centralized money control by governments and eliminate banking cartels. The historical roots of crypto-anarchy provide stronger evidence in defense of this claim.

The Crypto-Revolution Prior to Bitcoin

If one looks farther back than the white paper, it becomes clear that cypherpunks and early cryptologists already had a vision of what cryptography would accomplish.

Timothy May, one of the original crypto-anarchists, set the stage for cryptocurrency systems and other encryption-based technologies. In 1994, he wrote "Crypto Anarchy and Virtual Communities," where he explained the intended purpose of these technologies. May said:

> The combination of strong, unbreakable public key cryptography and virtual network communities in cyberspace will produce interesting and profound changes in the nature of economic and social systems. Crypto anarchy is the cyberspatial realization of anarcho-capitalism, transcending national boundaries and freeing individuals to make the economic arrangements they wish to make consensually.

He continued:

> Governments see their powers eroded by these technologies, and are taking various well-known steps to try to limit the use of strong crypto by their subjects. The U.S. has several well-publicized efforts, including the Clipper chip, the Digital Telephony wiretap law, and proposals for "voluntary" escrow of cryptographic keys. Cypherpunks and others expect these efforts to be bypassed. Technology has let the genie out of the bottle. Crypto anarchy is liberating individuals from coercion by their physical neighbors—who cannot know who they are on the Net—and from governments. For libertarians, strong crypto provides the means by which government will be avoided.

It was this early incarnation of crypto-anarchy and anarcho-capitalism that spearheaded philosophical, social, and technological development in encryption protocols. These ideas led to advancements designed to decentralize society and free people from the clutches of bureaucrats and banksters. Indeed, the crypto-revolutionaries anticipated the invention of bitcoin, along with the features it needed to incite peaceful anarchy (the absence of coercive rulers, not chaos or destruction).

So what are these features?

Cryptocurrency Features that Defy Authority: Push versus Pull System

Bitcoin is decentralized, peer-to-peer money. This feature implies that bitcoin does not have to be stored with third-party banks. Bitcoin is meant to be handled by the individual and used at his discretion. No other person should need to see or acquire that money unless the end-user allows it. This concept is called self-banking. It keeps money safe and prevents the user from dealing with the questionable practice of fractional reserve banking or direct seizure of funds as the cypherpunks intended.

This aspect of the technology is also referred to as a "push system" (as opposed to a "pull system"). This means people can only "push" money from within the wallet to others. No third party or person can "pull" money from an individual's wallet. There are plenty of market reasons why this is a valuable function, but it is particularly useful for helping a user guard against malicious governments or banks. It means he has total control over funds. He does not have to worry about organizations tampering with his money.

Pseudo-Anonymity, Blockchain, and Public-Key Cryptography

Another way bitcoin prevents tampering is by employing pseudo-anonymity through public-key cryptography, which is an encryption method based on algorithms and hash functions. This is the basic idea: When a person spends money, their public-private key combination is decoded by the recipient's public-private key. It is this form of encryption that prevents other people from interfering with the transaction or stealing the money. Public-key cryptography is the reason why governments cannot stop transactions on the blockchain.

But what is the blockchain?

It is a nearly impregnable public ledger based on a distributed consensus network. It records all transactions ever made in bitcoin. The technology is referred to as "Pseudonymous" because each transaction can still be tracked, but no one has to enter personal credentials or information to start a wallet. (There are ways to transact with more anonymity, but that is beyond the scope of this article.)

Pseudonymous methods potentially allow people to make transactions without government officials knowing their exact identity. They were supposed to be another layer of protection, but these mechanisms are not foolproof. The State has already employed the blockchain to track transactions and imprison people. This is part of how they claimed to prosecute the alleged Dread Pirate Roberts, aka Ross Ulbricht. But even though the technology is not fully anonymous, it still grants more privacy than traditional banking.

All of these fundamental bitcoin features allow people to dispense with the current system. However, none of this information addresses how bitcoin will stop the government from controlling money and ruling over the population.

Why Keeping Money Away from Government Is Good

Governments rely on money to subjugate the peasantry. Throughout the ages, politicians have conducted misdeeds and murdered, extorted, and hurt people because they have commandeered the money supply. They have held a monopoly on minting coins, managing central banks, and writing laws telling people what money they should use and how to use it.

But the easiest way government leaders oppress people is through minting and counterfeiting money—or printing it out of thin air. This activity causes inflation. When governments possess a central hold over money, they can inflate the currency in circulation without any consequences. If a normal person does the same thing, it is called "counterfeiting." Crypto-anarchists seek to free people from this kind of theft and level the playing field. Government is ultimately unnecessary and illegitimate.

Murray Rothbard elaborated in What Has Government Done to Our Money?.

> Counterfeiting is evidently but another name for inflation—both creating new "money" that is not standard gold or silver, and both functioning similarly. And now we see why governments are inherently inflationary: because inflation is a powerful and subtle means for government acquisition of the public's resources, a painless and all the more dangerous form of taxation.

Rothbard's book provided a complete view of the history and use of money and why governments take control of money to function. But this is also the weakness of the government. It is where bitcoin shines. Since bitcoin uses all of the features previously mentioned, especially decentralization, it is the first currency that moves beyond the reach of government. Politicians cannot stop the blockchain or control bitcoin. They can't turn it off, which is a huge advancement not only for technology but also for the sociopolitical and moral progress of humankind.

The Technology of Liberation

Bitcoin and other blockchain technologies will continue liberating humanity and spurring progress. The technology was built for this agenda. It was not meant to be a fluffy-bunny, cool form of money. It was geared to act as a monetary patriot, seeking to incite political change through crypto-anarchic means. It was constructed to do this because early crypto-anarchists recognized that money has been the epicenter of State power, and the State has likewise been the epicenter of evil.

Everyone should continuously remind each other of these truths. It is because of bitcoin that no one will ever have to grovel or genuflect at the feet of kings and tyrants. Therefore, bitcoin's purpose should not be rendered obsolete in the smokescreen of political correctness, kowtowing, and cowardice. The tool should be venerated. People should rejoice at its arrival. No one should ever deny why the protocol was written. It is the first iteration of absolute freedom—the first hint of peaceful anarchy. Let it be known.

Optimizing Anarchy for Optimism

March 30, 2015

Using the internet is like whispering into the void where minds congregate. It allows people easy, non-physical ways to connect with each other. The internet is a hyperspace highway used to channel various energies and draw them together. That is why it is such a powerful tool and why anarchists and hackers recognize its transformative power in society. Sadly, there are forces at work that want to condemn and undermine the internet because activities within its vast networks threaten those who harbor "power." Before, reality was the leash that enslaved people, but the quasi-reality of the internet allows unencumbered communication and transmission of various resources. Luckily, the good guys have already realized this, and they are taking full advantage of it at every turn—not to mention the deeper truths of the web have yet to be uncovered and used. P2P, TOR, and all deep web capabilities are only the start.

April 17, 2015

One of the greatest treasures of being human is our ability to change behavior. Unlike most other animals, we are not slaves to instinctual drives or conditioned responses. Though we may get stuck in certain behavior patterns, we can actively change our minds and consciously make new choices; we can become aware of our activity. If there is a truth behind "human nature," it is the fact that there is no absolute human nature, no specific behavior or goal we are predestined to follow and conform to. The beauty of humanity resides in our conscious will and the ability to manufacture new destinies. Never let the determinists persuade us into dismissing this beautiful truth.

October 11, 2015

I appreciate and admire people who build. I love innovators and creators. It does not matter what. It could be the next disruptive tech company. It could be the next marvelous oil painting. It could be a revolutionary, balls-to-the-wall social idea. It could be the next piece of medical technology or medical discovery. It could be the next emotionally jarring piece of literature. It could be the next movement in psychotherapy. It could be anything wonderful and spectacular, but it could also be subtle and clever.

In either case, I want superstars near me. I want movers and shakers. I want the kind of people with whom a desire to change the world resonates, who want to better this rock we live on. I seek to surround myself with motivated people, folks with an acumen for living well. No one should suffer having to bring people close to them who live dully and ineptly.

And I must say, so far, I am proud that the people closest to me possess these characteristics. It's what makes life interesting, entertaining, and beautiful.

February 8, 2016

For everyone to obtain psychological health, statism in all of its vectors needs to be abolished. The use of behavioral punishment must be condemned outright. Parenting with the use of positive punishment (spanking and hitting) needs to be stopped. Public schooling, with its focus on punitive measures, must be undone. Governments, with their focus on using violent discipline regiments, should be erased. Psychological health will be a myth until people stop being abused and tormented throughout their lifespan.

Currently, developmental psychology is the story of developmental torture. Only a handful of spirited and strong-willed individuals have been able to see the truth and quell the pain. Luckily, I believe more are coming to acknowledge all the culturally mandated abuses because anarchists continue to talk and siphon out the black bile. In this sense, anarchists and freethinkers are white blood cells in the diseased body of modern culture.

March 12, 2016

I am all about community-building. Nothing is as important for the promotion of liberty as anarchists who spontaneously organize and create networks. There is power in numbers—not forceful power but cultural power. It is the power to help people change by demonstrating the impact and popularity of voluntaryism. As more communities spring up, more people will be engulfed in the swirling vortex of peaceful communion. They will be swept away by it and ultimately transformed. This is the start of an anarchist renaissance, of a new era. Keep building. Keep working. We are here.

July 12, 2016

I take it as a good sign that there is now mainstream discussion about disbanding the police.

Nothing could be better for them or the community. If private security firms fill the demand for protection, leftover policemen who can work without the urge to murder people may have a job. Even if some of them possess a violent or psychopathic streak, the incentive to harm people while working for a private agency is almost nil compared to government positions. Further, the worst of the worst could be ferreted out rather easily with testing, but that is just one possible solution.

I can envision a smooth transition away from government-regulated police into community protection and defense squads.

In any case, I think the first step toward a more loving and compassionate civilization is the abolition of the police. This would at least be a positive movement toward stopping governments from modeling the idea that violent aggression is the answer to all our social ills.

October 31, 2016

I will never understand why anarchists fall for the allure of Trump or make arguments for voting. It blows my mind. We have all already learned a valuable lesson in the past: Presidential candidates do not keep their promises. They say what it takes to get elected while lying through their teeth. After they are elected, bombs continue to explode, police continue to murder, and the serfs remain in bondage. Politicians are equally vile—even if they come from a business background.

Furthermore, to vote for liars and maniacs means to justify democracy, to gleefully accept servitude via a failed system.

As anarchists, we know democracy is garbage. We know the system is built upon corruption and misdeeds. We have a thorough understanding of how the game of thrones functions, the psychology of the players involved, and the outcome of engaging in political rituals.

So why continue? Is Trump's rhetoric so different from past politicians? He is appealing to certain groups and "principles" and manipulating a coterie of admirers while ramping up fears for a variety of boogeymen.

The only path to freedom is working outside the system, educating people, engaging in civil disobedience, and living as freely as possible. The only course of action is pulling the fucking plug on this succubus system—this dead system, which long ago proved its rampant toxicity.

It's time to give up on the political "cure" and start growing grassroots anarchist organizations and cooperatives from the ground up. To suffer the system and pretend it can liberate and save us is a delusion that has played itself out. It is a carcass putrefying in the desert with vultures feasting on its remains.

December 14, 2016

The beautiful thing about the Internet is that you don't have to worry about third-party publishers to present new writing to the world. You can build your platform and share ideas with whoever will read them. This is an aspect of decentralization, and it's awesome.

December 14, 2016

Lots of protests with people bantering.

Lots of breaking, looting, and destruction.

Lots of animosity. Lots of hate. Lots of energy.

But what is being said? What is being accomplished?

I think all of this energy could be channeled into something much more positive and fulfilling. It could be transformed into energy that helps us create, solve problems, and heal society. Instead, the energy is aggressive, petulant, and attention-starved.

Can we not find more positive ways to heal ourselves and the world? Perhaps provide a reason for the malevolence other than the fact that there is a new ruler who happens to be rich and flamboyant?

Time for some introspection, critical thought, and redirection of energy. That's where the real activity for change and growth takes place.

March 9, 2017

The collapse of the State will be heralded by ginormous guffaws and laughs galore.

March 10, 2017

Who will build the roads?

The roads will be built with compassion, love, and sweat off the brows of undocumented, freshly migrated immigrants.

How Bitcoin Can Alter Our Psychology

11/06/2015

Money is a powerful drug. It is psychologically stimulating. It motivates and invigorates people. It also stresses them out. It can be the cause of great joy or staggering woe. It is pervasive. Yet it also resides underground, within the undulating ocean of the unconscious, to be left unappreciated or unacknowledged. Money is hated and condemned and at the same time cherished and celebrated.

Many people see money as outright evil. They see it as a catalyst for unending greed. It has thus assumed a suspicious character over time and been molded into a taboo topic. It has been considered so devilish it spurred Ayn Rand to eloquently rise to its defense. In *Atlas Shrugged*, through the voice of Francisco d'Anconia, she said, "Money is the material shape of the principle that men who wish to deal with one another must deal by trade and give value for value. Money is not the tool of the moochers, who claim your product by tears, or of the looters, who take it from you by force. Money is made possible only by the men who produce. Is this what you consider evil?"

Ayn Rand was onto something. Money cannot be considered evil. It is only a tool, resource, or object—a medium of exchange—yet it has suffered a tumultuous history. Many constantly express ambivalent feelings toward it.

But why is it considered taboo? Why is it hated and smeared as evil? Does the research buttress these claims? If money does cause angst and suffering, can bitcoin change the way people think about it? Maybe bitcoin can create new ways for people to relate to money.

However, the field of neuroeconomics is in its infancy. Almost no studies have been conducted on the psychosocial dynamics of bitcoin. In the past, neuroeconomics has focused on investment decision-making, but understanding mental and emotional reactions to various forms of money can also be of great significance.

The Pauper Effect

Western cultures altogether shun discussions of money. It is taboo. People in these cultures do not believe it is polite to divulge specifics about finance. They do not even chat with their children about it, as we shall see. Research suggests that economic inequality contributes to these negative views of money, and wealthy people are likewise painted as evil scrooges who do not give a damn about the poor. This is the consensus attitude. It betrays an underlying hatred of finance.

However, wealth can indeed corrupt a person. But it would be unfair to say that money corrupts only the wealthy. Even poor people suffer the psychological pitfalls of money. They deal with negative stereotypes of their own. I refer to the aforesaid view as the pauper effect. The pauper effect suggests that being poor can cause a bias against money and wealth.

Psychological Research on Money

Studies that examine how parents relay monetary information to their children illuminate why the pauper effect exists. One survey revealed that parents want their children to be financially and economically savvy but are unable or unwilling to share their knowledge.

In a *Psychology Today* article, money psychologist Adrian Furnham said, "Surveys show that over 90% of adults would like their children to know more about the financial reality of life than they currently do, but that they are not really confident enough to ensure their children are financially literate, sensible and mature."

Surveys like these demonstrate why people harbor such ambivalence and unconscious hatred toward money. Parents neglect to discuss it with children. On the other side of the coin, research has also shown that money can dampen a person's empathy response, yet another reason why people tend to dislike currency.

One study showed that there is a money-empathy gap. People who have accumulated wealth may treat the poor badly. Psychologist Paul Piff designed an experiment to prove this hypothesis.

In the experiment, two people were matched in a game of monopoly. Piff handicapped one of the players. The handicapped player would never make as much money nor gain as many properties. The "privileged" player reacted with disdain toward the handicapped or underprivileged player. The privileged player's facial expressions included sadistic smirks and other pompous gestures. Piff interpreted his experiment this way: People with more wealth tend to hold contempt or dislike for the underprivileged. Further studies have buttressed his research. People with more wealth and higher status do not have the same ability to empathize as poorer populations, thus making them more likely to be mean and cruel.

How else can the money-empathy gap research be interpreted? Just because people who have money may exhibit selfish and greedy behavior does not mean correlation equals causation, and to generalize would be premature and unscientific. But even if people agree that the consequences of the pauper effect have a basis in reality—that the rich truly are greedy and evil—could there at least be solutions to this problem?

Bitcoin Adoption and the New Neuroeconomics

Bitcoin offers a novel way to help people escape negative views of money and even alter their psychological predispositions. Oftentimes, early experiences with money are negative because families are not incentivized to save or talk about spending, as surveys demonstrate. Further, fiat currency is printed by a central banking cartel and controlled by people who want to keep it mysterious. They tend to make the processes behind printing and keeping money as obscure and inaccessible as possible. These power elites have even been known to steal from the people or arbitrarily print money to stuff their coffers.

No wonder discussions and honesty about money are discouraged. No wonder studies show that people hate money and rich people. No wonder talking intimately about it is considered taboo. No wonder money conversations involve tackling difficult moral issues and addressing entrenched psychological problems that uncover the truth about fiat currency: It is a tool for servitude and slavery. Most people probably recoil in horror upon realizing these truths, but they must eventually be addressed.

Since bitcoin is borderless and constructed on the platform of decentralized open-source software, it is a type of currency that instigates a new way of perceiving money. It could upend the old psychological paradigm and help pave a different path toward a new neuroeconomics. It could spur new options for people to learn and get excited about money. It could help diminish contempt for it. It could even imbue the rich with newfound empathy. The fact that bitcoin is not printed and controlled by a central entity can help people escape the idea that money is evil altogether and equalize the playing field. Perhaps people can even talk about it more frequently, which will help prevent money issues from slipping into unconscious awareness as repressed impulses and unfinished business. Perhaps the Ayn Rands of the world will not need to jump to the defense of money on every occasion.

For example, bitcoin enthusiast and journalist Jamie Redman of bitcoin. com is known as the family man of bitcoin. He chats with his children about money and the promise of cryptocurrency and does not despise either the rich or poor. His mentality may be unique, but it seems to foreshadow the idea that bitcoin is altering our psychology. *Vice* even wrote an article about his family-oriented ideals entitled "Meet the Bitcoin Family." These possibilities could mean things are changing for the better.

Conclusion

Still, I hate using "coulds" and "maybes." More research needs to be conducted on bitcoin and its global effects on psychological systems, especially the family system, culture, and governments.

Currently, studies suggest money highly affects the way people think and feel. But this is likely the result of the kind of money people use, how that money is acquired, and how various influences warp people's beliefs. Cryptocurrency, on the other hand, is a different animal. It is a currency that does not require faith in central bankers or monolithic governments. A person just needs to gain knowledge of the protocol that powers bitcoin to have a basic understanding.

Knowledge of cryptocurrency and experience with it have already altered the psychology around how people view money and wealth. This new monetary thinking has created a generation of millionaires who made their bitcoin riches from starting businesses or other ventures—hence why many people in the community do not harbor ill-will toward the wealthy, as is the case with Jamie Redman and his family. As a matter of fact, the bitcoin community is so tightly knit that they revere entrepreneurs as heroes.

My perspective is wholly anecdotal, but digital currencies provide a new psychological lens through which to view money. This evolved construction of currency could certainly begin to diminish the pauper effect and help eliminate the various biases toward money. Indeed, it is an innovation that could alter the course of neuroeconomics, behavioral economics, and humanity itself.

The Economics of Freedom

October 24, 2011

In my dream world, cigars would be the accepted medium of exchange. They're more valuable than the dollar, anyway.

December 3, 2013

Can someone tell me what a "livable wage" is? I've heard this term tossed around a lot lately, but no strict definition exists. Living conditions fluctuate from person to person. To me, "livable wage" implies that people want to force a certain business to pay higher wages just because they are larger. These anti-economic ideas are mostly nonsense masquerading as deep societal truths.

December 5, 2013

Arguing against property is inherently self-refuting. If you argue against property, logically you are arguing that you do not own yourself and that you are up for grabs.

Your body is the first form of property you will ever own.

July 8, 2015

Most people do not understand how the market works. They make judgments based on juvenile emotional reactions, hence why they believe business owners should be threatened with violence if they deny services to homosexuals or people of color. If a business owner chooses not to do business with someone for whatever reason, that is their choice, and they have to face the natural consequences of that decision.

There is no need to resort to waving a gun around and issuing orders because a businessman embraces homophobic or racist policies. There is nothing immoral about a business owner making these decisions, even if they are petty.

Also, there is no such thing as "emotional damage." Imagine if an already violent entity, like the government, tried to enforce all manner of "emotional damage." Everyone would be living in a cage for hurting feelings left and right.

That said, if there is an appreciation for African-Americans or homosexuals within society, the business owner who makes that decision is going to risk reduced business, strikes, negative press, and potential boycotts. There is no positive incentive for a business to come out as anti-black or anti-gay.

From a market standpoint, that is an amateur business strategy. People just need to realize this truth, as well as that pointing a gun at someone because of their business practices, is not taking the moral high ground unless that business physically harms or defrauds its customers or employees.

Bitcoin Is Not a Bubble

9/12/2017

The internet is replete with people referring to bitcoin as a "bubble." People are spreading fear, uncertainty, and doubt galore. They believe bitcoin's high price spells impending doom, but their criticisms move beyond mere skepticism. It seems they just hate cryptocurrency, yet many of these pundits do not fully grasp bitcoin—or even economics.

For anyone unfamiliar with what a bubble is, *Investopedia* refers to it as an asset driven by unwarranted but exuberant market behavior. It is basically a hike in price that has resulted in a lie or "false truth" about the actual value of an asset, and this, therefore, presages a massive selloff.

People Are Confused about Bitcoin

Commentators like Peter Schiff and others have routinely said bitcoin is a "bubble" and that it will collapse at any moment. They make these claims but do not seem to understand how bitcoin works. Everyone sees headlines like this all over the internet. "Bitcoin is a false truth, warns analyst," reads one, while another from *CNBC* claims "Bitcoin's nearly five-fold climb in 2017 looks very similar to tech bubble surge." There is even a site dedicated to collecting the FUD (fear, uncertainty, and doubt) and clickbait claims the mainstream media repeats.

In a recent *Chicago Tribune* op-ed article titled "Why Investors Should be Wary of Bitcoin," writer Gail MarksJarvis also compared the bitcoin boom to various historical bubbles.

> Do you remember the housing crash of 2008, when the innocents who bought homes thinking they'd make a fortune on soaring prices ended up losing 30 percent on plunging home values? Do you remember the technology stock bubble of early 2000? Until the technology bubble burst, people were euphoric about the pioneers of the fledgling Internet in the 1990s, and figured the gains in technology stocks would never end.

She went on to say that bitcoin is not special or different in this regard. She implied it is a "volatile bubble" that could burst at any time and leave investors gasping for air. Her comparisons—and all comparisons mentioned—are erroneous, though. The currency is not comparable to any of the aforementioned history lessons.

Bitcoin Is Special

Bitcoin is special. It is not a company that could lose profitability and fail. It is certainly not a speculative real estate scam that could crumble because of government and bank-induced chicanery. Bitcoin is another animal.

Its value is not increasing because of marketplace lies. It is increasing because it is a life-changing financial invention. It is increasing because more people are adopting it. The "network effect" is in full swing.

It is true that investors are eager to get on board and that this excitement is causing bitcoin's price to explode, but do not confuse this with an artificially inflated bubble based on a "false truth." Under the network effect, the more people continue to get involved with bitcoin, the higher the price will climb.

Basic Economics

Bitcoin is also growing in value as a result of basic economics. The supply is limited to 21 million units, and this necessarily makes bitcoin a scarce asset. When things are scarce and people want those things, their price will ultimately rise. This is supply and demand at work.

Thus, when economics and the network effect intermingle, you have a recipe for explosive growth within an asset. Bitcoin is not some new version of the 17th-century tulip bulb bubble. It is a groundbreaking advancement in accounting and money.

Bubbles versus Technological Failures

With that said, this does not mean bitcoin is guaranteed to succeed. The price could be affected if something bad were to happen to the protocol that underlies it. If this kind of event ever occurred, people would certainly lose faith in bitcoin, and its price would collapse.

However, this is not the same thing as an artificially hiked price or "bubble." It is the result of a technological or community failure, but not a market failure. For instance, bitcoin just upgraded to Segwit. However, Segwit does not necessarily align with Satoshi Nakamoto's vision that bitcoin should be a scalable, peer-to-peer cash system. Instead, it turns bitcoin into a settlement layer, which could harm the currency.

This illustration is not intended to spread panic. I am just saying bitcoin is susceptible to failures and crashes, but these potential crashes are not the result of a "bubble." They would occur because the community failed to make bitcoin economically viable. In either case, many people hope Segwit will work in the long run and that there will not be a technological failure.

Conclusion

Point being: If people want to call bitcoin a bubble, they ought to explain why exactly it is one instead of incompetently comparing it to past bubbles that do not share any characteristics with bitcoin other than a big price tag. If bitcoin were a bubble, it would be the largest one humankind has ever witnessed (not counting the 6,000-year-old gold bubble, of course). But that is unlikely. It is more likely that bitcoin is just an amazing creation. Its value and potential dwarf any fintech idea heretofore imagined, and the blockchain communities are just getting started.

Bitcoin Solves Runaway Inflation

6/7/2017

B ankers, governments, and other "trusted" centralized organizations require society to be steeped in runaway inflation. These fiduciary cartels thrive when they manipulate the money supply and cause drastic shifts in prices within the market economy. They believe the money supply must be regulated and controlled for the economy to function optimally lest society collapse as a result of too little currency injection.

Luckily, Bitcoin solves the dilemma of needing a trusted third party to control the money supply. Before delving further into why this is the case, everyone must possess a proper and clear grasp of inflation and deflation as economic concepts.

Inflation and Deflation Explained

Inflation refers to the rise of the cost of goods and services in a market environment and the decrease of the purchasing power of the prescribed currency. As *Investopedia* defines it, "Inflation is the rate at which the general level of prices for goods and services is rising and, consequently, the purchasing power of currency is falling. Central banks attempt to limit inflation in order to keep the economy running smoothly."

Conversely, deflation is the decline in the cost of goods and services resulting from the contraction of a money supply within an economic environment. Deflation generally causes an increase in the purchasing power of a currency in circulation. According to some economists, excess deflation can cause market actors to hoard money. However, inflation tends to be a more troubling and nefarious problem.

For example, if a currency is heavily inflated and you travel to the local supermarket to buy groceries, you may notice an upswing in the price of bread. This price "inflation" could be the result of the grocer arbitrarily altering the price, but it more likely occurs because of an inflated currency. In other words, too much printing and distribution of the currency would devalue its purchasing power and cause bread to appear more expensive. The bread likely has the same value as always, but the decreased value of the circulated currency provides the illusion that the bread is more expensive.

With a basic understanding of deflation and inflation clearly in mind, it might seem obvious that central money manipulators are needed to keep the economy grounded in a state of equilibrium where money is created with integrity and circulated for the betterment of society. However, there are several reasons why having a small, trusted group of elites control society's wealth is impractical, unnecessary, and dangerous—and why it has only instigated economic calamity.

The Problem of Central Money Manipulation by Fiduciary Cartels

In some places, governments and central authorities have caused such extreme runaway inflation that currencies have lost all their value and become worthless.

Recent examples include Venezuela and Greece. Mass currency devaluation through inflation likely also occurred in the United States, which led to the Great Depression. The Austrian economists have suggested that the creation of the Federal Reserve bank and its manipulation of the currency supply directly caused the depression, among other more recent economic catastrophes.

A *Mises Institute* article on Greece captured the effects of credit expansion and money manipulation, which was followed by runaway inflation.

> When currencies collapse, price inflation usually picks up. More units of the currency must be offered to acquire goods and services. What had started with credit expansion and distortions in the real economy, then, may well end up with high price inflation rates and currency reform. Another reason to avoid allowing a handful [of] people [to] control currency in a centralized manner is [that] it provides a subtle way for those individuals to "steal" value from everyone. Whenever central authorities inflate the currency supply, as mentioned, it causes the value or purchasing power of the currency to decline. This value is basically lost or "stolen" from the people.

> In other words, one group caused another group to lose their property's value. In most places, this activity by another name is called "destruction of property" or "theft." However, currency devaluation is such an esoteric and ingenious form of theft or destruction that it goes unnoticed and unexamined by the majority of the population.

A last major reason to reject central suppliers of money is more obvious and terrifying. When a small group of people has direct access to the wealth supply of whole economies, what prevents them from electronically keying that wealth into their own accounts? What stops them from making themselves richer and the rest of the world poorer? What stops them from taking that wealth and using it to start wars or harm people in the name of national defense or protection?

The short answer to these questions is nothing. Nothing stops them. These individuals can fill their coffers at a whim and control the rise and fall of whole countries by arbitrarily inflating and deflating a currency as they see fit, and the results of trusting these elite few have been devastating. It has led to mass warfare, mass exploitation of the population, and in some cases, runaway inflation, mass starvation, and death.

Thank goodness the solution to these problems is here. It is called bitcoin.

Bitcoin Solves the Problem of Runaway Inflation While Abolishing the Need for Centralized Trust

Bitcoin is a cryptocurrency that is automated by a consensus network algorithm. This algorithm, which was predetermined by creator Satoshi Nakamoto, has a set supply of bitcoins that will be distributed over the long term. This number is currently set to 21 million units of bitcoin.

This mathematically encoded number of bitcoin means no central group or fiduciary cartel can control the currency. In other words, they cannot inflate or deflate a currency to the detriment of the population. In this sense, bitcoin is naturally deflationary, or disinflationary. Bitcoin has utility in the sense that it neither inflates nor deflates on a whim. No human actor can make changes to the protocol without achieving consensus.

In this regard, bitcoin users have hedged themselves against control, against the small groups of "trusted" elites who can manage the flow or circulation of money across a population. When a currency like bitcoin is protected from artificial manipulation, this prevents people from using the creation and control of money to exploit and defraud others. It is the solution to the problem of runaway inflation and all forms of monetary control.

Some people think bitcoin is naturally inflationary as a result of its algorithm. The protocol indeed specifies the minting of new coins via mining, but this is not the same as arbitrary inflation that causes ungodly increases in the prices of goods and services. The protocol was built to create coins in such a way that it both heightens the value of bitcoin and also does not cause an excess in the market. It is enough to keep the market humming but not overburdened.

Bitcoin, then, is the most obvious solution to stopping the fiduciary cartels and other central entities from lording over everyone and causing massive undue harm to millions. It prevents runaway inflation. It stops theft through that inflation. It thwarts loss of monetary value caused by unscrupulous actors. It kills the evil of greed. It is the economic panacea *par excellence*.

It's time to open a cryptocurrency wallet and take the power back.

The Plight of the Individualist

April 26, 2010

Some people mistake weird for insane, but weird can often mean hyper-intelligent. This mistake causes us to label important people as lunatics. The problem is that if people do not fit cultural norms, we ostracize them. They're rejected because their behavior is too chaotic and doesn't mesh with stringent, anal-retentive values. We must change this social mindset. The day we venerate the weird is the day society advances because these "weirdos" remain imminently open to novel possibilities. They are the forgotten iconoclasts and the lost Teslas.

February 16, 2011

The greatest thing I can imagine in life is the absolute sovereignty of the individual. This is an ideal, possibly an unachievable one, but one that is worth harboring and holding close to your bosom as if it were an infant child.

March 3, 2014

I loathe the idea of "collective" anything. Does this mean I devalue group effort? No. It just means that group values can never trump individual values. Once the group overpowers the individual, utilitarian barbarism and bloodshed spread like wildfire, and I will not be a sacrificial animal. I will not purge every bit of my decency and humanity to be fodder for the sociopaths and sycophants. I will not kneel at the altar of abstraction and nihilism. Instead, I will live by my own conscience and self-reliance—for myself and those dearest and closest to me—of my own volition.

April 4, 2014

Some schools of psychology categorize people into one of two camps: introvert or extrovert. And people also tend to categorize themselves in one or the other domain. It's easy to do, and perhaps individuals fit snugly into one. However, I see this as a false dichotomy, as people exhibit vast irregularities and nuances of personality, at times fitting the gregariousness of the rockstar while at other times fitting the contemplative asceticism of the monk. The beauty of free will and conscious volition easily grants the addition of both traits, allowing the person to experience their true self however their personality exhibits itself to the world.

April 19, 2014

There's a certain design for living attached to the individualist philosophy: It's a blueprint that screams "I am *it*. I am what *matters*." Going away from this design and slumming toward shit that is beneath you is a recipe for disaster and death. It is the enemy's pride and joy because he knows he has duped you into believing you are something lesser. Don't fall for this malarkey. The individual is he who protects himself and his loved ones. The individual is he whose name resonates across the ages. The individual is he who destroys the lies perpetuated by religious groupthink. The individual is you, and you are designed to uphold your virtues, your friends, your family, and your desires— whatever *you want*. Don't let the naysayers and slave drivers drag you down into suffering and hell. Live as an individual. Be what matters. Scream it over and over!

February 9, 2016

I focus on the new and bold. I am apt to wander off the beaten path. I enjoy being courageous and blazing new trails. I feel like people get stuck in cultural ruts. That is why iconoclasts always need to come along to balance the equation, challenge the status quo, and help jar people from their trance.

That's the kind of person I am. I am not interested in doing the same things that don't work again and again, and I am certainly not interested in harming others because people living in this era say it's acceptable.

I have a penchant for truth. I want real insight. I don't want to be molded like clay and let loose in a putrid farm of cow zombies. I want to do shit differently in radical new ways that reshape the cultural milieu for the better. There are too many stuck in the coma culture, doing things the wrong ways for the wrong reasons.

What kind of person are you? Are you afraid to go against the grain? Do you prefer silent obedience to uproarious defiance? I choose to slam my fist down on the anvil of justice. I choose to leverage any talent I have to make this world better, and I plan on doing it as loudly and proudly as possible.

March 1, 2016

I live my own life. I pull myself up by the bootstraps. I reject political servitude and coercion. I will not be seen choosing "the lesser of two evils." I will not be seen degrading myself by begging political masters for scraps, favors, and gifts. The voting booth is a cancer ward, and everyone involved is terminal. I will keep my head raised high, live my life how I see fit, solve problems on my own, and cooperate with my fellow humans without resorting to rhetorically concealed violence. I will not vote for some chump who believes he knows what's best for millions of people. I will not waiver in my principles, and I will continuously decry this system of subjugation.

Act according to your own self-responsibility and human dignity. No one else is going to do it for you, though they may lie to convince you otherwise, as kings and dictators have done since time immemorial.

Don't vote. You have no say in their game of thrones.

December 15, 2016

It's okay to be unorthodox, opinionated, contrarian, odd, crafty, technical, and prone to all manner of eccentricities.

It's these quirks of personality that generally characterize people of vast depth, creativity, and intelligence. It's these weird people who help thrust humanity forward. They may discover a new philosophy, imagine a groundbreaking business, invent some gadget, write a beautiful novel, create some piece of emotionally compelling artwork, or take us to another planet. The strange and different are leaders of men. They are movers and shakers.

Treat all people well, but don't forget about or neglect these special individuals.

They keep the world alive with imagination and hope.

March 6, 2017

This is the nonsense I am having to read in my multicultural counseling class. This is the most judgmental, racist, and manipulative content I have ever had the displeasure of reading. This is not practical advice for soon-to-be counselors. This is politically loaded garbage that only makes counselors self-conscious and constantly concerned with possibly being racist. I love my classes, but this material is abusive and one-sided. Have a taste of it.

> First, it is clear that most Whites perceive themselves as unbiased individuals who do not harbor racist thoughts and feelings; they see themselves as working toward social justice and possessing a conscious desire to better the life circumstances of those less fortunate than they. Although these are admirable qualities, this self-image serves as a major barrier to recognizing and taking responsibility for admitting and dealing with one's own prejudices and biases. To admit to being racist, sexist, or homophobic requires people to recognize that the self-images they hold so dear are based on false notions of the self.

Sue, Derald Wing; Sue, David. *Counseling the Culturally Diverse: Theory and Practice* (p. 394). Wiley. Kindle Edition.

March 7, 2017

In my "diversity" and "multicultural" counseling class I made everyone giggle.

The professor said we need to recognize our "whiteness" to have what Carl Rogers called "unconditional positive regard" for all of our clients.

I said, "Sir, if I keep reading this book I won't be able to have unconditional positive regard for white people."

March 25, 2017

Hello neighbor, I want to speak with you about freedom.

You don't need a government to live your life. You don't need people telling you what to do. You don't need to be locked in a cage for eating candy or sniffing pixie sticks.

You just need your community, your connections, your family, and your dreams.

Sovereignty is right there waiting for you, within your grasp. You can feel it. Touch it. It has its own character and its own scent, and it is sublime and ecstatic. And once it has you in its grasp, you'll never let it go.

That's what I've done. But listen...if you don't like how I do it, you can try your own way.

April 20, 2017

Self-employment, entrepreneurship, and not doing the 9-to-5 grind make up the purview of anarchists, artists, iconoclasts, and forward thinkers. Freedom of intellectual movement is simultaneously the freedom to create and evolve. It is the freedom to live.

Economic Literacy Is Essential

March 21, 2019

To understand what's going on in the world, people must pursue economic literacy. I am not talking about the bastardized economics disseminated by ivory tower pseudo-intellectuals. I am talking about Austrian praxeology; I am talking about human action. It's through this conduit of knowledge that people internalize the vile and evil nature of governments.

An authentic economic education will provide people with insight into why so many things in society are broken—why the dollar continuously loses value, why the Great Depression happened, and why the housing bubble collapsed. It will provide people with insight into why cryptocurrencies are better money, and then they will begin to understand why money has value at all. They will come to terms with the nature of subjective value, and they will ultimately understand why morality is often studied alongside economic considerations.

The problem is that this awakening will come at a price. People will realize we are no longer on the *Road to Serfdom*, as F.A. Hayek pointed out. The road has ended, and serfdom is here—within, without, and everywhere around. This is because of government control, because of politicians' warped economic measures, and because vast ignorance makes up the collective psyche of humanity.

In this sense, awakening to these horrible economic realities will also be jarring, unsettling, and burdensome. It will be akin to Neo unplugging from the Matrix, and there will be a temptation to swallow the blue pill and go back to sleep.

That won't happen to most people, though. People who wake up come alive. They realize the vast problems in society, and then they begin to speak truth and connect with people, opening hearts and minds.

This is the power of economic literacy.

To Awaken Is to Live

January 29, 2011

To say something politically incorrect is one thing, but to live a politically incorrect life is satisfyingly dangerous.

August 3, 2013

Freedom is serious business, but to fight for freedom, people first must see the cage and realize they are slaves. The problem is that waking up is traumatizing and disorienting. It takes time and courage.

August 9, 2013

The real heroes are the peaceful parents who treat their children with dignity, and the cops, soldiers, and politicians who have quit their jobs because they realized the violent nature of them.

Heroes aren't the people assaulting and killing others. Heroes are the ones who stand in defiance of aggression and who practice nonviolence and peace in their day-to-day lives.

Power to the modern hero—the true hero.

November 7, 2013

It's the strong-willed people who see taxation as robbery. They're the kind of people who do not fall for collective guilt and who believe a person's earnings are his and that he can do what he pleases with them regardless of the sobbing and pleading going on all around, which are simply guns and threats veiled by emotional tantrums.

December 24, 2013

I speak strictly on anarchism and liberty because these ideas matter. These ideas are sparks intended to ignite the flame of a better society. Blabbering about irrelevant topics is a waste of my intellectual real estate and does nothing to change the world we live in. Regardless of how fascinating and intellectually stimulating other topics might be, they fail to actively alter people's thinking about morality and social organization. My goal is to not waste any more time and to follow my passion and conviction for liberty and truth. It is to get people motivated and inspired. Droning on about spacey topics will not accomplish my goals and will eventually lead to intellectual stagnation.

Matter of fact, anyone wondering about these things might also check their priorities. I am not suggesting you talk or think about what I want you to, but considering your own freedom and the fact that others have a perpetual gun to your head, changing your approach might kindle a rejuvenation of understanding and focus. Why waste time and energy philosophizing in a wasteland of moot points? Why not help address slavery and participate in making the world a better place? Why not engage in moral evolution? Why not work to unleash everyone's greatest potential as humans?

We do not accomplish anything by speculating on Anatolia, Bigfoot, lizard-men, space elves, panspermia, mushroom trans-dimensional travel, or the exact cause of language in our species. It's all really interesting and neat stuff, but it is wholly useless until we have the freedom to work without having to dodge all the violence, bullying, controls, and douchebaggery.

Here is why I focus on anarchism, first principles, and freedom: I want to heal society and free myself, not get lost in the mental masturbatory hallucination of intellectual snobbery and pomposity.

December 31, 2013

Use whatever skill or ability you possess to express freedom and bring it to its logical conclusion. Don't surrender or let naysayers, petty tyrants, or brow beaters thwart your activity. The desire for freedom is powerful enough to bring the brilliance in anyone bursting forth regardless of barriers. Let your absolute freedom shine through. You cannot let yourself down. The future depends on it.

January 18, 2014

My fiancé posted an article on Facebook earlier. It was about Missouri lawmakers who want to institute the firing squad as an acceptable death penalty. In the comments section, people had all kinds of colorful ideas about how to mutilate evildoers, including beheading, hanging, drawing and quartering, etc. This disgusts me, and not because I feel sorry for anyone who might have done a horrendous deed but because of people's urge to see and use the most despicable forms of violence. It shows the internally cruel and barbaric nature of many people.

However, my experience reading that article allowed me to acknowledge the spiritual kinship of my fellow anarchists. We aren't searching for the kill or living vicariously through the cannibalistic and vampiric urge to feed off heinous and grotesque violence.

Instead, we are trying to purify life, simplify it, and not drown in the blood of past mistakes and darkness. Together, we calculate the least violent formulas for living and dealing with people, and we always refer to the sanctuary of reason as our North Star.

None of us are perfect, but we do everything in our power to undercut the brutal Freudian unconscious of an abused species and work toward healing all. The voluntaryist philosophy is something I am proud to be part of and belong to. Dwelling on ways to hurt people just shows a lack of decency, dignity, sophistication, and originality.

January 24, 2014

I am not certain what changed or what has gotten into me, but the fire and passion for moving forward intellectually and doing something positive for the growth of anarchism have really struck and overwhelmed me. It's like an understanding of the emotional and positive side of the movement has filled me with ideas, and I just want to spread them. I want people to realize that anarchism warrants everyone's attention because it allows us to experience the world in all of its splendor and goodness. People just have to see it, and I believe I can show the anarchist's love to people and still maintain the reason and logic embedded in the philosophy. Let the love of anarchism free the world from the shackles of darkness and evil. Let us immerse ourselves in its poetry and ecstasy and bestow that on our fellow humans forever.

January 28, 2014

To incite change, you must rock the philosophical boat from time to time. This is mandatory because people are so resistant to change. You can only allow yourself to be stuck in vicious cycles of abuse for so long. It is now time for humanity to start questioning, awakening, and changing its thought process. Too many have suffered for too long at the hands of stupidity and evil. Acknowledge your chains, and you shall be free.

January 29, 2014

Too many people want to argue for the sake of arguing, as if to satisfy an ego drive. Grow beyond this mindset. Have passion. Have conviction. Argue because you advocate truth. Argue because you want peace. Argue because you want motherfuckers to get the gun out of your face. There's too much at stake to waste on personal insecurities. Push the truth and change people. Change the world. The morning has barely broken, so make the day count.

February 3, 2014

The iconoclast must live dangerously on the edge at every moment. She must express the grandeur of her mind and spirit, which is indicative of absolute freedom regardless of the nincompoop, pedantic petty tyrants who hover over issuing warnings, threats, and commands.

February 13, 2014

The liberty community seems enticing because there is such fierce intelligence radiating within it. But it is not just Intelligence that draws one in; it is also the charisma, eloquence, and persuasiveness of these individuals. They debate and argue with such confidence and knowledge that it is almost impossible to dismiss them or pretend any other logic is stronger.

Eventually, you yield to it not because of any physical force but because these beautiful and persuasive individuals seize you with the power of love and honesty, and you freeze up and suddenly know that freedom and anarchy are for lovers and that the other possibilities reek of incomplete logic, shallow verbiage, and outright violence. And so, people easily say "fuck that" to these other Stone Age, troglodytic philosophies, and they accept a hard but well-earned truth.

February 17, 2014

Want change? Make waves. You may piss a few off in the process, but if your aim is true, it will be better for them—for everyone.

Life is too short to stand by and grit your teeth. Get in there, balls deep, and show them what you are made of.

This is how whole truths are stumbled upon, how collections of people wake up, and how everyone rejoices at the courage it took from you—from everyone.

Live beautifully. Live dangerously. Live truthfully.

They'll see and come alive with spirit—even the haters and the villains.

February 21, 2014

The greatest thinkers wield intellectual courage. If you are not using your thoughts to break the mold and create change and are instead speaking in riddles or beating around the bush, you are wasting precious time. Do not be afraid to go out there and speak the truth. The world will be better for it. There are too many ivory tower hypocrites out there comfortable with the status quo and keeping people anesthetized and dumbed down. Let us reinvigorate the spirit of revolt together!

May 13, 2014

The State is nothing but a floating abstraction. It's nothing but a figment of the imagination. It's a myth embedded in the mind of the everyman. The truth is much more absurd than the myth: The State is nothing but a group of buffoons who believe they have power. Fuck this. Forget this. Remember that only you have power; only you have authority. Only you have absolute sovereignty over yourself and rightness over your own volition and decency. Remember that you are the one, the arbiter of your humanity and destiny.

Shed the manacles and live and die as a free man above the myths and false prophets of power.

January 15, 2015

If you are going to do one thing in life, stand for something positive and meaningful. Help to heal the world, if only a little.

March 8, 2015

I love that anarchists are so far ahead of the curve. Most recognize the following truths: They understand that government is just a larger mafia and do not sugarcoat that fact and pretend statism is necessary. They acknowledge that taxation is straight-up robbery. They recognize that fiat currency is just printed monopoly money with enforced value. They realize that the drug war is just modern-day witch-hunting. They know that culture is poisonous because it reinforces Stone Age dogma and violence. They admit the family teaches people that violence is an acceptable method of solving problems.

Above all, they realize the importance of individualism over governmental systems and socialist philosophies. They have withdrawn their consent and support for the current social paradigm, and they fight for the greatest positive change humanity has seen—greater even than the abolition of slavery or recognition that the earth is round and circles the sun.

Anarchists and voluntaryists have entered the fold and fight for a whole new epoch in the forward march of human evolution. The question remains: Will you choose to be on the right side of history, or will you cower before all things evil and antiquated? Anarchy is rising with or without you.

July 21, 2015

You can see the evolutionary nature of anarchism. Anarchists are picking up on where the digital age is guiding humanity, and they are running with it. Why would you not want to be a part of this? If you are still living in the mental age of statism, you are behind the times. You are like the people who denounced Newton and Galileo. You still believe that the earth is the center of the universe and that the sun circles it. Wake up and look around. Humanity is on the verge of yet another epoch.

September 5, 2015

I am enjoying living in these times. You know how some people seem like they were born into the wrong era? I feel like I was born into the right one. I feel naturally disinclined to the idea of authority. I gravitate strongly to property rights and the propertarian mentality. This is the reason I am enjoying watching consciousness and culture shift toward these ideas.

It looks like respect for police and their brutality is starting to wane as more folks wake up to the idea that jackbooted thugs are unneeded in society. People are decrying and disobeying police regularly, which I hope will lead to the complete abandonment of authoritarian lifestyles. Lack of respect for police is emerging on such a broad scale that politicians are whining about it and calling for their "constituents" to support them, but I am seeing a lot of "fuck offs," which is great.

Of course, too many people are still blinded by political preoccupation and the rhetorical alchemy that flows from bad ideas, but this, too, will subside. More people are starting to embrace sharing economy lifestyles and submit to the will of their own being rather than the rulers who play the game of thrones.

It is a beautiful time we live in, and if you share my vision and ideals, you should be as excited as I am. Indeed, we may not see freedom in our lifetime, but we can push for it and watch the sociopaths and petty tyrants squirm as they attempt to consolidate power and issue their threatening and ugly invectives.

The days of the politician and king are coming to an end, and the rise of the individual and community is nearing its birth. It is truly a wonderful age even amid the violence and power-whoring.

Are you ready to continue raising your voice and speaking passionately about the truth? Soon, we may all need to use the pulpit and bullhorn. Keep freedom growing and spreading. We are one, but we are also many.

December 12, 2015

Everyone's consciousness should be overwhelmed with revelations of anarchism. If they are not saturated with thoughts of anarchism, they haven't broken open their heads and unleashed satori.

Anarchism is like a psychedelic drug. It is a mind-manifesting agent that works to dispel old dogmas and release negative energies. It is the tree of life growing up through the body, branching out in the musculature and flowering within the seat of the soul. Anarchism is the poetry and music of life because it is a hymnal that soothes, calms, and puts a person on the path to awe. It is a permanently altered state of consciousness, a kind of sensual orgasm that gives an individual rapturous access to the forbidden truths of the world.

Once the anarchophany has been witnessed, there is no going back. There can only be a joyful rollicking and rolling in the felt ecstasy of interpersonal freedom replete with visions of an unfettered world. Anarchism is the hybridization of personality with everything. It is the crucible of all dignified existence, then and now.

December 17, 2015

Some people might wonder why I do it—why I incessantly talk "politics" and freedom. Here is why: We live in a world of totalitarian madness. We muster energy every day to survive in a slave state that has violent police enforcers everywhere and sociopath politicians searching all around with their panopticon gaze, hunting for people to abduct and punish for paltry reasons.

Most folks languish in a business-as-usual stupor, blind to the depredations of government and the fact that they praise and worship their fetters. So, I trumpet this truth to bring people out of their careless comas. I speak to bring down the light of reason and compassion onto the choir of the careless. I want to create communities of active acolytes for freedom, something formidable enough to foment a cultural shift. I loathe the notion that people must be collectivized, controlled, corralled, costumed, and consumed. This is an absolute shame, a pockmark on the face of human history and anathema to everything decent and dignified. And my dire reasoning for wanting this to change is simple.

It is not the nihilistic painting of human nature that causes wanton bloodshed and slavery. Humankind is not doomed to it any more than it was doomed to Aztec-style human sacrifice. It is that people get too comfortable in their cultures and their systems. Like cardboard characters, they believe governments must be allowed to run roughshod over the population for protection. They fear change. But such atrocities are in their twilight and sounding their death knell. The day of conformity and numbed deliberation is over; it is bleeding out on the pavement. The new life is beckoning everyone forward, sounding its beautiful tones. The reverberation of truth and justice is shimmering like the North Star. It is the guiding light bringing peace into the fold regardless of the defeatism of naysayers and their primitive hatred, their reliance on the lizard brain, and their denial of higher things—of wisdom.

Yes, anarchism grows strong while the thugs and thieves clamor for relevance. The liberty laborers continue to acknowledge truth, to grasp the North Star, and to obtain their divining rod of justice. The new world is right there between the eyes, a destination delivered upon us in this time of desolation and damnation. Let's rise in haste, then, and smash all fetters forever.

January 26, 2016

Part of being an anarchist means having spine and flair. It means adhering to principles and values regardless of cultural trends. The political and social milieu we live in is saturated with political correctness and feel-good manipulation. It is driven by the most evocative but baseless ideologies, and these pseudo-philosophies are advertised like costume jewelry on infomercials. The anarchist realizes this, but he does not tuck his tail and run. He does not arbitrarily agree with people for the sake of social solidarity. Instead, the anarchist acknowledges and understands the psychological implications of the current system, but he remains strong and argues his points without buckling. Of course, he also picks and chooses his battles. If he has to retreat for strategic reasons, he does so. But when he stands his ground, he intensely defends the position and argues it as eloquently as possible. This is the calling card of the mature and polished freeman. If he maintains his principle and spine, more people are likely to respond to his declarations. This means his integrity and ability are respected. It demonstrates poise and confidence, and this is, in part, how more anarchists are minted.

March 5, 2016

Current society is founded on dangerous ideas and superstitions that cause harm to many people living within the system. The anarchist can clearly see what needs to be done to make repairs. In this sense, when the anarchist talks to people, plants the seed of freedom, and attempts to convince everyone to remove their shackles, they are helping rewrite how people think about traditional culture, how they perceive the world, and what they imagine to be right and wrong.

The anarchist is thus introducing new programming into a system set to self-destruct. The anarchist's social inputs are a kind of fail-safe, a reboot disk, or a natural reaction to the ringing of cultural alarm bells of impending disaster. It is therefore no surprise that the figure of the anarchist has emerged most heroically in recent days. Society's reliance on sleeping people with umbilical cord attachments to government has come to a head, and now the anarchistic scream is acting as the natural emergency reaction to a culture that has buried itself beneath its own shit.

Now, the anarchist frantically applies the defibrillator to the heart of a dying society, hoping to resuscitate it. The question is whether people want to be brought back to life.

April 21, 2016

Don't be afraid to speak up about the failed system. Don't be afraid to condemn it with every ounce of heart and soul you can muster. Let your rage fly, and make all sycophants, cowards, and leeches tremble. More voices will amplify yours. More love will find you. It is time our choir of peace penetrated all minds and restored virtue worldwide. Those who defend the system are out of arguments. They have failed, and now the power of their lies is diminishing. Anarchy is ascending as people continue to lose faith in their masters. We are now crossing the event horizon. Governments have entered the terminal stage of their sickness. Death becomes them, and light is breaking. A new voyage is beginning, and more and more anarchists will arise to meet our call. Change is around the corner. Never falter.

July 25, 2016

I commend and congratulate all the vocal anarchists.

Speaking for liberty and speaking out against the injustices of the political system takes real courage. Every day, these unique individuals sacrifice a little of their social livelihood and risk being ostracized and punished for their views. They have more gumption than almost every public official, celebrity, or "political" activist. It takes no grit to work within the system or promote government solutions.

To strike at the root of evil, however, takes real guts. It takes a real leader and iconoclast. When people work within the system or attack businesses, they have next to no repercussions to fear because they are playing by the rules; they are playing the sociocultural game.

Anarchists, on the other hand, are tearing the game down and exposing the truth that it is rigged. Thus, they face ridicule and persecution. That is why I give the utmost appreciation to these people, as well as my undivided attention and support.

Thank you for your courage. Thanks for going out on a limb to make this world better each and every day.

July 30, 2016

It amazes me how many people blindly go along with the law simply because a politician wrote it down. It never even occurs to many people to question its legitimacy or morality. Disobedience is not part of their language or heritage, and this makes me sad; it is a tragedy. But hopefully, as society continues to erode because of government, we can help shake people from their stupor of subservience. We can help break their bonds and build their character. We can finally instill in them the joy of living unfettered and free. That is why anarchists are as much healers as they are dissidents. They are providing people with the wherewithal and hunger to question their masters.

August 22, 2016

Anarchists are a special class of people. They are a branch of individuals with unique brains; they are part of the neurodiversity movement insofar as they think differently and shun cultural trends like the idea that government is necessary. This is certainly "fringe" contemplation, but it is based on first principles, knowledge of human psychology, and rational self-interest.

It is also true that many fringe movements grow large enough to foment change. It is this unique and gifted segment of the population that may appear "odd" or "crazy" but possesses the insight and knowledge to make the world a better place. In this regard, I would encourage hearing the plight of the anarchist and internalizing the ideas.

Anarchism has been a fringe movement for years and years, but with the advancement of internet communications and the strengthening of the philosophy, anarchist communities are blossoming, and they are effectively creating more neurodiversity and more uniqueness as the preeminence of the individual overcomes the brutality of the collective.

August 26, 2016

I am pretty good at articulating ideas, but I don't think I can communicate the sheer profundity of what anarchists have already accomplished. I am going to try like hell, though.

Most people talk about anarchism in terms of the future, about *how* it will achieve a freer society. They ask rhetorical questions as if anarchism were a wet dream, but I find this amusing and ironic. Anarchists have already won. It's just that the total consequences of their efforts have not come to fruition just yet.

Anarchists have already created freer societies bustling with decentralized micro-economies. Crypto-cultures exist across the web and function in their entirety beneath the radar of government intervention. There are also new devices that are anarchistic in nature and already reshaping society—like the Defense Distributed Ghost Gunner.

There is a veritable smorgasbord of anarchist influence ballooning outward across society (many of which I have not even heard of), and this huge growth largely owes its success to the tireless efforts of modern anarchist thinkers, entrepreneurs, philosophers, and activists.

I seriously cannot underscore how proud I am to be part of this new wave of anarchistic revolutionaries. I will say with pride that being part of this culture of visionaries has improved my life in so many ways, many of which I had not fathomed were possible.

I just hope I can keep contributing in the little ways I can and continue providing my communication skills to help enlighten even more people to the imminent global paradigm shift.

If you run in anarchist circles, you already know what I am talking about, and I thank you from the bottom of my heart.

September 12, 2016

One of the most tragic things about the world is that authority is expected to exist.

People are expected to fall in line.

There is an expectation there should be rulers and serfs.

Everyone who is not in power is expected to bend the knee.

These expectations are universal and based on broken psychology and fear— fear of social revolution, fear to change the system, and fear of being an individual against all odds. This is a pervasive, encompassing fear that keeps people tethered to silence.

The expectation for silence is unwritten but ubiquitous. The depravities of culture are supposed to continue without counteraction, without someone interfering in the mundane movement of the levers and pulleys of the system.

But now there is a new expectation.

That expectation is for a transformation of society, a focus on the beauty, peace, and nonviolence of the anarchists who have disavowed the contaminated social norms and expectations.

The anarchists won't give in to convention and consensus myopia.

Now we will speak, allowing the thunder of our voices to boom, reverberate, and destroy the banality of everyday evil and workaday violence.

No more will there be the cowardice of silence. Against all odds, we will speak, rise, and convene in a rapturous throng in the thrall of absolute freedom.

Be with us. The expectations of old are no longer the expectations of the new.

December 17, 2016

I am proud to be an anarchist. I am proud to say I don't accept the idea that rulers should control my life. I am glad I don't have to make excuses for politics and politicians. I don't have to worry myself about which tyrant got elected and which did not. I am ecstatic to be free from the religious ritual of statism. I am thankful to have finally found compassion, solace, and understanding.

And if you have not accepted anarchism, I hope you can soon discover the same feeling of mental and emotional freedom.

January 4, 2017

It takes special people to speak out against the system and strive for anarchism. The people who have taken this path are the cream of the crop. They are courageous and authentic. They are visionaries who will stop at nothing to create a new, better world for everyone.

However, the task of combating the system is not an easy one. Anarchists face constant threats. They are chastised, alienated, ostracized, threatened, harassed, and scapegoated for their beliefs and principles. They will be hated, and sometimes the consequences of their actions will be dire.

I have risked jobs, my life, and my livelihood for my convictions. I have dealt with scrutiny from those close to me all because I think government is garbage and freedom is good.

Nonetheless, I keep pushing forward because peace, love, and freedom are ideals I cherish deeply and keep close to my heart. Things may get worse before they get better, but I am going to keep on keeping on. I suspect many anarchists will also continue down this path because they believe the ideal is worth the effort. They believe a new world is possible.

No matter what maelstrom of malicious nonsense from government cronies and sleeping sadists they have to deal with, they will not break in the face of fear. They will not stop because people issue threats and condemnations of anarchy. No. They will persevere through all difficulties.

This is because anarchists are not like any other political group. Their ideas, principles, and personalities are not shaped by any goddamn television program, school curriculum, or religious ideology. Their ideas ultimately come from within, from a voracious hunger to live outside the system— to be free of festering tyranny and all the godforsaken violence.

This is why these people are special. They are freethinkers. Free lovers. They are unique. Bold. Enthusiastic. Forward-thinking. Compassionate. Kind. Strong.

Without anarchists and similar iconoclasts, the world would be rife with sycophants and succubi, and the forces of good would be nowhere. All the world would be drowning in damnation without a single voice crying out for dignity and decency.

January 16, 2017

When society has forgotten decency, compassion, and freedom, it is up to anarchists to help everyone remember.

January 18, 2017

Don't be afraid of change.

Anarchism, like all philosophies, can evolve and grow. There is no padlock that bars intellectual innovation and the development of ideas. Being a traditionalist is antithetical to the spirit of anarchism. This philosophy is about rebellion, revolution, and spontaneous mutation.

Without this spirit of innovation and creativity in anarchist circles, anarcho-capitalism would not have been fully fleshed out as an anarchic philosophy. The traditionalists—the left anarchists—would have kept anarchism locked away in a box with their limited vision of the philosophy like they still do to this day.

But luckily, renegade philosophers worked their magic and augmented the philosophy to fit their values, logic, and objective reality. They didn't let the traditionalist anarchists dictate how anarchism should be. They didn't capitulate to dogmatic pressures to conform.

No. They rejected the Marxist perspective of anarchism. They ignored appeals to tradition, and they worked instead. They heaved and hoed. They pushed forward and advanced the philosophy for the good of humankind.

Indeed, I hope anarchism never stops growing. I hope one day someone builds a version that is more palatable to the everyman but still jibes with the spirit of a stateless, rulerless society. I hope further development of the philosophy creates even more widespread adoption.

February 12, 2017

Anarchy is not only a moralistic philosophy but is also a human potential movement.

March 17, 2017

Anarchism is not only a philosophy but also a profound feeling. The cognitive liberty it delivers brings a person closer to God, whether such a thing exists. The mere feeling of being next to divinity is rapturous, and anarchism is the holy sacrament that confers this type of ecstasy. In this regard, it's about the feeling and the inspiration. It's about the beauty and the poetic grammar of unobstructed freedom.

April 2, 2017

I want to take this moment to show mad respect to all vocal anarchists. It takes courage to speak up about freedom in all the different ways we do. When we express our disdain for government violence, we risk attacks from all angles.

People will try to contaminate our character, spoil our reputations, frame us, whine about us to other people, or otherwise use their fear to undermine our philosophical quest.

They will do whatever it takes to prevent the inevitable escalation of liberty from breaking their urban trance.

Well, I have good news. This means our output for freedom is making an impact. Our words are so powerful they are upsetting people. Our words are resonating with those who have never bothered to think outside the box or imagine anarchism as anything but unbridled mayhem. We have planted anarchist ideas right into the bosom of culture, where we can continue to water them and cause the pain of truth to grow inside the sleeping multitudes.

Don't fear, for we are the harbingers of truth. We are the voices of the future. It is our utterances of abolition that will bring this decadent society out of its stupor and into the light of liberty.

We only live once. Keep pushing. We are change.

You and I: Discovering Our
Natural Opposition to Authority

Bear it aloft, O roaring flame!
Skyward aloft, where all may see.
Slaves of the World! Our cause is the same;
One is the immemorial shame;
One is the struggle, and in One name —
Manhood— we battle to set men free.
"Uncurse us the Land!" burn the words of the Dead,
Written-in-red.
—Voltairine de Cleyre

Me

I am naturally opposed to authority; it is in my bones. But I did not always know. It was buried alive deep inside of me and I had to coax it out. It just took time and experience to expose this truth. But once I grasped it, I was forever changed. Now, I do not see the world in the same hazy, drunken stupor. I no longer harbor the lemming mindset. If I come marching down streets, I come with my fist raised and head held high.

If someone tries to tell me how to live without my consent, they will have a bad time. If they try to command me to do as they wish, I will indulge the opposite. If they try to make me get down on bended-knee and genuflect, I will mock them. If they try, resistance they will meet.

I *am* sovereign.

I will fight against their dictatorial malice with every fiber of my being. I do not believe in the concept of a ruler, king, or president. I acknowledge self-responsibility and self-ownership. I believe standing on my own with pride and dignity is the only way to live. Catering to psychopaths who believe they have the right to tell everyone how to live and solve problems is not only a degradation of rights but also an insult to the very spirit of humanity.

To bow to those who claim to be my master just for the sake of it means sacrificing myself. It means being something less than human, something pitiful and dead. There is nothing lowlier than thinking I must be led around by noose and chain. I want to make my own decisions and choices and have the opportunity to fail and succeed of my own volition. I am not afraid to trod through life's difficulties and risk everything. That is the nature of being, and no one is truly existing if they are restricted by fetters. It is slavery. It is the icy negation of life—absolute zero.

I discovered this natural opposition to authority by examining the world around me and experiencing the brutality of authority firsthand. Then I began to question the systems that perpetuate this nonsense, which caused a boiling rage to erupt within me. I now wonder why I ever believed I had to follow. I wonder why I imagined someone had the right to rule and control me.

I just hope you can understand my anger and see the control freaks who attempt to lord over us. I hope you will join me.

You

I want to help you find your inner defiance. I want you to realize that you are not a creature of burden. You are a human being; you are alive. You radiate beauty and dignity. You are not the property of any president, council, oligarch, or board member. You possess your soul and its unique characteristics. Why feel the need to obey psychopaths?

They make you believe they can guarantee safety and security, that they will protect you and make you happy. But government puts you in peril. It only provides the illusion of safety and security.

The politicians, cops, and kings soil your freedom and cause you to pull the sheets over your head at night. These people start wars, exploit the weak, tell you how to live, enslave everyone, and murder children in their cribs. Government is the absolute antithesis of freedom and safety—it is the betrayal of love and trust.

A memory may help you realize this truth. It may help spur an epiphany. Recall your run-ins with political authority figures. Look back on the biased news stations. Consider things from the standpoint of the old man cops shot in the back. Contemplate the babies murdered overseas by drone strikes at the behest of politicians. Look deep into the souls of those innocent victims of the drug war who smoked a plant and were entombed inside concrete and barred cages filled with monsters and rapists.

Think about all the people fucked and tortured by authority. Peer into the oculus and return with a knowledge of democide. Know that government has been the largest perpetrator of injustice known to mankind.

Let sovereignty thus embrace you. You can see all the evils of the world. You know what must be done. Let the experiences of the evil done to you and others flow through you and change your thinking. Reject the fetters and shackles.

You and I are one.

We are in this together. I want you to be here with me through this—in the maelstrom of suffering, this hell erected by human indifference. It is time to know that our humanity begs us to return to the idyllic state of nature.

You are naturally free. You are opposed to slavery. You are against those who wish to hold you down and pin you to this life of servitude. Will you see reason as I did? Will you let it bloom in you, the yearning for a peaceful world? Will you spit in the face of those who command everyone to kneel and suffer and die before them? Will you let the spirit of your humanity rise from the ashes, rejuvenated and rekindled with love for truth and wisdom?

I say do it. Join me. You and I are naturally opposed to government. We are kindred spirits in liberty. Do not wait. Do not falter. Embrace your knowledge and trust your heart.

Live free.

Sterlin Lujan is an author, innovator, futurist, and crypto-anarchist philosopher.

Sterlin travels the world, speaking at blockchain and voluntaryist events.

He works full time in the fintech ecosystem with Cryptospace, a trading platform and exchange desk.

Sterlin lives with his lovely wife Cecillia and two dogs.

Discovery
Publisher

Discovery Publisher is a multimedia publisher whose mission is to inspire and support personal transformation, spiritual growth and awakening. We strive with every title to preserve the essential wisdom of the author, spiritual teacher, thinker, healer, and visionary artist.

www.ingramcontent.com/pod-product-compliance
Lightning Source LLC
Chambersburg PA
CBHW011539260326
41914CB00043B/2061/J